MAKING SENSE
OF TASTE

Food & Philosophy

Carolyn Korsmeyer

Cornell University Press
Ithaca and London

First published 1999 by Cornell University Press.

Printed in the United States of America.

Library of Congress Cataloging-in-Publication Data
Korsmeyer, Carolyn.
    Making sense of taste : food and philosophy / Carolyn Korsmeyer.
        p.   cm.
    Includes index.
    ISBN 0-8014-3698-2
    1. Food—Philosophy. 2. Food—Sensory evaluation. 3. Food—Aesthetics.   I. Title.
    B105.F66   K67   1999
    664'.07—dc21
                                                            99-16165
                                                            r99

Cornell University Press strives to use environmentally responsible suppliers and materials to the fullest extent possible in the publishing of its books. Such materials include vegetable-based, low-VOC inks and acid-free papers that are recycled, totally chlorine-free, or partly composed of nonwood fibers. Books that bear the logo of the FSC (Forest Stewardship Council) use paper taken from forests that have been inspected and certified as meeting the highest standards for environmental and social responsibility. For further information, visit our website at www.cornell.edu

Cloth printing   10 9 8 7 6 5 4 3 2 1

for David, Chris, and Jonathan

Contents

Illustrations

Acknowledgments

Many people were helpful with advice, support, and useful information during the time I was writing this book. I thank in particular members of my writing group, unfailing sources of useful criticism: Ann Colley, Betsy Cromley, Rosemary Feal, Claire Kahane, Liz Kennedy, Isabel Marcus, Suzanne Pucci, and Carol Zemel. Susan Feagin and Phil Alperson both read the entire manuscript at a crucial time and offered substantial advice. Others who generously read portions of various chapters include Dabney Townsend, Larry Shiner, Dominic Lopes, David Hills, and Jorge Gracia. I also thank for other advice and help Margaret Holland, Gloria Zúñiga, Hilde Hein, and Barbara Sandrisser; and Peg and Myles Brand for their hospitality when I was doing research at the Lilly Library. The staff at the Lilly were prompt and helpful, and I also thank Daisy Stroud at the Albright-Knox Gallery and Simon Taylor at Art Resource for help in obtaining the pictures that illustrate Chapters 4 and 5. Thanks to Kerry Grant, dean of the College of Arts and Sciences at the University at Buffalo, for his generous support of the reproduction of images in this book. Late in this project I learned from Emily Brady of Frank Sibley's unpublished work on taste and smell, and I thank John Benson for sending me this work in manuscript. And finally, I thank my editor at Cornell University Press, Roger Haydon, for his judicious advice and help in bringing this book to publication, and Barbara Salazar for her wise and elegant editing of the manuscript.

Portions of this book have appeared as "Taste as Sense and as Sensibility" in *Philosophical Topics* 25.1 (Spring 1997). I thank the journal's editor, Christopher Hill, for permission to use that material here; and I thank Pauline von Bonsdorff and Arto Haapala, editors of *Aesthetics in the Human Environment*, International Institute of Applied Aesthetics series 6 (Lahti: International Institute of Applied Aesthetics, 1999), for permission to use parts of "Food and the Taste of Meaning" in Chapter 4.

I have enjoyed the task of researching and writing this book tremendously, not least because the subject matter has led me to read widely in areas in which I am not especially trained. This is both the pleasure and the risk of interdisciplinary work. I have relied on friends and colleagues to flag missteps when I ventured beyond the edges of philosophy, and if errors remain, they are my own.

I dedicate this book to my husband, David, and our sons, Chris and Jonathan.

C. K.

Buffalo, New York

MAKING SENSE
OF TASTE

Introduction

This book is a philosophical investigation of the sense of taste. Usually when a philosopher addresses this subject, discussion moves rapidly to issues of aesthetic discrimination regarding objects of art and to questions about relative preference and standards for artistic judgments. But it is literal taste—that is, the kind that takes place in the mouth—that is the focus of my interest. The literal sense of taste has rarely caught the attention of philosophers except insofar as it provides the metaphor for aesthetic sensitivity. If this sense in its gustatory role is considered at all, it is only briefly, often to be dismissed as unworthy of extended examination. I intend to dispute this presumption and argue on behalf of the experiences availed by the sense of taste and its familiar but little-understood operations.

As with any functioning sense, we exercise taste daily. It affords intense and immediate sensation, and thus it can be pursued for escape, relaxation, and pleasure. This very pleasure, however, is often cause for misgiving. Not only may taste enjoyments be tempting and diverting, but tastes can be indulged, abused, depraved, and even perverted. Philosophers have generally concurred that pursuit of taste for pleasure alone seems an unfit preoccupation for a being whose higher capacities require the efforts of rationality. Moreover, it seems a frivolous pursuit permitted only a leisured few: those who have plenty to eat and to drink. For eating is a physical necessity; its privation brings death. So closely are taste and eating tied to the necessities of existence that taste is frequently cataloged as one of the lower functions of sense perception, operating on a primitive, near instinctual level. Taste is associated with appetite, a basic drive that propels us to eat and drink. Its role in sheer animal existence is one of the factors that has contributed to its standard neglect as a subject of philosophical inquiry.

By long tradition, philosophers have assumed that this sense affords little of theoretical interest. Too closely identified with the body and our animal nature, it seems not to figure in the exploration of rationality or the development of knowledge. Therefore taste is omitted from epistemology's discussions of sense perception, in striking contrast to vision, which receives a great deal of attention for its delivery of information about the world. Most ethical theories assume that taste presents base temptations that in a moral life must be controlled. Although aesthetics exploits the metaphor of taste in theories of aesthetic perception and evaluation, the variety of preferences observable in taste choices have long served as a paradigm for subjective relativity that resists systematic understanding. "De gustibus non est disputandum," as the saying goes: "There's no disputing about taste." Of that which we cannot dispute, we also apparently cannot philosophize. Philosophers have interpreted taste preferences as idiosyncratic, private, and resistant to standards. What is more, they have not considered taste sufficiently important to worry about or to delve into very deeply. I intend to look closely at the way taste has been understood—and misunderstood—in the Western intellectual tradition. The common assumption that taste presents no interesting philosophical problems is a deep-seated error that banishes a potentially fascinating subject from the scope of philosophical inquiry.

Because as a rule what is tasted is eaten or drunk, this book is also an investigation of the objects of taste and of the activity of their consumption. We cannot fully understand the character and importance of the sense of taste unless we also consider what is tasted and the circumstances that surround the exercise of this sense. Taste, food and drink, and eating and drinking—the sense, its objects, its activities—are too complex to be considered from any single perspective, and in the course of this book I shall make use of the discoveries of both laboratory and field scientists, as well as investigate what can be learned about food from the roles it serves in visual and narrative arts. Though I shall explore ideas from a variety of disciplines, my method and focus remain philosophical. Not only does the history of philosophy harbor the roots of the way we think about taste, but established philosophical concepts concerning the senses continue to shape our understanding of taste, food and drink, and their governing appetites.

Since classical antiquity, studies of human perception have noted five external senses through which the mind receives information about the world: vision, hearing, touch, smell, and taste. The foundational texts of Western philosophy consistently rank these senses in a hierarchy of importance. Vision comes first because it is the sense considered to have the greatest significance for the development of knowledge. Though it is followed closely in the hierarchy by hearing, sight receives far and away the most attention in philosophical studies of perception. (Indeed, the very word "perception" can connote visual perception alone.) The remaining three senses, smell, taste, and touch, are treated more briefly, and the order of their importance varies according to which aspect of sense is stressed. If the role of sense in learning about the world is in question, then touch is usually seen as cooperating with the cognitive operations of vision. If the role of the senses in the development of moral behavior is under scrutiny, then both touch and taste figure as the senses that require the most control, since they can deliver pleasures that tempt one to indulge in the appetites of eating, drinking, and sex. Pleasure and pain are intimately, sometimes inescapably, connected with the sensations delivered by taste, smell, and touch, making these senses a cause for concern because of the seductive diversions they represent.

Philosophers who study perception have concluded that the cognitive developments made possible by sight and hearing are so superior to the other senses that both may be labeled the "cognitive" or "intellectual" senses—or in short, the "higher" senses. They provide more of the sensory information necessary for the exercise of the rational faculties, and they permit the development and communication of human knowledge. Vision and hearing are senses that are less involved with the experience of pleasure and pain in their exercise and thus appear comparatively detached from experiences that are phenomenally subjective—that is, that are felt as sensations in the body. One sees a cat at a distance, not in one's eyeballs; its meow is perceived as coming from the cat. But one pats its fur and feels the softness in the tips of one's own fingers. Similarly, though odorous objects may be at a distance, smell is experienced in the body's olfactory passages. Taste requires perhaps the most intimate congress with the object of perception, which must enter the mouth, and which delivers sensations experienced in the mouth and throat on its way down and through the digestive track. The degree to which the body is experienced as involved in the operation of the senses contributes to the value assigned their objects. Sometimes we develop artifacts for delight of the eyes and of the ears that achieve the status of works of art; objects of the other senses are valued more for sensuous pleasure, such as the enjoyment of perfumes or of food and drink. For this reason, only vision and hearing are traditionally considered genuine aesthetic senses. In short, taste, touch, and smell constitute the "bodily" senses, a station that also merits the designation "lower" senses.

For all the theoretical disdain directed at taste on the part of philosophers, it affords experiences that have inspired others to sing its praises. Writing about food is so extensive that it constitutes a virtual genre of its own, including not only recipe books but also extended encomia to eating, its purposes, and its pleasures. Clearly, the caution prescribed by moral philosophy does not appeal to everyone. What is more, this writing is not merely in praise of taste pleasures, for it also takes seriously the preparation, serving, and function of food. It implicitly acknowledges what social scientists bring to light in their research: the fact that eating is an activity we freight with significance considerably beyond either the pleasures it affords or the nutritional sustenance it provides. It is an intimate part of hospitality, ceremony, and rituals religious and civic. What features of taste and eating dispose foods to be employed in these ways? Answering this question will reveal common threads between foods and cultural products customarily given greater esteem: works of art.

Although my special interest is the sense of taste, a focus on taste requires attention to the other lower senses as well. In modern (though not ancient) science, smell is linked with taste as one of the chemical senses, and indeed it is virtually impossible to conceive of a full-fledged taste sensation that does not have an olfactory component. This coordination has led some researchers to consider taste and smell together as a single sensory operation, but we need not stop there. Touch nearly always accompanies the sensation of taste, especially if one extends tasting beyond the isolations of laboratory experimentation and considers actual eating, including biting, chewing, and swallowing. Therefore an emphasis on taste will include at least selective consideration of the other bodily senses as well. Indeed, all five senses contribute to some particularly rich eating experiences.

I start from the assumption that eating, food, and drink—and by extension the tastes of ingested substances—do indeed have an importance in life that invites philosophical investigation, whether one speaks of individual experiences of eating or of social patterns of behavior. To reveal the character of this "importance" I shall skirt the usual consideration of the sheer enjoyment of the sensations of tastes, even though most advocates of taste and of eating have standardly concentrated attention on the pleasures of the table and the development of sophisticated cuisines. Despite the undeniable appeal of gustatory pleasures, however, emphasis on this aspect of taste will not reveal what is of greatest philosophical salience for this sense and its objects: namely, tastes convey meaning and hence have a cognitive dimension that is often overlooked. Foods are employed in symbolic systems that extend from the ritual ceremonies of religion to the everyday choice of breakfast. Perhaps most obviously, eating is an activity with intense social meaning for communities large and small. A study of taste and its proper activities thus takes us into territory involving perception and cognition, symbolic function and social values. I believe that the values and meanings of tastes, foods, and eating are all around us and are readily revealed by reflection upon life, practices, and habits. A nascent philosophy of taste and of food is, as it were, already under our noses, to borrow an image from a kindred sense modality. I hope to clear promising paths along which a robust understanding of these subjects may be discovered.

The branch of philosophy that is potentially the most inviting to a theoretical understanding of taste, food, and eating is aesthetics and philosophy of art, partly because the sense of taste has long provided a provocative comparison for theories of aesthetic perception and discrimination of artistic qualities, and also because of certain parallels between food preparation and artistic creativity. Therefore, my chief frame of analysis is derived from this area of philosophy. Additionally, I consider the contributions to the understanding of taste available from disciplines such as psychology and anthropology, fields that have provided empirical understanding of taste by studying, respectively, the physical operation of the sense and the development of cuisines and eating patterns across the globe. The multiple meanings assigned to foods in visual art furnish further evidence of its aesthetic import, as do literary narratives that reflect upon the values manifest in appetite, eating, and food.

I begin by considering the reasons why the senses have been classified into higher and lower orders. In the first two chapters I examine the traditional grounds that support a distinction between intellectual and bodily senses and investigate the conceptual systems that justify and perpetuate this way of thinking. It is an excursion into some of the originary texts of Western philosophy which, in spite of the intervening centuries, continue to exercise influence over our thought because of the power they have wielded to determine issues of philosophical interest and to organize inquiry according to a recognized set of questions. Chapter 1, "The Hierarchy of the Senses," opens with a discussion of the influential writings of Plato and Aristotle, for both these giants of Greek philosophy offer an early categorization that distinguishes between the distance senses of vision and hearing and the bodily senses of smell, taste, and touch. Examining these philosophies reveals an elaborate system of values supporting a hierarchy of the senses within which one can also discover a marked gender dimension, for the higher senses turn out to be those the exercise of which develops "masculine" traits and virtues. Here we see at work a conception of philosophy itself that has precluded serious attention to taste and to the other bodily senses, in part because they have been lumped into a category of "the feminine" that traditionally has never contained much of interest to philosophers. In spite of the passage of two millennia, the terms establishing philosophical investigation that we see in ancient theories still cling tenaciously to contemporary ways of thinking and account in large part for philosophers' continued neglect of taste. Attention to gender recurs from time to time throughout my discussion, especially as the question of appetite arises, for appetite is often conceived as a twin drive for food and for sex.

Eighteenth-century theorists developed "philosophies of taste," theories of the perception and appreciation of beauty that form the foundation for contemporary philosophies of art and aesthetic value. These are the subjects of Chapter 2, "Philosophies of Taste: Aesthetic and Nonaesthetic Senses." The literature about aesthetic taste and perception again concentrates on two senses: vision and hearing. Despite the parallels between literal and aesthetic taste that prompted the choice of this sense as a metaphor for the perception of beauty, gustatory taste is expelled from formative theories of aesthetic taste such as Kant's. Taste is also excluded from among the senses that have arts as their objects. Philosophers such as Hegel articulated concepts of fine art that elevate the "arts of the eyes and ears" above the activities of the bodily senses. At the same time, the concept of aesthetic taste continues to exploit parallels with gustatory tasting to refine the notion of aesthetic discrimination. (It is interesting to note that taste serves as an aesthetic metaphor not only in European theories but also in the much longer tradition of Indian aesthetics.) Certain features of gustatory taste dispose it to comparison with aesthetic discrimination, such as the immediacy of pleasure or displeasure (dis-gust) attending experience. Paradoxically, this same feature also distances literal taste from aesthetic discrimination because of the ties of the former to sensuous, bodily pleasure. There is thus an abiding tension in aesthetic theories between the idea of taste as a sense pleasure and taste as a discriminative capability: fine discernment is accomplished by means of the pleasure, yet the pleasure itself is too sensuous to count as aesthetic. I argue that while the tension between aesthetic and gustatory taste reveals differences between arts and foods, the tenacity and aptness of this aesthetic metaphor indicates the tremendous complexity and subtlety of the literal sense of taste and the vivacity and power latent in the bodily intimacy of this sense.

The neurochemistry of the sense of taste, mysterious until recently, is now understood in greater detail thanks to research on the part of psychologists and physiologists, whose work is reviewed in Chapter 3, "The Science of Taste." Though even scientific studies of taste have been influenced by presumptions about the hierarchy of the senses, this research provides empirical evidence for the discriminative capacities of taste and for constants and variables in its development. After presenting a sketch of how the sense of taste functions, I consider several common disparagements often directed against the acuity of this sense, including the claims that smell is the actual contributor to gustatory enjoyment, that there are really only four basic tastes, and that taste and smell are "primitive" senses. The latter charge is countered by evidence documented by sociologists and anthropologists, who have devoted much attention to the phenomena of eating and food preparation. If tastes were simply "natural," they should not vary any more than does binocular vision. But food practices and attendant taste preferences exhibit strikingly different patterns in different societies. Cross-cultural studies provide additional evidence that taste, far from being simply a natural receptivity, in fact varies in the scope of its exercise and its preferences across the globe, evidence that is inconsistent with the standard philosophical assumption that food and taste do not occasion interesting theoretical questions about the relativity and objectivity of perception. One such question examined here concerns what we might call the phenomenology of taste. I analyze the multiple components—physiological, cultural, and individual—that contribute to taste experiences. Once the components of taste are outlined, I reassess the traditional claim that this sense is too "subjective" to admit rational deliberation, criterial assessment, or philosophical theorizing.

Our understanding of the sense of taste is complete only if the full context of its exercise is taken into account. The next chapters turn attention to the objects of taste: food and drink and the circumstances of their consumption. I investigate the nature of the aesthetic value of food and of the experiences that taste provides. By "aesthetic value" I intend something of far greater scope than the usual meaning of "tastes really good" that generally attaches to the advocacy of sophisticated eating. In Chapter 4, "The Meaning of Taste and the Taste of Meaning," I argue for a cognitivist view of the aesthetic—that is, a position that holds that the appreciation of works of art and similar objects requires a certain understanding and insight that constitute aspects of the pleasures they deliver. Food, if valued at all in aesthetic terms, is usually regarded only as a gourmet item of particular delectability. I acknowledge the powerful sensory pleasure of eating and the refined discrimination that can be developed for food and drink. As sole foundation, however, these are meager grounds on which to establish aesthetic features of tasting and eating, especially in comparison with the symbolic significance that foods and their consumption achieve. These cognitive dimensions are what actually make foods most comparable to works of art. Foods qualify as symbolic and meaningful in a host of ways, for they are representational and expressive. These functions are exploited in some of the most important social rituals, such as religious ceremonies and commemorative occasions, and we can also see their operation in the common and familiar acts of eating we engage in every day. I adapt Nelson Goodman's theory of the symbols that operate in art in support of this contention, for I claim that food (while not art itself) performs many of the same symbolic activities as works of art.[1] This enterprise is designed not to slight the pleasures of eating but to pull sensation and sense pleasures more fully into the purview of aesthetics by claiming that the pleasure they deliver is often an enhancement or even a component of their cognitive significance.

Further exploration of the cognitive dimensions—the systems of signification or meaning-making—of food are continued in the final two chapters. We can discover many of the meanings attached to tastes and foods by considering how these subjects are represented in art. Artistic renderings permit discovery of yet more dimensions of meaning that food and eating can attain, although these meanings may be only implicit in everyday practice, since the artistic presentation of taste, food, and eating often exceeds what is practical or even tolerable in acts of actual eating and food preparation. The focus of investigation now moves from philosophical texts to two venues of art: visual art, especially painting, and narratives. Chapter 5, "The Visual Appetite: Representing Taste and Food," surveys depictions of the senses and of foods and eating in visual art, where pictures indicate the potential for foods and flavors to assume an enormous diversity of meanings. The values of the sense hierarchy itself enter into the systems of signification that are reflected upon and explored in the depiction of food and, perhaps especially, of appetite, in which representations of gustatory and sexual desires impart complex gender meanings to visual art. However instinctually driven, eating and sex are activities that are inflected with social meaning. What is exploited as an apparently natural connection becomes far more than that, for both sorts of appetite are not only culturally coded but elastic in the meanings they take on in artistic renderings.

We find in paintings devoted to matters of the kitchen and the table an echo of the sense hierarchy that has demoted the sense of taste to a mere bodily necessity.

---

[1] Nelson Goodman, *Languages of Art* (Indianapolis: Hackett, 1976) and *Ways of Worldmaking* (Indianapolis: Hackett, 1978).

Just as taste has been considered a "low" sense, so has the class of painting dedicated to depicting subjects such as foods—the genre known as still life—been designated a lesser form of painting among theorists of art. The history of art contains a continuous denigration of still life for being preoccupied with mundane and trivial subjects. This low esteem derives in part from the value accorded so-called history painting, which features heroic, dramatic stories and events rather than matters pertaining to everyday life. By contrast, still life painting, with its laden tables and kitchen detritus, seems to concern only mundane, everyday affairs. The art historian Norman Bryson argues against the detractors of still life on behalf of the serious moral insight and artistic profundity of that genre. Far from being occupied with trivial subject matter, he asserts, the repetitive world of necessity and bodily maintenance represented in still life is a reminder of values often denied by the more heroic concepts of art: the leveling effects of time and mortality.[2] This reclamation of value for still life painting suggests an instructive parallel for insertion of taste into philosophy. For similarly, the exercise of the bodily senses reminds us of mortal, quotidian aspects of life that have traditionally been deemed unworthy of philosophical attention.

But we may go even further, and I shall claim that the immense complexity and variety with which matters pertaining to food and to appetite have been represented in art betoken the depth and flexibility of meaning that these phenomena acquire. The depiction of food in art extends from the base and gross to the most profound spiritual dimensions, and images of foods range from the decorative to the horrible. Artists have employed foodstuffs in contexts sacred and profane; to whet appetite and to keep it at bay; to immerse the viewer in a lusty sensuousness and to catch us unawares with reminders of mortality; to tempt and to sicken. Depicted foods may lead the mind to God or to sensuous indulgence. They may mimic real meals and stun us with their illusory charm, or they may be so abstracted from actual eating as to appeal to the intellect alone. Granted, one must be cautious while navigating the similarities and differences between actual and depicted foods; nevertheless, the presence of such profusion of meanings in visual art testifies to the elasticity and richness of the roles of food and eating in our lives.

I stated earlier that the values of taste, of food, and of eating are evident all around us, whether in daily routines whereby appetite is satisfied, in customs of hospitality, or in ritual acts of commemoration. To explore this observation more deeply, in the final chapter I turn to narratives in which eating has a particular meaning, narratives that distill the messy complexities of life into stories. This method has been adopted usefully by many philosophers, especially by those inclined to explore

[2] Norman Bryson, *Looking at the Overlooked* (Cambridge: Harvard University Press, 1990).

the particularities of ethical situations.[3] I find that it offers much scope for considering the values and meanings to be found in eating, though to be sure, not all those values are pleasant or easy to confront. One of the most significant roles of food is social: eating is part of the rituals, ceremonies, and practices that knit together communities. This process takes place over time, and the temporality of a narrative, whether written, dramatic, or cinematic, permits extended reflection upon the ways eating serves (or severs) communities. Because of their narrative form, stories lead the reader imaginatively to a discovery availed through a taste, an act of eating, or a reflection upon food.

This exploration begins by continuing a theme raised at the end of Chapter 5: the horrible, disgusting, and brutal aspects of eating. While eating is often praised for its role in hospitality and formation of community, the sustenance of social bonds through shared eating occurs against a backdrop of disturbing moral significance, for eating consumes its objects and appetite is a drive that must destroy in order to be appeased—a fact that Herman Melville elevates to a moral problematic in *Moby Dick*. The brutish and even predatory aspects of eating are dramatically demonstrated with Stubb's macabre feast, as the second mate of the *Pequod* competes with sharks for the best cut of whale.

More positively, and perhaps also more frequently, one finds narratives that portray the role of foods as components of civility, community, and friendship, though even these positive values, seemingly remote from Stubb's savage appetite, presume the destructive necessities he relishes. A story such as Isak Dinesen's "Babette's Feast," for example, explores the fellowship that a meal can provide, using the delectable flavors of haute cuisine as a gateway to heightened awareness of love and divine kinship in a religious community and refuting with gentle comedy the fear of bodily pleasures that permeates the sect's doctrine. A related example is the dinner party that is the centerpiece of Virginia Woolf's *To the Lighthouse*. The dinner party unifies, however temporarily, the affections and interests of the disparate characters and the scattered pieces of experience that would be but a jumble of sequential episodes were it not for the structure with which such a meal frames experience and memory. These and other narratives of eating, both literary and cinematic, will be used to explore the ethical and social dimensions of taste and its objects and to complete the picture of the philosophical significance that food achieves.

In effect, this book falls into three sections. The first two chapters review and analyze the historical roots of the sense hierarchy and the reasons why the sense of taste has a dubious, even disreputable standing in philosophy, reasons that have been hugely influential in the popular ways in which the bodily senses and their

---

[3] For example, Martha Nussbaum, *Love's Knowledge* (New York: Oxford University Press, 1990) and *Poetic Justice* (Boston: Beacon, 1995).

pleasures are regarded. The middle two chapters begin to repair this account of taste by reviewing how the sense actually functions and the factors that come into play with the development of food preferences and practices. Here I mount a brief for a "philosophy of food" that defends the aesthetic character of taste and eating and draws parallels between foods and arts in terms of their symbolic, cognitive functions. Having established grounds for understanding the meanings and uses of tastes and foods, in the final two chapters I pursue certain examples of art to deepen the case made earlier and to indicate the breadth and profundity of meanings that all the phenomena of eating attain. It is a demonstration of the complex world of taste and food and eating, of the meanings that we take into ourselves daily. While the middle two chapters dispute the traditional ranking of the senses and argue that taste fully qualifies as a cognitive sense of aesthetic significance, the sense hierarchy cannot simply be criticized and dismissed, for it is ingrained in the deepest conceptual frameworks with which we organize sense experience. Indeed, some of the meanings of eating depend on the hierarchy itself. The last two chapters acknowledge its influence and the ways in which its values are incorporated into the representation of foods and appetites.

Recent years have witnessed a period of revaluation of the discipline of philosophy and its traditional assumptions, and this book takes a place with others that now question the reliance of Western philosophies on the distal sense of sight and models of detachment and objectivity to characterize the ideal relationship of the perceiver to the object of perception.[4] Many philosophers have begun to turn away from their discipline's venerable preoccupation with the "mind" over the "body" and with matters of universal concern over particular experiences. Attention to the bodily bases of experience not only provides balance to the traditional preoccupation with reason and the mind that has characterized philosophy, it also quickens awareness of physical being itself. Consideration of foods and of eating, I believe, is ripe for contribution to this intellectual direction and to an increased understanding of the roles of bodily experience in knowledge, valuation, and aesthetic encounters. The experience of tasting takes us to the most intimate regions of these phenomena.

[4] Indeed, as Martin Jay has remarked, an entire generation of French philosophy can be regarded as such a critique: *Downcast Eyes: The Denigration of Vision in Twentieth-Century French Thought* (Berkeley and Los Angeles: University of California Press, 1993).

CHAPTER 1

The Hierarchy of the Senses

The tradition that ranks the sense of taste as among the lowlier attributes of human beings has roots that run long and deep into the history of philosophy. Plato and Aristotle not only laid down some of the major alternatives for philosophical thinking but helped to determine the grounds on which an issue should be considered worthy of philosophical consideration at all. The sense of taste is among those subjects that have received only cursory theoretical attention on the part of philosophers. Even in earlier times when philosophy and science were indistinguishable, taste and its cousin smell were given short shrift in comparison with the "higher" senses, especially vision. This relative neglect is especially noticeable in investigations of the abilities that represent the highest achievement of human effort: knowledge, morals, and art. Taste is early placed on the margins of the perceptual means by which knowledge is achieved; its indulgence must be avoided in the development of moral character; and it perceives neither objects of beauty nor works of art. I hope to correct some of these judgments by pointing out that philosophical investigations have by and large overlooked the significance that taste and the related activities of eating and drinking actually (and sometimes rather obviously) have. The first step in this direction is to discover the origin of the conceptual frameworks that distort our understandings of these subjects.

I begin therefore by considering some of the early philosophies that examine the senses. As is the case with so many issues in the Western philosophical tradition, Plato and Aristotle are a good place to begin, not only because of their remarkable influence on subsequent philosophy but also because both left fully developed philosophies of value that underwrite the hierarchical ranking of the senses and partially account for its persistence.[1] We shall see not only how a hierarchy among the senses is early determined but also how it has helped to select the standard content of philosophy altogether, leaving taste and its bodily kin largely out of range of the philosopher's eye.

---

[1] This remains the case even though we are today less confident of generalizations such as that of the Grecophile Bruno Snell, who declares approvingly that "European thinking begins with the Greeks": *The Discovery of Mind: The Greek Origin of European Thought* (1948), trans. T. G. Rosenmeyer (New York: Harper Torchbooks, 1960), p. vii.

The Senses and the Body: Plato and Aristotle

The most basic distinction that separates sight and hearing from smell, taste, and touch concerns the apparent degree of involvement of the body in the operation of the senses. Early Greek philosophers were curious about how the senses work, how they manage to take in the information peculiar to them, how sensations from the different sense organs are synthesized and coordinated. Somehow or other, they surmised, the object of perception must reach the organ of sense. With touch and taste this process is not so mysterious; the object appears to be in direct contact with the skin or with the tongue—that is, with a part of the body. Smell occurs with some space between the nose and the odorous object, for one smells an object when at a distance from it, though usually one needs to be fairly close. Sometimes the emanations that stimulate the sense of smell are themselves perceptible, as in the case of smoke, and one can observe their progress toward the nose, at which point contact is presumably achieved. Vision and hearing are different. While it was agreed that some kind of interaction is necessary to stimulate the eyes and the ears, there is no evident contact between the perceived object and the organs of perception. There is a distance, sometimes considerable, between these senses and their objects, and just how they operate was debated for centuries. In virtually all analyses of the senses in Western philosophy the distance between object and perceiver has been seen as a cognitive, moral, and aesthetic advantage. The bodily senses are "lower" in part because of the necessary closeness of the object of perception to the physical body of the percipient.

A number of pre-Socratic philosophers formulated theories of the senses and their operation, so by the time Plato and Aristotle joined the discussion, the identification of the senses and the outline for certain terms of debate were already under way.[2] Plato presents a fairly extended discussion of the senses in the course of outlining the speculative cosmology of the *Timaeus*. In this dialogue one Timaeus, conversing with Socrates, examines the probable origins of the universe and of life. The language of the dialogue is poetic and sometimes fanciful, and the discussants acknowledge that many of the questions they consider do not admit of certain answers. Nonetheless, their purpose is also scientific, and empirical questions mingle with cosmological matters. How do living creatures fit into the physical world? How do they move around and flourish? How do they learn? Specifically, how do living bodies interact with things outside themselves? This latter question introduces consideration of the senses, those attributes of living organisms that are designed to receive information about objects in the world around.

---

[2] A useful treatment of Greek theories of the senses remains John I. Beare, *Greek Theories of Elementary Cognition from Alcmaeon to Aristotle* (Oxford: Clarendon, 1906).

Plato's metaphysics conveys an immediate caution regarding the reliability of the information provided through bodily experience. According to the parable of this dialogue, the creator brought souls into being and assigned a star to each as its first and native home (*Timaeus* 41e).[3] Souls are eternal. Upon the birth of a new human being, however, a soul enters into a body, which is mortal. Flesh itself is an encumbrance to the soul, which forgets its divine knowledge at birth and must recall it in the process of learning, which, ideally but rarely, culminates in apprehension of the eternal Forms. (This view is familiar from dialogues such as the *Meno, Republic,* and *Symposium* as well.) Bodies require senses and emotions in order to preserve their existence, and this need sets up an immediate tension within the composite being that is the living individual: the rational soul must conquer—or at least govern—the senses and emotions of the body if it is to achieve wisdom and virtue.

Recognizing the conflict between soul and body, the creating gods designed us so that our most divine part is at a safe remove from the most corrupting. The head, which houses rationality, is above and separated from the trunk, which contains the grosser machinery of appetite and passion (44d, 69d–70a). (Plato selected the brain as the seat of reason; Aristotle—usually the better scientist—chose the heart.)[4] The soul has three components. Rationality is the divine element of the soul and is immortal; but both the energetic, passionate soul associated with anger and courage and the appetitive soul that seeks pleasure die with the body. It is the immortal soul of intellect that occupies the top floor of the body—the head. The spirited element of passion resides in the thorax and stands guard there on behalf of the intellect in defense against the appetites, seated in the lower part of the midriff.

An immediate complication to this picture of the hierarchical arrangement of the body is that the chief organ of taste, the tongue, also resides in the head, as does the organ of smell. This is not evidence of a design flaw, however, for the substances that are the objects of taste soon leave the head for lower regions. Plato is probably speculating about the visible papillae on the tongue when he observes that when food is taken into the mouth, it dissolves and penetrates the "small veins which are the testing instruments of the tongue" (65d), making its effects felt by dilations and contractions of these veins or ducts. Remarking on the problem of finding a common language for taste sensations, Plato notes that several basic tastes have received names. He singles out the four tastes commonly recognized by modern physiology: bitter, sweet, sour (or acid), and salt; to these he adds harsh, astringent, and pungent

---

[3] All quotations from Plato are taken from *Plato: Collected Dialogues,* ed. Edith Hamilton and Huntington Cairns (Princeton: Princeton University Press, 1963). The translation of the *Timaeus* is by Benjamin Jowett.

[4] The location of the command center for mental operations moved about in ancient science. Alcmaeon of Croton was an early proponent of the brain as the locale for the reception of sensations. See Beare, *Greek Theories,* p. 5, and D. W. Hamlyn, *Sensation and Perception: A History of the Philosophy of Perception* (New York: Routledge & Kegan Paul, 1961), p. 6.

(65e–66c).[5] The objects of perception for the tongue, however, do not remain in the diviner residence of the head, nor do they have their principal effects on the intellectual soul. Sapid particles—that is, substances that have flavor and can be tasted—dissolve and make their way through the veins of the tongue to the heart. What is more, the chewed food itself descends through the isthmus of the neck into the stomach and thence to the lower regions of the bowels. The organs housed within the rib cage, the heart and the lungs, are as it were sentinels that in a virtuously functioning person are ready to muster passion in the service of the reason and to quell the potential rebellions of the appetites (70b–d).

The image Plato conjures of the digesting stomach is instructive and vivid: the stomach is a manger for the ravening appetitive soul, that part of the soul whose job it is to sustain the bodily creature. Appetite is a powerful, relentless force that must be kept chained like a wild animal lest it overtake the whole being. He presents this picture of internally warring factions:

> The part of the soul which desires meats and drinks and the other things of which it has need by reason of the bodily nature, [the gods] placed between the midriff and the boundary of the navel, contriving in all this region a sort of manger for the food of the body, and there they bound it down like a wild animal which was chained up with man, and must be nourished if man was to exist. They appointed this lower creation his place here in order that he might always be feeding at the manger, and have his dwelling as far as might be from the council chamber, making as little noise and disturbance as possible, and permitting the best part to advise quietly for the good of the whole and the individual. (70e–71)

Note that while it is a man—a human being—who is being analyzed in toto, the composite of mind and body that must eat in order to survive, in this passage it is also "man" in a narrower sense who is chained up with the "wild animal" that needs food.[6] This latter "man" alludes to the person's distinctively human qualities of rationality, and this usage highlights what in Plato's view is the discomfort of the combination of rational soul and animal body. This is not the first time in the course of

[5] Astringent and pungent are also basic taste sensations noted in Sanskrit and Hindi treatments of taste. See Sylvain Pinard, "A Taste of India: On the Role of Gustation in the Hindu Sensorium," in *The Varieties of Sensory Experience,* ed. David Howes (Toronto: University of Toronto Press, 1991), p. 222. Attempts have been made to isolate a set of basic tastes for as long as this sense has been investigated. Aristotle chose seven and toyed with their kinship with seven basic colors. Theophrastus selected eight basic tastes: sweet, oily, bitter, harsh, pungent, sour, astringent, saline. See George Malcolm Stratton, *Theophrastus and the Greek Physiological Psychology before Aristotle* (New York: Macmillan, 1917), pp. 44–45. I discuss basic tastes further in Chapter 3.
[6] This use of "man" refers generically to persons of either sex. But see below for some complexity regarding Plato's assessment of women.

an analysis of the human creature that Plato has distinguished certain composite parts of him as really separate from his essence. Another famous image of like import occurs in *Republic* IX, 588c–e, where the tripartite soul is described as having three components: a many-headed beast (the appetites), a lion (the spirited element), and a man (the reason). Such images reinforce the inferiority of the mortal being with its passions and appetitive senses, for the nonrational elements of the living creature are interpreted as incidental to the valuable, essential attributes that make him human.

Aiding in the control of the beast at the manger is the placid liver, which is also the seat of divination, a backhanded compliment, since Timaeus notes that one does not prophesy except when out of one's head.[7] Another crucial aid is the intestines, which act as a storage house for surplus food. Without them the appetite would so overwhelm the hapless person with its gluttony that the soul would have no time to exercise its higher faculties. As Timaeus surmises:

> The authors of our race were aware that we should be intemperate in eating and drinking and take a good deal more than was necessary or proper, by reason of gluttony. In order then that disease might not quickly destroy us, and lest our mortal race should perish without fulfilling its end—intending to provide against this, the gods made what is called the lower belly, to be a receptacle for the superfluous meat and drink, and formed the convolution of the bowels, so that the food might be prevented from passing quickly through and compelling the body to require more food, thus producing insatiable gluttony and making the whole race an enemy to philosophy and culture, and rebellious against the divinest element within us. (72e–73a)

Here gluttony is posed as a clear enemy of philosophy, the love of wisdom. This is not by itself an indictment of taste, for one can obviously argue that overindulgence in an appetitive pleasure is a misuse rather than an inevitable outcome of the exercise of this sense. However, by implication taste is regarded as complicit in the dangers of appetite. It does, after all, provide much of the enjoyment of eating, and such enjoyment is a temptation to indulgence and gluttony.

Moreover, there is another sense that is singled out as serving philosophy and balancing the desires of appetite, and that is vision. The delights of visual experience are not ones that tempt one to overindulgence in pleasure, though to be sure this sense is prone to illusion and mistaken perception and thus cannot be relied on by itself. However, vision in this dialogue is put forth as a sensible companion to intellectual activity. Timaeus observes:

---

[7] See also Socrates' objections to the inspiration of the performing rhapsode in *Ion*.

The sight in my opinion is the source of the greatest benefit to us, for had we never seen the stars and the sun and the heaven, none of the words which we have spoken about the universe would ever have been uttered. But now the sight of day and night, and the months and the revolutions of the years have created number and have given us a conception of time, and the power of inquiring about the nature of the universe. And from this source we have derived philosophy, than which no greater good ever was or will be given by the gods to mortal men. (47a–b)

Exactly why vision is supposed to foster philosophy is a little obscure. Plato is fond of visual metaphors and images to explain knowledge of the disembodied world of intellect. His most famous parables involve visual images, such as the allegory of the cave in *Republic* VII, in which the sun is equated with the Form of the Good. Its light makes sight of the world possible and prompts the intellect to grasp the reality of the Forms. Plato calls vision "the most sunlike of all the instruments of sense" (*Rep.* 508b)[8] In the passage above, Timaeus seems to be referring to the fact that visual experience can cover a vast sweep of objects, thereby enabling rational inquiry, which includes naming and classifying all that can be seen. An experience such as a survey of the night sky is an example of the cooperation of visual experience and intellectual inquiry, for the perceiver is curious about the objects of perception, many of which are distant. The stars are distinct from one another and can be both numbered and named. Visual experiences of this sort thereby foster the development of mathematics and language. Vision takes in the finest, purest element of light, screening out grosser particles (45c). Least encumbered of all the senses in its attachment to the body, sight may aid or support the intellect in the eventual apprehension of the Forms.[9]

Plato surmises that sight is composed of the basic element of fire.[10] Noting that light is required for vision to take place, Plato speculates that the eye sends out small rays of fire that reach toward the object of perception. It in turn emanates its own rays (or more exactly color—the proper object of vision—sends out rays) and the

---

[8] Links between vision and cognition abound in a variety of theories, and many languages employ visual metaphors for knowledge. See Martin Jay, *Downcast Eyes: The Denigration of Vision in Twentieth-Century French Thought* (Berkeley and Los Angeles: University of California Press, 1993), Introduction.

[9] Eva Keuls discusses the dual role of vision as a metaphor both for the world of the senses and for the discovery of reality in *Plato and Greek Painting* (Leiden: E. J. Brill, 1978), chap. 2.

[10] Many Greek thinkers chose the four elements of Empedocles—earth, air, fire, and water— in various combinations as components of the senses. There is nothing very clear or consistent about this aspect of their theories, as Aristotle's struggle to assign senses to elements illustrates (*De Sensu*, sec. 2; *De Anima*, bk. 1). See Hamlyn, *Sensation and Perception*, p. 20.

two meet in the medium of light, itself composed of fire. The visual rays are conduits that bring sensations to the mind, the seat of intellect, whereas the other senses convey their information to the lower portions of the body.[11] Importantly, visual experience is distinct from experience that involves a change of bodily state, as is the case with the contact senses of taste and touch.

Even though vision, like any sense experience, may produce illusions, it is comparatively free from the pull of appetites that plague the bodily senses. This is another feature of the fact that there is a distance between object and organ of perception. This distance fosters the impression of the separation of mind from body and the potential freedom of mind to explore worlds of intellect and diviner regions where bodies cannot travel. Vision permits us to cultivate intelligence by aspiring to the divine; thus it is also a sense that fosters moral improvement. Timaeus continues: "God invented and gave us sight to the end that we might behold the courses of intelligence in the heaven, and apply them to the courses of our own intelligence which are akin to them, the unperturbed to the perturbed, and that we, learning them and partaking of the natural truth of reason, might imitate the absolutely unerring courses of God and regulate our own vagaries" (47c).

Although the language of vision dominates Plato's images, he acknowledges similar benefits attending the other distance sense, hearing. He extends the potential intelligence of vision to hearing, though his treatment is comparatively brief, more or less an addendum to the encomium to sight: "The same may be affirmed of speech and hearing," he says. "They have been given by the gods to the same end and for a like reason" (47c). He adds that not only does hearing contribute to the development and exercise of language, but it also is the sense by which we perceive harmony and rhythm in the form of music. Hearing and its related activity, speech, are favorably contrasted with taste and eating in this description of the mouth: "For that is necessary which enters in and gives food to the body, but the river of speech, which flows out of a man and ministers to the intelligence, is the fairest and noblest of all streams" (75e).

There is moreover a striking contrast between the affinity with intelligence of the two higher senses and the corruption and danger of the sense of taste, mired as it is in the maintenance of the flesh. This treatment is consistent with values expressed elsewhere in the dialogues. The philosophic life for Plato requires that the body be transcended as much as possible during life, so that the intellect may ascend to the apprehension of the ideal world of permanence, where truth may be glimpsed. The dinner guests who assemble in the *Symposium* have gathered for a celebratory banquet; but while they stay for philosophical disquisitions about love, to aid their

---

[11] Beare discusses indeterminacies regarding the seat of sensations in Plato. See *Greek Theories*, pp. 274–76.

minds they refuse food, drink, and the entertainment of the flute girl.[12] As Socrates remarks in the last hours of his life, a philosopher must be concerned with neither food, drink, nor sex (*Phaedo* 64d). Indeed, in some of his writings Plato goes so far as to suggest that only after the death of the body may the soul rejoin the Forms and fully recollect its lost knowledge. To be sure, such declarations recommend dissociation of the soul from all sensations, including those of hearing and sight (*Phaedo* 65c); by itself no sense yields knowledge because it is never free from error and because its objects occupy the physical world of appearance. The senses of hearing and vision, however, may also be sensory aids in the development of wisdom, while the proximal, bodily senses tempt one to detours of pleasure that impede progress toward knowledge. (Plato's *Philebus* contains an argument against pleasure generally in support of wisdom as the foundation of the good life.) Again, the distance that obtains between the objects and organs of sense seems to be a strong factor in this ranking. While the visual and auditory senses never substitute for the activity of the intellect (in fact, by themselves these senses may mislead even more radically than the lower ones), they do not engage the body so potently as smell, taste, and touch. This is also why vision is a suitable sense to employ in metaphors for the disembodied wisdom of true philosophy.

Aristotle's treatment of the senses, which is less guided by idealism, less prone to ascetic interpretations, more scientific and pragmatic, provides a somewhat more complex view of the sense hierarchy. Part of the difference between the two philosophers stems from a difference in metaphysics: Aristotle insists that souls require bodies just as form requires matter. Flesh cannot be described as stuff that simply gets in the way of the operation of the rational soul. Again unlike Plato, Aristotle maintains that knowledge must have as its object both universals and particulars. Knowing the former does not guarantee knowing the latter, for which the experiences of the senses are indispensable (*De Anima* 424a18ff).[13] Senses are also sources of pleasure, and pleasure is an important dimension of human goodness when it functions as a component of practical wisdom. But Aristotle concurs that knowledge is part of the proper end of human endeavors, and again sight and hearing are singled out as the highest and cognitively most important senses. In the famous opening lines of the *Metaphysics*, Aristotle declares, "All men by nature desire to know. An indication of this is the delight we take in our senses; for even apart from their use-

---

12 William J. Slater, ed., *Dining in a Classical Context* (Ann Arbor: University of Michigan Press, 1991), contains essays on the symposia—festival drinking parties—of the ancient world.

13 Discussions of Aristotle's views on sensation, perception, belief, and knowledge may be found in Deborah K. W. Modrak, *Aristotle: The Power of Perception* (Chicago: University of Chicago Press, 1987), and R. J. Sorabji, "Intentionality and Physiological Processes: Aristotle's Theory of Sense Perception," in *Essays on Aristotle's "De Anima,"* ed. Martha C. Nussbaum and Amelie Oksenberg Rorty (Oxford: Clarendon, 1992).

fulness they are loved for themselves; and above all others the sense of sight. . . . The reason is that this, most of all the senses, makes us know and brings to light many differences between things."[14] Sight is superior to all the other senses insofar as it permits apprehension of the most information about the world when it is called upon to act alone. "The faculty of seeing, thanks to the fact that all bodies are coloured, brings tidings of multitudes of distinctive qualities of all sorts" (*Sense and Sensibilia* 437a5–10). No sense by itself is fully adequate, however, and hearing is just as important as vision when one considers the long process of learning that a human being must undergo in the quest for knowledge. In fact, hearing is a greater aid to education than all the other senses because of its role in speech and communication (437a10–15).

De Anima, or *On the Soul,* which includes analysis of the animating principles of life in all its forms, systematically enumerates five external senses. The senses are distinguished from one another by the incommensurability of their proper objects of perception; that is, each sense is receptive to a type of quality that cannot be sensed by any other means. Color, says Aristotle, is the proper object—or special sensible— of vision and cannot be sensed by any organ other than the eyes; sound is the special sensible of hearing; flavor of taste; odor of smell; and tactile qualities such as rough, soft, hot, cold are the proper objects of the sense of touch. Aristotle notes that the objects of touch may be further categorized as to texture and temperature, and he wonders whether touch might be a combination of sensory receptivities.[15]

In addition to proper objects of sense or special sensibles, Aristotle recognizes that some properties of objects may be perceived by more than one sense. These— such as movement, number, figure, magnitude—he calls "common sensibles." Sight is especially informative about these objects, for "it is through this sense especially that we perceive the common sensibles, viz. *figure, magnitude, motion, number*" (*Sense and Sensibilia* 437a5–10). Touch is a companion to vision in its apprehension of common sensibles. Because these sensibles are perceived by more than one sense, they require coordination of their reception, which ability he terms the "common sense."[16] The common sense is also responsible for relating together the data from all the senses and producing an impression of an entire object.

---

[14] Quotations from Aristotle come from *The Complete Works of Aristotle,* ed. Jonathan Barnes, 2 vols. (Princeton: Princeton University Press, 1984).

[15] See Cynthia Freeland, "Aristotle on the Sense of Touch," in Nussbaum and Oksenberg Rorty, *Essays on Aristotle's "De Anima"*; Richard Sorabji, "Aristotle on Demarcating the Five Senses," in *Articles on Aristotle,* ed. Jonathan Barnes, Malcolm Scofield, and Richard Sorabji, vol. 4 (London: Duckworth, 1979).

[16] This is a simplified account. Hamlyn offers a critical analysis of Aristotle's treatment of the senses and their objects, pointing out several inconsistencies and incoherencies, in *Sensation and Perception,* pp. 17–30. A detailed critical analysis of the complexities of Aristotle's notion of common sense is provided by Charles H. Kahn, "Sensation and Consciousness in Aristotle's Psychology," in Barnes, *Articles on Aristotle,* vol. 4.

It is important to note that this analysis of the senses is not focused exclusively on human perceivers. Aristotle is investigating life in general and the stations of different living creatures in the hierarchies of nature. Indeed, he begins with what he considers the lowest sensory level, touch. "Lowest" here does not mean that the sense functions poorly; in fact, Aristotle remarks that the sense of touch is more acute in humans than in all other creatures and that our excellence of touch means that we are the most intelligent of all animals. (He remarks obscurely that soft-fleshed men are smarter than hard-fleshed [callused?] men [*De. An.* 421a25]). However, touch represents a lowest common denominator of sorts. It is the most basic sense in that any living, sensing creature must possess it. Plants live but do not sense; even the lowest animal senses by touch and hence has basic capacities for pleasure and pain, attraction and aversion, and can use its animal motility to respond to such feelings.[17]

Taste comes next in his list, for several reasons. Because any creature must nourish itself to survive, taste is closely associated with the sense of touch as a tool for locating and ingesting food, for that which nourishes must be tangible. (He goes so far as to label taste the variety of touch that serves nutrition.) The method by which the sense works also puts taste and touch in the same category, for in both cases there is proximity, even contact, between the organ of sense and the object sensed. There is some ambiguity in Aristotle's treatment of this matter; the tongue is referred to sometimes as the organ of taste, sometimes as the medium. The skin similarly is treated ambiguously as the organ or medium of touch. It is necessary that the object of taste dissolve slightly before the taste sensation appears; but while the sapid object must be moist, water is not itself the medium of transfer for sensation. Strictly speaking, according to Aristotle, the tongue is an internal medium for taste, and flesh is the internal medium of touch. The true organs of these senses, he speculates, reside in the region of the heart. But Aristotle often speaks in more familiar terms, calling the tongue and the flesh or skin the organs of these senses. From either analysis it is clear that Aristotle believed there to be no interposed external medium that is required for the sensations of taste and touch to occur. Touch and taste are contact senses, whether the point of bodily contact is understood as an organ or a medium. Thus the body is directly involved, even subtly altered, in the operation of these two senses.

Sight and hearing are both senses that require not bodily contact but a separating medium to function (*De An.* 419a10–25). In the case of vision, light is the medium that, when appropriately disturbed in the presence of an object, conveys disturbances to the eyes. (Aristotle rejected the idea that the eyes give off rays of their own

---

[17] Aristotle of course does not have microscopic organisms in mind. It is interesting to note that taste and smell, now classified together as chemical senses, are today sometimes regarded as the most "basic" senses because even microorganisms respond to chemical stimuli, as we shall see in Chapter 3.

that reach to the object of vision.) Air is the medium for sound; when disturbed it produces the sensation of hearing. Water may also serve as a medium for sound, and in the case of aquatic animals also holds the light that permits vision. Aristotle located smell in an intermediate position. Like sight and hearing, it functions at a distance from its object; unlike them, it does not serve well the development of rationality. He viewed it as a sort of bridge between the proximal senses of taste and touch and the distal senses of hearing and sight (*Sense and Sens.* 445a5–8).

The superiority of sight and hearing over taste and touch (and smell, insofar as one is ranking the senses for cognitive operation) he establishes on several grounds. First of all, the quality of information received from vision is superior to that received from the other senses insofar as more of the "form"—the defining qualities—of an entire object is available to sight than to hearing, smell, taste, or touch. We perceive only form, never matter.[18] As Aristotle defines a sense and its activity, "we can say that a sense is what has the power of receiving into itself the sensible forms of things without the matter, in the way in which a piece of wax takes on the impress of a signet-ring without the iron or gold" (*De An.* 424a18–21).

The distance between object and percipient is part of what makes possible the discriminative complexity of vision. Since it puts the observer at a remove from the object, a survey of that object in its entirety is more readily made, and more of the common sensibles are in evidence. An equally important factor is that the distance of both sight and hearing occasions less distraction away from the objects of perception to the state of one's own body. Therefore the distance senses are directed outward to the world outside, while the bodily senses—particularly smell and taste—have the more limited scope of the subjective state of the percipient. While touch can deliver important objective information, its pleasures can be just as distracting as those of smell and taste, and they similarly focus attention on the condition of one's body.

As with Plato, acknowledging the role of the physical body requires consideration of moral implications for the contact between organ and object of perception, and the alteration of both body and mind that may ensue. Plato and Aristotle concur that the pleasure accompanying the taste of good and healthful foods is an aid to nutrition, though Aristotle is far less squeamish than Plato about bodily pleasures in general. Indeed, sensory enjoyment is a kind of virtue in a complete, good life. But only to a point. Taste and touch are senses that one may overindulge to the degree that the activity becomes a vice. Thus temperance or moderation, one of the Greek cardinal virtues, is a characteristic that must be cultivated particularly to protect

---

[18] We can note an apparent anomaly with the operation of taste, however: though it may be only an object's form—that is, its sensible qualities—that is tasted, clearly the entire package of form and matter is ingested, masticated, swallowed, digested.

against the dangers of these two senses. Vision and hearing actually appear to be senses that cannot be overindulged.

> If one sees a beautiful statue, or horse, or human being, or hears singing, without any accompanying wish for eating, drinking, or sexual indulgence, but only with the wish to see the beautiful and to hear the singers, he would not be thought profligate any more than those who were charmed by the Sirens. Temperance and profligacy have to do with those two senses whose objects are alone felt by and give pleasure and pain to brutes as well; and these are the senses of taste and touch, the brutes seeming insensible to the pleasures of practically all the other senses alike, e.g. harmony or beauty. (*Eudemian Ethics* 1230b31–1231a1)[19]

In the *Nicomachean Ethics* Aristotle observes that while the bodily senses are the ones that most tempt indulgence, the distance senses may admit of their own obsessions, and "it would seem possible to delight even in these either as one should or to excess or to a deficient degree" (1118a2–6). Plato, too, had noted that the distance senses may be wrongly valued for the sensory pleasures they afford. These are inferior to the intellectual advances hearing and sight may accomplish and amount to a misuse of these higher senses (*Tim.* 47d).[20] (One supposes that this would be the reply both would make to a theorist such as Freud, for whom vision is as erotic and tempting a sense, indulgent in its own way, as any other.)

Pleasure, however, is the special danger of the senses of taste and touch. Because of the necessary if slight alteration of the body that occurs with the exercise of both, pleasure or pain always accompanies these senses, if only to a small degree. Taste when indulged leads to gluttony or drunkenness, and touch to everything from gluttony (again, since taste is akin to touch) to sexual debauchery. Aristotle is no ascetic, and this is emphasized in his doctrine of the mean of virtue. According to his reasoning, good qualities are likely to be destroyed by excess and deficiency. This he took to be an empirically sound observation, not without exceptions, but true in enough cases to yield a rule of guidance for the person attempting to develop prac-

[19] Władyslaw Tatarkiewicz cites this passage as evidence that Aristotle recognized but did not name the phenomenon so important in modern theories of the aesthetic: disinterested pleasure. See *A History of Six Ideas: An Essay in Aesthetics,* trans. Christopher Kasparek (Warsaw: Polish Scientific Publishers, 1980).
[20] The elevation of the eye as a conduit to the mind and its intellectual pleasures, in contrast to sensory visual pleasures, is familiar in Renaissance and early modern theories of painting, which were heavily influenced by Neoplatonism. After quoting Boccaccio's distinction between "those who painted rather to delight the eyes of the ignorant than to please the intellect of the wise," E. H. Gombrich notes, "This contrast between a low kind of art that appeals to the eyes of the simple-minded and a 'higher' form that can be appreciated only by the cultured, becomes a commonplace of criticism in the sixteenth and seventeenth centuries": *Meditations on a Hobby Horse,* 2d ed. (London: Phaidon, 1971), p. 17.

tical wisdom and thereby a virtuous character. One of the easiest ways to see the truth of this generalization is with examples of diet. Food is a functional good. It is needed for health and maintenance of energy and strength. But too much food sickens, and too much food over a long period of time is detrimental to health. Too little food weakens the body and in extreme cases causes death. So properly speaking it is the right quantity or "mean" amount of food that is good for a person. Because food is measurable, it is also a convenient example for Aristotle to demonstrate that the proper mean between extremes—the virtuous point for activity—is not always the same for all people. Milo the wrestler, he observes, requires a mean of great quantity, one that would be an extreme of excess for a person of sedentary habits (*Nic. Eth.* 1106b1–5).[21]

Even the most ascetic philosopher recognizes that one must eat in order to live. Eating a moderate amount is in a sense making a virtue of necessity. But Aristotle is also attuned to the psychology of pleasure and pain in his ethical theory, including pleasures and pains of the senses; and the development of a virtuous character requires learning to manage pleasures and pains so that one is pleased by the right things (*Nic. Eth.* II, 3; VI, ll; X, 1). Gluttony is indulgence not only in the pleasures of taste but in the sheer quantity of food. Construing the sensation in the throat as a species of touch, he notes that "brutes" care more about swallowing than tasting: "Therefore gluttons pray not for a long tongue but for the gullet of a crane" (*Eud. Eth.* 1231a15–16). But moderation also advises a judicious pleasure taken in eating and drinking. The man who fails because of a deficiency of pleasure in the appetite may be called insensible. Though lack of sense pleasure is a fault, Aristotle believed that the natural human tendency is to overindulge in pleasures of the body. For this reason, the mean for eating is likely to be closer to the extreme of deficiency than excess (*Eud. Eth.* 1222a22–40).

Aristotle frequently compares the functions of the senses in humans and in nonhuman animals, and the differences concern a mixture of natural, developmental, and moral issues. As far as their acuity is concerned, our lower senses of touch and taste are the most discriminating, in comparison with the same senses in other animals (*De An.* 421a17–20). And our higher senses, hearing and sight, are inferior to the hearing and sight of animals such as hawks, owls, dogs. Yet it is these higher senses that are the most important for human cognitive development and are the chief sensory feeders for the faculty that is uniquely human: the intellect. Knowledge is an achievement, not an ability that is born in human beings, as the senses are. Some of the senses more readily team up with rational faculties to develop

[21] Theodore Tracy details the extent to which the idea of a mean pervades Aristotle's thought and Greek philosophy generally in *Physiological Theory and the Doctrine of the Mean in Plato and Aristotle* (The Hague: Mouton, 1969).

knowledge, whether theoretical or practical; in this way sight is usually the most developed sense. (That is, assuming that all five senses are functioning normally. Because of its importance in speech and learning, hearing is crucial for the development of intelligence, an assumption that leads Aristotle to remark that people born blind are more intelligent than those born deaf [*Sense and Sens.* 437a10–15].) The upshot of these differences is the conclusion that the senses that do not foster the intellect should not be indulged by the virtuous person, not just for the sake of the mean but also because the exercise of these senses does not yield the development of any particularly human trait of knowledge.[22] "Neither for the pleasure of eating or that of sex, if all the other pleasures were removed that knowing or seeing or any other sense provides man with, would any man value existence, unless he were utterly servile, for it is clear that to the man making this choice there would be no difference between being born a brute and a man" (*Eud. Eth.* 1215b31–36; viz. *Nic. Eth.* 1118a–b).

The pleasures of the lower senses are not exactly the same in animals and humans, for a human being can reflect upon the pleasures of these senses—can, for example, relish taste sensations like an epicure. But this distinction is not sufficient to lead Aristotle to reverse the judgment that even the most refined gustatory savoring remains a pleasure of the sense, and as such it is lower than the intellectual pleasures available from sight and hearing. This is why the arts of the eyes and the ears are superior to lower sense arts such as perfumery and cooking.[23] Vision and hearing develop mimetic arts and present portrayals of human life and moral character. The finest cuisine in principle falls short of these achievements.[24] In the *Hippias Major* Plato also defines as beautiful the pleasures that are received from hearing and sight, but not from the other senses (297e). Thus the moral suspicion with which the sense of taste is regarded extends to an equally important reservation about its aesthetic possibilities. These observations distinguishing the arts of the different senses are in keeping with the distinction that will play an even larger role in modern philosophy: that between the beautiful, which can be perceived by eyes and ears, and the pleasant or agreeable, enjoyable sensations from the other sensory organs.

In summary, here are the various considerations that Plato and Aristotle advance to support the ranking of bodily senses such as taste below the higher, more rational or cognitive senses: Sight and hearing operate with a distance between object and organ of perception, and as a consequence they serve to draw attention away from

[22] I am glossing over distinctions among sense experience, perceiving, knowing that would be germane to a study of Aristotle's epistemology. For a treatment of these issues, see Modrak, *Aristotle*.
[23] Aristotle has passing remarks on this subject; see, e.g., *Nic. Eth.* VII, 1153a25. Plato argues in the *Gorgias* that cookery is not an art but something like a routine.
[24] See David Summers, *The Judgment of Sense: Renaissance Naturalism and the Rise of Aesthetics* (Cambridge: Cambridge University Press, 1987), pp. 54–62.

the body of the perceiving subject to the object of perception external to the body. (Modern theorists sometimes make this point by observing that there is a less discernible distinction between sensation and perception with sight and hearing.)[25] The senses of taste, touch, and smell, in contrast, are experienced as "in" the body, locatable in the fingertips, the mouth, the olfactory passages. While all three senses are experienced phenomenally in the body of the percipient, the degree of subjectivity of bodily sensations varies. Pains, for example, are actually locatable in the body and travel with it. Smells reside in the locale of odorous objects.[26] Tastes appear somewhat in between; one can carry around a taste in one's mouth, but the taste is also experienced as of the tastant. In spite of these variations, sight and hearing remain by comparison phenomenally objective.[27]

A related point is that sight and hearing are sources for "objective" information; that is to say, what is learned concerns the world external to the body of the percipient. This does not preclude the possibility that the body influences the information received, of course. Judgments about the objects of sight and hearing are often relative to the perspective and position of the percipient. The information, as opposed to the pleasures, delivered by touch also directs attention to objective qualities. Like the other two bodily senses, however, touch inescapably reminds one of the facts of embodiment. While from the experience of the distal senses one may even share Plato's fantasy and aspire to leave the senses behind and ascend to purely intellectual understanding, the proximal senses keep the percipient in a state of awareness of his or her own flesh.[28]

The information delivered by sight and hearing, especially sight, lends itself to reflection and to the abstraction that yields knowledge of universals. (It is the intellectual activity of knowing that permits this generalization, not the sense experience itself, which only gives one acquaintance with particulars.) Because attention is directed outward rather than toward the particular state of the body, the mind is disposed to generalize about its objects. They may be counted and assigned number; their qualities may be summarized in categories such as color and shape. Because the truths arrived at concern the external world, the language developed to refer to them is common, shared. By comparison, the information delivered by the bodily senses is particular, specific, pertaining to the here and now.

The role of pleasure in the exercise of the senses is another feature of distance or its absence that contributes to the ranking of the senses. Experience of the cognitive

[25] Nicholas Humphrey, *A History of the Mind* (New York: Simon & Schuster, 1992), chap. 4, and Hamlyn, *Sensation and Perception,* chap. 1.
[26] Paul Grice, "Some Remarks about the Senses," in *Studies in the Way of Words* (Cambridge: Harvard University Press, 1989).
[27] Subjectivity and taste are analyzed further in Chapter 3.
[28] Vision need not lead one to imagined disembodiment, as Maurice Merleau-Ponty demonstrates in *Phenomenology of Perception,* trans. Colin Smith (London: Routledge & Kegan Paul, 1962).

senses is not necessarily accompanied by pleasure and pain; that of the bodily senses has some pleasure-pain valence. For this reason, taste, like sexual pleasure, is prone to be overindulged; hence vice is a constant danger with this sense, and with its cousin, the sense of touch. Self-control or moderation must be developed particularly to guard against the temptations offered through these senses. And finally, as a result of all the foregoing considerations, it is customary to think of the objects of the cognitive senses as those that also may be beautiful; but objects of the bodily senses are at best pleasant or sensuously enjoyable, even in their most sophisticated and refined forms.

The Sense Hierarchy and the Continuity of Tradition

Though these features of the hierarchy of the senses are here extracted from classical antiquity, they persist in philosophies of perception through the centuries that follow.[29] While the science of the senses has changed, the hierarchy is consistently apparent in theories of perception and evaluation in the entire tradition. The eye continues to be the symbol for intellect, "as if the eye were a spy of the intellect and of all intelligible things," as Leone Ebreo vividly put it.[30] Concerns about the dangers of the lower senses reached an extreme of sorts in some varieties of thinking, such as that of the Stoic Marcus Aurelius, who counseled virtual contempt for food and matters of the body. The influential writings of Thomas Aquinas disseminated Aristotelian ideas throughout the medieval Christian world ("it is clearly impossible that human happiness consist in pleasures of the body, the chief of which are pleasures of the table and of sex").[31] Such ideas are not manifest only in philosophy; the history of painting is another venue for extolling the sense of sight. Leonardo advanced painting as a universal language, superior to speech, since while the comprehensibility of speech depends on fluency in a particular language, the eye grasps information universal to human nature.[32] Nor is the hierarchy a preoccupation only of the world of scholars and artists. It is evident in writings aimed at a popular understanding of science and art, such as we find in Henrie Peacham's pronouncement that "the eye is the most excellent organ of the noblest sense."[33] Descartes echoes the

---

[29] See Jay, *Downcast Eyes,* and Humphrey, *History of the Mind,* for discussions about the primacy of vision in Western philosophical theories. Summers, *Judgment of Sense,* is a detailed study of the continuity and interpretation of Platonic and Aristotelian ideas about the senses from classical through early modern European theory. See also Michel Jeanneret, *A Feast of Words,* trans. Jeremy Whiteley and Emma Hughes (Chicago: University of Chicago Press, 1991).

[30] Quoted in Summers, *Judgment of Sense,* p. 33.

[31] Thomas Aquinas, *Summa Contra Gentiles,* trans. English Dominican Fathers (New York: Benziger, 1928), vol. 3, pt. 1, p. 67.

[32] James Ackerman, "Leonardo's Eye," *Journal of the Warburg and Courtauld Institutes* 41 (1978).

[33] Henrie Peacham, *Graphice* (London: Printed by W. S. for John Browne, 1612), p. 65.

sentiment in his study of optics: "The conduct of our life depends entirely on the senses, and . . . sight is the noblest and most comprehensive of the senses."[34] The British empiricists, those philosophers dedicated to showing that all knowledge derives from sense experience, devoted most of their attention to vision. And contemporary philosophy of perception is almost invariably focused on visual perception—and for many of the reasons advanced by Plato and Aristotle.[35] The chief reference work for anglophone philosophers for several decades contains this statement:

> Our visual experience . . . is not of seeing with our eyes. We can imagine a disembodied mind having visual experiences but not having tactile ones. Sight does not require our being part of the material world in the way in which feeling by touching does. . . . The directness of seeing when contrasted with hearing, its noninvolvement with its object when contrasted with feeling by touching, and its apparent temporal immediacy when contrasted with both hearing and feeling by touching are features that may partly explain the belief that sight is the most excellent of the senses.[36]

Note that this philosopher does not even consider smell and taste as candidates for excellence.

Even more important than the elevation of sight to the top of the sense hierarchy is the fact that the reasons advanced to distinguish sight from the other senses—even hearing—are also reasons that determine philosophical issues, that select questions to pursue because of their theoretical interest. Hans Jonas, a twentieth-century phenomenologist, articulated this point in a 1954 essay that sought to disclose and defend the reasons why sight has always had such a central role to play in philosophy. It is an instructive essay not only because of the topic but because Jonas's position in the mid–twentieth century demonstrates the continuity of certain assumptions about philosophy.

Jonas titled his essay "The Nobility of Sight," thus echoing an encomium that had been common for centuries. Three features of vision distinguish it from the other senses, Jonas observed. First, there is the simultaneity of the contents of the visual experience. What is seen before us is laid out all at once. Sight, unlike hearing or

---

[34] René Descartes, *Optics,* in *The Philosophical Writings of Descartes,* trans. John Cottingham, Robert Stoothoff, and Dugald Murdoch, 3 vols. (Cambridge: Cambridge University Press, 1985), 1:152.
[35] There are exceptions. Jay, *Downcast Eyes,* chap. 5, notes that not every European philosophy is so bound up with sight. The German hermeneutic tradition, for example, tends to valorize the sense of hearing.
[36] G. Vesey, "Vision," in *Encyclopedia of Philosophy,* ed. Paul Edwards, 8 vols. (London: Macmillan, 1967), 8:252.

touch, does not depend on temporal sequence for its operation: "It does so in an instant: as in a flash one glance, an opening of the eyes, discloses a world of co-present qualities spread out in space, ranged in depth, continuing into indefinite distance, suggesting, if any direction in their static order, then by their perspective a direction away from the subject rather than towards it."[37]

The other senses require a sequential experiencing of an event over time, which hinders detachment: "These more temporal senses therefore never achieve that degree of detachment of the signified from the sign, of persistent existence from the transitory event of sense-affection, which sight offers."[38] Jonas illustrates his points with contrasts to hearing and touch, which he believes are the only senses that are interestingly compared with sight. Smell and taste do not even come in for mention. Hearing is a more passive sense than sight, Jonas observes, because the percipient must wait for sound to occur. There is no equivalent of letting his gaze wander over a field of material already "out there."[39] Touch shares with hearing the fact that it requires sequential sensation over time. The objects of touch, shapes, are constructs that the mind must put together. Transience and time are the essence of "now," whereas sight presents an "extended present." This has profound effects on the congruence of this sense with philosophical ideas: "Indeed only the simultaneity of sight, with its extended 'present' of enduring objects, allows the distinction between change and the nonchanging and therefore between becoming and being. . . . Only sight provides the sensual basis on which the mind may conceive the idea of the eternal, that which never changes and is always present."[40]

The second feature of sight that distinguishes it from the other senses is "dynamic neutralization": one can see something without entering into a relationship with it. (Jonas has in mind a relationship of some physical intimacy, for the viewer does bear a relationship to the object of vision, such as "being in front of.") The thing seen does not need to affect the percipient in order to be seen. The contrast here is especially with the sense of touch. Touch requires a degree of force, at least pressure, against the skin. Sight is contemplatively uninvolved. And finally, Jonas invokes the significance of the spatial distance over which sight operates. Distance makes the first two features of vision possible. Sight is the "ideal distance sense," the only sense in which advantage lies with lack of proximity between percipient and object. In his conclu-

---

[37] Hans Jonas, "The Nobility of Sight," *Philosophy and Phenomenological Research* 14.4 (1954): 507. See the comments on this essay by Jay in *Downcast Eyes* and by Evelyn Fox Keller and Christine R. Grontkowski, "The Mind's Eye," in *Discovering Reality,* ed. Sandra Harding and Merrill B. Hintikka (Boston: D. Reidel, 1983).

[38] Jonas, "Nobility of Sight," p. 508.

[39] This characterization of auditory perception, questionable in any case, is challenged by the work of composers such as John Cage.

[40] Jonas, "Nobility of Sight," p. 513.

sion Jonas reiterates the features that not only elevate sight as the noblest sense but also outline its congruence with the interests that determine philosophical subjects:

> We even found, in each of the three aspects under which we treated vision, the ground for some basic concept of philosophy. *Simultaneity of presentation* furnishes the idea of enduring present, the contrast between change and the unchanging, between time and eternity. *Dynamic neutralization* furnishes form as distinct from matter, essence as distinct from existence, and the difference of theory and practice. *Distance* furnishes the idea of infinity.
>   Thus the mind has gone where vision pointed.[41]

If hearing and touch are thus disqualified as "philosophic senses," how much more useless for the intellect are the senses of taste and smell! They too demand time to experience, and they require intimate practical commerce with their objects in order to function. Practice is so requisite in the operation of taste that the very idea of a division between theory and practice is hard to conceive. Even more than touch, taste involves the body. The objects of taste must actually enter the body, and in most instances, they are actually devoured. Jonas's conception of philosophy requires that it maintain a level of abstraction that is as detached from singular bodily experience as possible.

Of course, philosophy itself has undergone some scourging critiques since Jonas wrote, many of which have called into question his assumptions about the importance of being over becoming and of theory over practice. This is one reason why reading a philosopher who both is a relative contemporary and represents an older set of assumptions is instructive in assessing the nature of the bodily senses and why they have figured so little in philosophy. Shortly I shall raise some questions about the intuitive adequacy of these judgments for the nature of taste. But in advance of that line of thought, and in preparation for it, let us put the ranking of the senses in another context. The conceptual framework that ranks the senses has aroused critical examination by philosophers whose projects have prompted revaluation of many of the ideas that Western intellectual tradition has come to take for granted. In fact, one can reassess the very analysis of vision that Jonas links to the framework of philosophical inquiry, and use it to argue that the sense hierarchy has blinkered philosophical investigation, causing it to screen out matters of considerable interest because of a skewed picture of what sorts of issues count as philosophical. A key to discovering what philosophy has omitted from its purview is provided by a consideration of gender.

---

[41] Ibid., p. 519.

On the most general level, the conventional ranking of two of the five senses as superior on epistemic, moral, and aesthetic grounds is congruent with several other basic presumptions employed widely in philosophy.[42] As we see from the reasons Plato and Aristotle advance in their studies of sense experience, this hierarchy accords with the elevation of mind over body; of reason over sense; of man over beast and culture over nature. It also lines up with another ranked pair of concepts not yet mentioned: the elevation of male over female and with "masculine" traits over those designated "feminine." It is significant that there is a gender dimension to the presumptions to be challenged here, for gendered concepts are often components of tenacious intellectual frameworks. In moral theory, philosophy of science, metaphysics, and epistemology, feminists have repeatedly traced a taproot back to the concept of reason, that faculty of the mind that both distinguishes human from nonhuman activity and supposedly elevates male over female. The result for many epistemologies is that the paradigmatic rational knower is male, while the female is regarded as more governed by the senses and by emotion. In moral theory, the model of responsibility and hardheaded justice is male, the female the image of vacillation and forgiveness. In politics the sphere of the male is public and abstract, associated with "mind"; that of the female, domestic and associated with the "body."[43] The pernicious effects of this binary conceptual structure include not just the value judgments involved in ranking one term of each pair over the other but also the comparative theoretical neglect of everything that is categorized with the inferior terms. We can see a specific variation of this way of thinking in theories of the senses.

In some respects Plato might be expected to be an exception to this general claim about philosophy, for his famous argument in *Republic* V that women of the ideal state should have equal standing with men is out of step not only with reigning Greek views of women but also with a good deal of later political theory.[44] While equality between the sexes is reaffirmed in the opening passages of the *Timaeus*, however, at the same time women are treated as inferior types of human beings, though the reasons are only implicit. Plato imagines that the earth was populated by a sort of reverse Darwinian evolution: First the gods created men, then from the reborn souls of men who lived poorly were produced women. Other creatures came into being through successive devolution, such as birds (lyrically, from light-minded

---

[42] Some of the ideas of the next few pages I first developed in "Gender Bias in Aesthetics," *American Philosophical Association Newsletter on Feminism and Philosophy* 89.2 (Winter 1990).

[43] The line of argument that discovers gender in putatively universal, neutral theory is familiar in feminist writings. Some sources include Genevieve Lloyd, *The Man of Reason: "Male" and "Female" in Western Philosophy* (Minneapolis: University of Minnesota Press, 1984); Luce Irigaray, *Speculum of the Other Woman* (1974), trans. Gillian C. Gill (Ithaca: Cornell University Press, 1985).

[44] For some feminist analyses of Plato, see Nancy Tuana, ed., *Feminist Interpretations of Plato* (University Park: Pennsylvania State University Press, 1994). Eva C. Keuls describes the pervasive misogyny of classical Athenian society in *The Reign of the Phallus: Sexual Politics in Ancient Athens* (Berkeley and Los Angeles: University of California Press, 1985).

men who occupied themselves too much with vision and were deluded into seeking truth in visual appearances) and quadrupeds (who live no longer by the mind at all but only the nonrational drives), and so on down to the creeping things of the ground and the seabeds (91a–92c). According to the sort of reincarnation of souls that Plato envisions, if a man does not lead a good life the first time around, he gets to try again in the lesser incarnation of a woman (42b). Conduct of one's life in an irrational manner is what warrants this demotion. Irrationality may be manifest in an excess of an ignoble emotion such as fear (producing cowardice) or an excessive indulgence in appetites. If those who so indulge merit punishment by being made to live again in a body whose inferiority suits the earlier wrongdoing, we may reasonably infer that women are considered inferior in powers of rational control and more apt to give in to the appetites and to the pleasures of the lower, bodily senses.

In other words, implicit in Plato's view is the belief that the ability to transcend the body, to govern the senses, to gain knowledge, is a masculine ability that when exercised well will keep one embodied as a male. There is, therefore, an implicit gendering of the use of the senses themselves, with the higher, distal senses of sight and hearing paired up with the controlling intellect of a virtuous man, and the lower, proximal senses with the appetites and the dangerous pleasures that are in one way or another associated with femininity. This is not a simple association, however. Women with complete faculties also obviously have all five senses, and rarely is it suggested that their senses actually function differently. The implausibility of applying such judgments to the class of real males and females indicates that we already have a split between some rather vague concept of "femininity" associated with the bodily senses and actual females—a split that is responsible for a great deal of incoherence in conceptual frameworks where gender lurks.

The presence of gendered reasoning in Aristotle's treatment of the sense hierarchy is apparent in a series of parallels and (only) apparently incidental claims. That Aristotle consistently denigrated females on metaphysical, epistemic, moral, political, and biological grounds is widely acknowledged. One commentator goes so far as to credit him as the single most influential thinker on this subject in the Western tradition: "Aristotle . . . was the first philosopher to develop a completely consistent set of answers to questions about sex identity that previous philosophers had raised. . . . Aristotle argued that differences between women and men were philosophically significant and that men were naturally superior to women."[45]

Aristotle defines the sexes in opposition to each other, building on the Pythagorean table of opposites that he summarizes in *Metaphysics* X. Whereas men are active, women are passive; men are hot, women are cold; men are fertile and perfect in human form, women are infertile and imperfect; men contribute the form to

---

[45] Prudence Allen, R.S.M., *The Concept of Woman: The Aristotelian Revolution, 750 B.C.–A.D. 1250* (Montreal: Eden Press, 1985), p. 83.

the development of embryos, women contribute only the matter. And so on. In short, "Aristotle grounded this relation of hostile opposition between women and men within the most fundamental of his metaphysical categories."[46]

The significance of gender for the senses emerges with Aristotle's view about how pleasures are managed. Unlike Plato, Aristotle wastes no time with the speculation that women and men might be equals within social classes. Women are by nature less competent than men because their rational faculties are less able to govern their appetites and emotions. With many of the binary relations, the first term designates the proper ruler over the second. This governing function inevitably imports social meaning into epistemic and metaphysical principles, for the proper ruler in the most intimate society, the family, is the husband and father. In the virtuous man / human being, the reason instructs the emotions and the appetites. The particular virtue of males in a family is to rule (taking the position of reason), and the particular virtue of a woman is to obey (taking the position of emotion and appetite). Once again, it seems that the distance senses are suited for the activities of men, the bodily senses for those of women.[47] It helps to add—as Aristotle and many others do—that the minds of women are less inclined to apprehend knowledge in an abstract, universal form, more inclined to particular judgments of sense.[48] Vision feeds the intellect and its universalizing abilities; the bodily senses are not calibrated for this activity but occupy one with the particular state of the body at the moment of sensation.

Another of Aristotle's peculiar tenets suggests grounds for doubting the reliability of women's sense of sight: Aristotle held that the gaze of menstruating women clouds mirrors and other reflecting surfaces. "For in the case of very bright mirrors, when women during their menstrual periods look into the mirror, the surface of the mirror becomes a sort of bloodshot cloud; and if the mirror is new, it is not easy to wipe off such a stain, while if it is old it is easier" (*On Dreams* 459b28–30). It would seem therefore that males and females have eyes that function somewhat differently a good deal of the time, and that the eyes of females are affected by a phenomenon that is distorting to the image seen. Aristotle did not invent this bit of folklore, but he did incorporate it into his systematic science and thereby lent his authority to its dissemination. (In 1612 the Englishman Henrie Peacham makes the same observa-

---

[46] Ibid., p. 89.

[47] "Throughout dominant Western religious and philosophical traditions, the 'virile' capacity for self-management is decisively coded as male": Susan Bordo, "Reading the Slender Body," in *Body / Politics: Women and the Discourses of Science,* ed. Mary Jacobus, Evelyn Fox Keller, and Sally Shuttleworth (New York: Routledge, 1990), p. 101.

[48] Though occasionally such conceptual arrangements remain only theoretical, they have practical consequences. For example, this view of the female mind has affected the kinds of education considered appropriate for women. Whitney Chadwick notes that the assumption that women were inept at mathematics prevented much education in linear perspective and affected the participation of females in the development of Renaissance painting. See *Women, Art, and Society* (London: Thames & Hudson, 1990), pp. 66–67.

tion, citing Aristotle.) Pliny the Elder added ivory and marble to the list of items that could be damaged and clouded by a woman's sight.

Thus we have in the basic hierarchy of the senses articulated by its theoretical originators an unexpected twist: certain senses are regarded as functioning in the development of traits assigned a masculine character, and others, sometimes by default, are considered feminine. Not because it is assumed that the senses actually operate differently in males and females (Aristotle's comment above notwithstanding), but because the virtues and achievements of the distance senses are considered masculine virtues on account of their contributions to the development of rational nature. And the weaknesses of the bodily senses by implication fall into the category designated "feminine." Of course, scientific studies of the senses have moved miles away from the speculations of the ancients. What relevance, therefore, do they have for our own understanding of the senses? When the senses are functioning in their ordinary, quotidian way, gender hardly surfaces. It is when they are used emblematically to signify something of social or cultural value that their gender dimension emerges. It is the value structure embedded in the sense hierarchy that persists beyond the ancient science of the senses. Plato and Aristotle are instructive because they both were so explicit in spelling out values that they saw following from the ways the body is involved in experience. Greek analyses of the senses were revised long ago; the value structure they employed has been naggingly persistent.

Where might these observations lead? If the cognitive, distance senses are framed in terms of achievements designated masculine, does this mean that bodily senses encompass a domain of retrievable "feminine" talents? While some have tried to argue this case, pursuing this route requires an exaggeration of the gendering of the senses, as well as a tendentiously selective treatment of their characteristics. For example, those who assume that there are early erotic drives that shape psychic development have linked philosophical with psychoanalytic modes of analysis and have questioned the emphasis that Freud placed on specular activity. Criticism of Freud's theories of the role of sight in psychosexual development, for example, leads Hélène Cixous to call vision the sense of a voyeur. Freud and Lacan emphasize the presence or absence of the signifier—penis or phallus—that can be seen. "A voyeur's theory, of course," quips Cixous, for a spectator can assume a viewing position at a safe distance from the object of his interest.[49] The sweeping survey of sight that Jonas praises as a mark of its nobility emerges here as furtive surveillance and a refusal of direct participation and involvement in the bodily senses. Luce Irigaray comes to a similar conclusion and singles out touch as a feminine realm with her statement: "Within this logic, the predominance of the visual, and of the discrimination and individualization of form, is particularly foreign to female eroticism. Woman takes

---

[49] Hélène Cixous, "Sorties," in Cixous and Catherine Clément, *The Newly Born Woman* (1975), trans. Betsy Wing (Minneapolis: University of Minnesota Press, 1986), p. 82.

pleasure more from touching than from looking, and her entry into a dominant scopic economy signifies, again, her consignment to passivity: she is to be the beautiful object of contemplation."[50]

Robin Schott and Susan Bordo have also found in values of epistemic objectivity and the distance of vision so prominent in those theories a masculine fear of the feminine world of particularity, birth, death, and impermanence.[51] The binary that consistently associates male with rationality and female with nonreason can be argued to underlie virtually all modes of organizing thought. Cixous sees this as a "subordination of the feminine to the masculine order, which gives the appearance of being the condition for the machinery's functioning."[52] She and Irigaray infuse a gendered analysis into what Martin Jay sees as a general tendency to reject the primacy of sight in twentieth-century French thought, amounting to a critique of what he whimsically calls "phallogocularcentrism." It has a sweeping relevance to the issue of the hierarchy of the senses. As Irigaray says, "Investment in the look is not as privileged in women as in men. More than any other sense, the eye objectifies and it masters. It sets at a distance, and maintains a distance. In our culture the predominance of the look over smell, taste, touch and hearing has brought about an impoverishment of bodily relations."[53]

However, while a web of gendered opposites subtends some of the deepest regions of philosophical analyses, including theories of the senses, it would be a mistake to flatten out the many roles of the senses and assign them gender too categorically. There are further accounts of gender and of the senses to consider. Evelyn Fox Keller and Christine Grontkowski are more sympathetic to the idea that knowledge finds an apt metaphor in vision. They argue that the problem of gender bias enters into discourse when the bodily eye is replaced by the notion of the "mind's eye," with its insistence that knowledge demands lack of involvement with the object of perception. They therefore suspect that insofar as there is bias in such theories, it has to do with the values of objectification and the suppression of desire, rather than with the mere employment of vision as the sensory metaphor for knowledge.[54]

In addition to such cautions regarding the sense of vision, the ascription of touch to a feminine domain ignores its complex employment. Touch may be considered feminine if certain erotic kinds of touching constitute the image conjured of this sense. It is certainly feminine if we romanticize the gentle touch of a mother. (Irigaray claims that the woman's desire for touching is given reign in maternity and in

[50] Luce Irigaray, *This Sex Which Is Not One* (1977), trans. Catherine Porter with Carolyn Burke (Ithaca: Cornell University Press, 1985), pp. 25–26.
[51] Robin May Schott, *Cognition and Eros: A Critique of the Kantian Paradigm* (Boston: Beacon, 1988); Susan Bordo, *The Flight to Objectivity: Essays on Cartesianism and Culture* (Albany: SUNY Press, 1987).
[52] Cixous, "Sorties," pp. 64–65.
[53] Luce Irigaray quoted in Jay, *Downcast Eyes*, p. 493.
[54] Keller and Grontkowski, "Mind's Eye."

caressing an infant.) But obviously touch may be violent as well as gentle. Even more important for the sense hierarchy are the similarities between touch and the two distance senses, such as the fact that their objects can be organized syntactically. Like vision and hearing, touch has objects that are discrete, repeatable, and organizable into complex wholes. This is the basis for Braille, a linguistic system that employs touch. As we have already seen, vision and touch are coordinate senses that come closer than others to apprehending objective qualities, a feature that has often been noted in the history of philosophy. Both vision and touch, for example, apprehend the Aristotelian common sensibles of dimension and shape. Augustine allied touch with sight and hearing insofar as each of these senses could be used to explore a public object that could thereby be a focus of common experience. By contrast, he noted that taste and smell take unique portions of their objects into the body, making the sensory event more private. ("When the palate tastes something pleasant, no matter how small a portion it is, it claims this for itself once and for all, and makes it become part of the body's nature.")[55] Brian O'Shaughnessy has argued that touch deserves to be considered first among the senses because of its direct contact with its objects and its indispensability for bodily experience, which yields a primacy for the knowledge it provides of the world at large. (He also observes without argument that "pretty plainly, by almost any yardstick smell and taste must share fourth and fifth position.")[56]

None of these considerations boosting the importance of touch suggest it may be appropriated as notably feminine. Nor indeed can any sense be. However, because of the linkage of intellect and cognition with the senses that may deliver common, public information about objects, I believe that the deeper potential for gender analysis resides with the two remaining bodily senses. So far, however, we have little more than a suggestive series of parallels and analogies between the lower senses and appetites and that vague conceptual dumping ground that has come to be labeled "the feminine."

What do we do with a set of analogies and comments that associate women with the less rational aspects of life and ipso facto to the lower senses? In particular, how do philosophers' comments about gender affect their thinking on the sense of taste? In short, what do these widely noted "associations" amount to? There are several speculative routes that more or less accuse philosophy of a systematic oversight. It could be the case, for example, that linking women with senses such as taste causes the latter to be denigrated in relation to the sight and hearing faculties. Or perhaps the converse is even more likely: the recognition of the lesser power and value of the lower, bodily senses causes them to be linked with femininity because it is the lesser

---

[55] Augustine, *The Free Choice of the Will,* trans. Robert P. Russell, O.S.A. (Washington, D.C.: Catholic University of America, 1968), p. 128.
[56] Brian O'Shaughnessy, "The Sense of Touch," *Australasian Journal of Philosophy* 67.1 (March 1989): 37.

valued term of that pair of opposites. It is likely that patterns of social life account for the linkage to some extent, for in many historical periods and societies there is a public–domestic distinction that figures as another binary set. Thus if the business of preparing meals is the job of women, servants, slaves (and of course women are in all those categories), then food, the sense of taste, and gustatory appetites reside in the wrong social place to merit much notice.[57]

On a more theoretical level, we can also see how the content of traditional philosophical discussion has been strongly affected by gender considerations. Rationality standardly defines man and distinguishes his capacities above those of other animals, which are considered to share other faculties such as passions and appetites.[58] Insofar as dispositions regarded as characteristic of feminine weakness are believed to fall short of rational excellence, they are less interesting objects to study in an effort to comprehend the important and unique traits of human nature. Therefore, major attention is directed only to the "masculine" subjects. (Commonplaces about women, female nature, and the feminine tend to be repeated but not to be examined as the central point of a theoretical investigation. In fact, in many writings the remarks regarding women and "the feminine" do not really amount to theories at all— just to conventional stereotypes that attach to conceptual systems so deep they appear self-evident truths that do not require skeptical scrutiny.) When not simply ignored, the bodily senses are actively denigrated for their base nature and danger. Identifying certain senses both as superior and as serving the particular defining characteristics of humanity brings about a neglect of the other senses.

Moreover, the great treachery of the body is that it is not always governable. Whatever is awry scientifically with Platonic or Aristotelian psychologies, each presents its own vivid picture of a soul divided against itself, of character tendencies in conflict. Plato's image of the beast in the belly threatening to overtake the mind doubtless overrates the intellect and separates intelligence from the body in ways that suffer under scrutiny. But still his image vividly captures a familiar phenomenal truth: the war between what one knows one ought to do and the overwhelming power of what one wants at the moment. While desires may have many kinds of objects, when their control is required they invariably refer to the two dangerous appetites: for food and for sex. And the commonly employed figure of temptation for sexual desire is the body of a woman.[59] Everything associated with bodily desires

---

[57] See also Sherry Ortner's argument in "Is Female to Male as Nature Is to Culture?" in *Women, Culture, and Society,* ed. Michelle Zimbalist Rosaldo and Louise Lamphere (Stanford: Stanford University Press, 1974).

[58] Often included in the faculties that are designated "animal" are emotions. Emotions are immensely complex intentional states, however, and all but the very basic emotions such as fear and anger are arguably as unique to human beings as rational deliberation.

[59] This generalization is complicated but I think not refuted by Greek homosexuality, for the ideal homosexual union was with a person of equal intellectual virtue and social status. The temptation a woman

that might overrule reason requires control. All these factors contribute to—indeed overdetermine—a general neglect of the sense of taste and its complicated objects: meals, feasts, rituals, and routines.

The neglect is not easily mended. One cannot simply add taste and the other bodily senses to philosophy as it has evolved and correct theories accordingly to be more comprehensive in their treatment of sensory worlds. Jonas's reasons for why sight is the noble sense make this clear: philosophy is (or at least used to be) built upon attention to the eternal over the temporal, to the universal over the particular, to theory over practice. Taste is a sense that is not suited to advance the first term of any of these pairs. (In fact, one philosopher has speculated that if an activity such as cooking were the focus of attention for theorists, the distinction between theory and practice might not evolve at all.)[60]

Philosophy contains some gaps that are only now visible, having been previously hidden because the assumptions about what constitutes a philosophical question were so widely shared as to have become invisible. These omissions and distortions have led theory to develop in ways that overlook important beliefs and practices and that ignore living values. Theoretical treatments of the sense of taste frequently contravene the ways we actually employ that sense and its objects, which is one symptom of the fact that working, practical beliefs and theories are seriously divergent.

Is the territory of taste really so bereft of interesting philosophical questions of its own? Or rather, have theoreticians prematurely dismissed complex issues because they were already assuming the unimportance of the bodily senses and the baseness of their pleasures? The elaborate objects of taste alone should lead one to reject the simple judgment that this sense yields no interesting philosophical problems. We use our taste sense with immense complexity. The remarkable thing is that it has been left so innocent of theoretical exploration.

Long ago a Mexican nun pondered the activities that prompt philosophical thinking and observed how often her own mind was stimulated in the kitchen. While Sor Juana Inés de la Cruz did not herself pursue food or its taste as a topic for study, perhaps she was right when she remarked, "Had Aristotle cooked, he would have written a good deal more."[61]

---

represents is only bodily. Kenneth J. Dover, *Greek Homosexuality* (Cambridge: Harvard University Press, 1978), discusses this complex social practice. For contrast between homosexual attraction and relations between men and women, see esp. pp. 12, 103–4, 106, 149.

[60] Lisa Heldke, "Recipes for Theory Making," in *Cooking, Eating, Thinking: Transformative Philosophies of Food* (Bloomington: Indiana University Press, 1992).

[61] Sor Juana Inés de la Cruz (1648 or 1651–95), *The Answer / La Respuesta,* ed. and trans. Electa Arenal and Amanda Powell (New York: Feminist Press, 1994), p. 75

CHAPTER 2

Philosophies of Taste:
Aesthetic and Nonaesthetic Senses

Although the hierarchy of the senses has resulted in scant attention directed to the literal sense of taste, there is a great deal of philosophy concerning taste of a metaphorical sort: aesthetic discrimination. The use of the term "taste" to refer to an ability to discern beauty and other aesthetic qualities is intriguing and paradoxical, for literal, gustatory taste is by and large excluded from among the chief subjects of the theories of taste that become prominent in Enlightenment European philosophy. The sense of taste provides the language, indeed the conceptual framework, that fosters theoretical understanding of aesthetic appreciation of works of art. That sense itself, however, is eclipsed as the concept of the aesthetic develops philosophical rigor and depth. In fact the earlier ranking of the intellectual or distance senses over the bodily senses now expands to include a distinction between aesthetic and nonaesthetic senses that confirms the same hierarchy. Moreover, this classification prompts a parallel distinction between sense experiences that permit the development of art forms and those that do not. The objects of taste, food and drink, are presumed to be only items of nourishment, necessary for bodily sustenance but too ephemeral to merit theoretical address in the way that works of art demand.

Since we shall now be dealing with both literal, gustatory taste and analogic or metaphorical, aesthetic taste, the terms distinguishing the two are apt to become cumbersome with modifiers. Therefore in this chapter I shall skip the qualifying adjectives and simply use "taste" with a lowercase *t* when I refer to the actual sense of taste, and "Taste" with a capital *T* to refer to aesthetic Taste—that type of Taste signified in the expression "philosophies of Taste" or the "philosophical problem of Taste."

"Taste": From Literal to Analogic Usage

Philosophers occasionally take note of the degree to which their theories make use of metaphoric language.[1] Plato may have been the first to call attention to the heuris-

---

[1] This use of the term "metaphor" is its general connotation, whereby systematic comparisons are structured into a variety of linguistic expressions. It does not distinguish among analogy, simile, metonymy, metaphor in the stricter sense, etc.

tic use of sensory images to illuminate the world of abstractions, but twentieth-century thinkers have been particularly reflective on the subject. Metaphors, remarks Iris Murdoch, are "fundamental forms of our awareness of our condition: metaphors of space, metaphors of movement, metaphors of vision." Philosophical systems, she believes, can often be understood as explorations of centrally important images. Indeed, it seems to her "impossible to discuss certain kinds of concepts without resort to metaphor, since the concepts are themselves deeply metaphorical, and cannot be analysed into non-metaphorical components without a loss of substance."[2] Mark Johnson agrees and observes that discoveries in cognitive science provide empirical evidence for claims about metaphor that previously were largely intuitive, namely, that "metaphor is not merely a linguistic phenomenon, but more fundamentally, a conceptual and experiential process that structures our world."[3]

If these observations are correct, then metaphoric language is not simply the colorful application of terms from one domain in another for decorative or rhetorical purposes, such that the basic things that positively need to be said can be uttered without the use of metaphor. Metaphors constitute parts of the webs of meaning from which conceptual frameworks emerge. If metaphoric language is so crucial to developing the sorts of systematic relations among ideas that we call philosophies, then the choice of images to serve as theoretic metaphors calls for judicious reflection.

Philosophy frequently employs *sensory* metaphors in the conduct of its conceptual exploration, as though this most abstract of endeavors requires grounding in familiar perceptual experience. More specifically, as we saw in Chapter 1, the degree to which philosophy relies on metaphors of *vision* is striking. Murdoch herself, following Plato, employs the notions of looking, of the gaze, of the sun, of attention outward to describe the progress of moral understanding. More critically, Jacques Derrida observes that all philosophical discourse (though he has in mind metaphysics in particular) comprises "metaphorical contents of the sensory type." He adds—ironically for aesthetics—that "thus one does actually speak of visual, auditory, and tactile metaphors (where the problem of knowledge is in its element), and even, more rarely, which is not insignificant, olfactory or gustatory ones."[4] Aesthetic theory, in almost unique contrast to the other labeled subfields of philosophy, does make heavy use of the sensory model of *taste*. Even aesthetics, however, embraces gustatory language reluctantly, for within most theories aesthetic Taste seeks to attain the detachment and contemplative distance of vision, leaving the literal sense that provides the metaphor behind. Parallels and tensions between aesthetic Taste

---

[2] Iris Murdoch, *The Sovereignty of Good* [1970] (London: Routledge, 1991), p. 77.
[3] Mark Johnson, "Introduction: Why Metaphor Matters to Philosophy," *Metaphor and Symbolic Activity* 10.3 (1995): 157.
[4] Jacques Derrida, "White Mythology," in *Margins of Philosophy*, trans. Alan Bass (Chicago: University of Chicago Press, 1982), p. 227.

and the gustatory sense are especially dramatic in the formative period of aesthetic theory.

A distinctive approach to perception, pleasure, beauty, and art emerges in eighteenth-century European philosophy. These writings make central the notion of Taste, conceived as a sensitivity to fine distinctions and an ability to discern beauty, and in this period the concept is widely developed in writings sufficiently different from their predecessors that a new field with its own name comes to be distinguished within philosophy: aesthetics. As Luc Ferry remarks:

> The birth of aesthetics as a philosophical discipline is permanently linked to the radical mutation the representation of the beautiful undergoes when the latter is thought of in terms of *taste* and, therefore, using as starting point that which in the human being soon comes to seem the very essence of subjectivity, the most subjective within the subject. With the concept of taste the beautiful is placed in a relation to human subjectivity so intimate that it may even be defined by the pleasure it provides, by the *sensations* or sentiments it provokes in us.[5]

As the discourse of aesthetics develops, there comes a period when the sense of taste stands right next to aesthetic Taste in philosophical writings. Indeed, at certain points it almost seems to be invited into the company of recognized philosophical subjects. Though I shall argue shortly that taste is eventually excluded from philosophies of Taste, let us begin by noting how observations about taste furthered the growing field of aesthetic theory. For the first point to make about taste as it appears in the intellectual tradition of early modern philosophy is a positive one: of all the senses, the gustatory sense seems most disposed to employment in aesthetic contexts. While examples of the apprehension of beauty are frequently drawn from visual experience (the sight of a flower, a design, a well-executed painting), the actual operation of the appreciative reaction is compared to the savoring of a flavor in which perception and pleasure merge. Taste comes to provide the chief analogy by which the apprehension of the beautiful and of fine artistic qualities and even social style is explicated.

The English term "taste" has had several meanings in its history, all of which relate in some way to the idea of intimate acquaintance with an object by means of one's own sensory experience.[6] Precursor terms include usages that mean to touch, to smell, and to test. Also of relevance is the fact that a "taste" of something has a quantitative connotation—a very small amount, one that requires careful discern-

---

[5] Luc Ferry, *Homo Aestheticus: The Invention of Taste in the Democratic Age,* trans. Robert de Loaiza (Chicago: University of Chicago Press, 1993), p. 19.
[6] Oxford English Dictionary (1971), s.v. "Taste."

ment even to notice. And of course "taste" also refers to personal dispositions and preferences, as in the expression "to have a taste for" something, whether a food or an activity or a type of object. The sensation of tasting seems to carry a virtually inescapable affective valence: tasting involves registering the sensation as pleasant or unpleasant. Therefore this sense provides a suitable analog for judgments of the quality of experience by means of immediate, subjective approval.

The metaphor of Taste fosters interest in unique qualities of objects that seize attention because of their fine character, summed up in the term "beauty." Beauty is an elusive concept. Objects found to be beautiful display so much variety that it is impossible to specify what constitutes beauty in general. While some writers thought they could identify an objective correlate to beauty, few argued that the presence of beauty could actually be inferred from correlative qualities. Moreover, not every percipient is able to make the particular judgment of Taste, for such discernment requires the development of a special sensitivity. This becomes an important theoretical meaning that Taste carries when it assumes centrality in aesthetic theory: an ability to judge the fine points of an individual object, the presence of which cannot be inferred from principles or rules. "Taste" designates a type of apprehension that does not yield knowledge about the causes of sensation or about the principles that govern the phenomenon, but rather provides an evaluative assessment about the immediate object of experience, perceived directly through firsthand acquaintance and the subjective feelings that arise in response.[7] This capacity comes to be seen as a type of good judgment whereby one responds appropriately to art and beautiful objects of nature.

The language that governs discussions about beauty and art was established well before the eighteenth century. The connection between taste and appreciative judgment can be found as early as the fifteenth century, but it was in the seventeenth century that the usage spread.[8] In Spanish, Italian, English, French, German, the practice spread of using literal taste (*gusto, goût, Geschmack*) analogically to describe an

---

[7] Some of these generalizations about the operation of the sense of taste are questionable, and indeed can be seen to reflect the typology of the lower senses as somehow more "natural" and less rational than the higher senses. Here I am accepting this classic characterization of taste because of its role in the historical debate, but in the next chapter some of these claims will be challenged.

[8] Comprehensive analyses of this development include David Summers, *The Judgment of Sense: Renaissance Naturalism and the Rise of Aesthetics* (Cambridge: Cambridge University Press, 1987); Jeffrey Barnouw, "The Beginnings of 'Aesthetics' and the Leibnizian Conception of Sensation," in *Eighteenth-Century Aesthetics and the Reconstruction of Art,* ed. Paul Mattick, Jr. (Cambridge: Cambridge University Press, 1993); Dabney Townsend, "Taste: Early History," in *Encyclopedia of Aesthetics,* ed. Michael Kelly, 4 vols. (New York: Oxford University Press, 1998), vol. 4; Giorgio Tonelli, "Taste in the History of Aesthetics from the Renaissance to 1770," in *Dictionary of the History of Ideas,* ed. Philip P. Weiner, 5 vols. (New York: Scribner, 1973), vol. 4. For an account of the earlier philosophy leading up to theories of Taste, see Umberto Eco, *Art and Beauty in the Middle Ages,* trans. Hugh Bredin (New Haven: Yale University Press, 1986).

ability to discern what eventually would be designated aesthetic qualities. (Both Addison and Voltaire remarked that this dual meaning of the term was widespread in many languages.)[9] Taste is construed as the ability to perceive beautiful qualities and to discriminate fine differences among the objects of perception, differences that might escape notice by someone without Taste. The terminology of early theories centers on beauty, though many types of aesthetic discrimination tend to be lumped together under Taste, whether the subject be delight in the beauties of nature or the appreciation of complex artistic compositions. ("Taste" also refers to social sensitivity and is thus a term of manners as well.) As the eighteenth century advances, other qualities become equally important, such as novelty, sublimity, harmony, the picturesque, and so on; eventually the language of theory takes refuge in the unity possible with a general concept of aesthetic pleasure.

Along with the exploration of the taste metaphor, the very term "aesthetic" also appears in modern philosophy. It was adapted from the Greek term referring to sense perception by Alexander Baumgarten, who employed "aesthetic" to refer to a science of sense perception. He contrasts *aestheta,* or things perceived, to *noeta,* or things known, which make up the content of intellectual knowledge and are objects of logic.[10] Baumgarten was especially interested in poetry, which he argued presents particular representations vividly, though it does not provide a general understanding of the ideas it presents, which would require the logical faculty of the intellect.[11]

Certain philosophical questions are already apparent in the analogical use of taste for a faculty that discerns artistic qualities and makes value judgments of beauty. One of the first issues of debate concerns the mental status of Taste. Is this capacity related to the use of reason? Or—as the metaphoric expression would suggest— does it signal a more immediate reaction akin to a sense experience or a sentiment? Whether Taste is a function of rational faculties or of sentiment is a matter for debate

---

[9] Joseph Addison, "Pleasures of the Imagination I," *Spectator,* no. 409 (1712); Voltaire, entry on "Goût" ("Taste") in Diderot and D'Alembert's *Encyclopédie* (1757).

[10] Alexander Baumgarten, *Reflections on Poetry* (1735), trans. Karl Aschenbrenner and William B. Holther (Berkeley and Los Angeles: University of California Press, 1954) p. 78. In Baumgarten's 1750 work, *Aesthetica,* the term "aesthetic" became particularly associated with beauty. In the *Critique of Pure Reason* (1781) Kant used "aesthetic" to refer to sense perception; in the *Critique of Judgment* (1790) he employed it to refer to judgments of Taste, or the judgment that something is beautiful. The term "aesthetic" was not used in English until the nineteenth century.

The distinction drawn between *aestheta* and *noeta* relates to debates about clear and distinct ideas and to the philosophies of Descartes and Leibniz and their followers. Baumgarten argued that *aestheta* were clear but confused; that is, not analyzed and classified according to their representation of universals. *Noeta* are both clear and distinct. *Aestheta* provide particular knowledge, which is inferior to the general knowledge attainable by the intellect. See Benedetto Croce, *Aesthetic as Science of Expression and General Linguistic,* trans. Douglas Ainslie (New Brunswick, N.J.: Transaction, 1995), pt. 2, chap. 4, for a critical exposition of Baumgarten.

[11] Although the aesthetic faculty is inferior in its knowledge to the intellectual faculty, aesthetic experience is still a type of cognition. As we shall see shortly, this cognitive element of the notion of the aesthetic temporarily disappears from theoretical view as the discipline develops.

in the seventeenth and eighteenth centuries, with sense, sensibility, or sentiment (the terminology varies) gaining the edge, at least until Kant's complicated solution of the *Critique of Judgment*. This triumph of sensibility over rationality diminishes acknowledgment of the cognitive elements of aesthetic enjoyment in the most influential theories of eighteenth-century philosophy.[12] Nonetheless, a feature of taste that makes it an appropriate metaphor for aesthetic Taste is precisely that it *is* a sense, and as such it is understood as a disposition to respond to qualities immediately perceived.

Not only is gustatory taste the comparative foundation for judgments of aesthetic Taste, in certain ways the sense of taste seems to work just like aesthetic Taste. The literal taste experience, like the discernment of aesthetic qualities, requires individual experience. One cannot judge the taste of a stew without tasting the actual stew to be judged; nor can one infer from reading the recipe that this particular meal is successful. (One can say that the recipe sounds as if it will be good, but the proof of the pudding is always in the eating.) Just as a particular painting or poem must be actually experienced before it can evoke the subjective response indicative of beauty, so food must be chewed and swallowed in one's own mouth, its flavors released against one's own tongue. Both aesthetic objects and food and drink are "savored" or "relished" as part of the assessment, and gustatory metaphors continue in this choice of language. And—importantly—both are intensely bound up with pleasure or pain reactions. Disapproval is more than an intellectual judgment; it involves distaste—again both literal and metaphorical. (Particularly strong aversions evoke disgust.) This is another aspect of the fact that they are importantly subjective—constitutively a response of the subject him- or herself. The alleged subjectivity of taste will be the focus of more exacting scrutiny later. For now, let us see how taste was embraced as close kin to the appreciation of beauty in some of the formative texts of modern aesthetics.

Early in the eighteenth century the abbé Dubos appealed to gustatory taste in his argument that aesthetic judgment is based on feeling rather than reason:

> Does one reason in order to know if a ragout is good or if it is bad, and does it ever occur to anyone, after having posed the geometrical principles of flavor and defined the qualities of each ingredient which makes up the composition of foods, to discuss the proportions of their mixture, in order to decide if the ragout is good? One never does this. We have in us a sense designed in order to know if the chef has followed the rules of his art. One tastes the ragout, and without knowing the rules, one knows if it is good. It is the same in some re-

---

[12] This historical development is criticized at length by Hans-Georg Gadamer, *Truth and Method*, trans. Joel Weinsheimer and Donald G. Marshall (New York: Continuum, 1989), pt. 1.

spect with the works of the mind and with pictures made in order to please and move us.[13]

Voltaire's short essay on Taste in Diderot and D'Alembert's *Encyclopédie* follows a long entry on taste of the literal sort by the chevalier de Jaucourt. Both authors make note of the ease with which "taste" switches between a sense for flavors and a liking for art. ("Taste in general is the excitation of an organ that delights in its object. . . . One has taste for music and painting, just as for ragouts," observes Jaucourt, appealing again to stews.) Voltaire pursues the comparison further, finding the two species of taste similar not only in the immediacy of their responses but also in their need for education. Taste, asserts Voltaire, "is a quick discernment like that of the tongue and the palate, and which, like them, anticipates reflection; like the palate, it voluptuously relishes what is good; and it rejects the bad with loathing; it is also, like the palate, often uncertain and doubtful . . . and sometimes requires habit to help it form."[14] Learning good habits through proper education is an indispensable qualification that enters into the development of the ability called Taste. Like the sense organ, Taste presumes a natural disposition to notice the qualities that give rise to aesthetic enjoyments; but this disposition needs to be trained and refined in order that good Taste be the outcome. *L'homme de goût*—the ideal man of Taste—is a product of careful cultivation.

Though the focus here is the development of the aesthetic concepts of Enlightenment Europe, it is worth noting that the sense of taste is employed as a term of aesthetic discrimination in other philosophical traditions as well. Probably the most elaborate theoretical placement of taste in aesthetic theory occurs in the Indian tradition, in which *rasa* designates a host of experiences and qualities in both foods and arts. The simplest and most literal sense of *rasa* refers to the juice of plants, but there are multiplied meanings that build upon this basis. It connotes the distilled essence of a thing, its taste or flavor, the relish a perceiver takes in encountering it. And as a quality of a cultivated object, including a work of art, *rasa* designates the heightened state of aesthetic awareness and enjoyment of a perceiver or audience. Thus Indian aesthetics refers both to the *rasa* of an object—the qualities to be appreciated—and to the experience of *rasa*. The term also designates the expressive power of art; the capture of emotional states in works of art may be likened to the combination of spices and foods in fine cooking. Bharata, who discussed the concept of *rasa* some nineteen centuries ago, remarks: "How is *rasa* tasted? [In reply] it is said that just as well-disposed persons while eating food cooked with many kinds of spices enjoy its

---

[13] Abbé Jean-Baptiste Dubos, *Réflexions critiques sur la poésie et sur la peinture* (1719; 2d ed. 1770) (Geneva: Slatkine, 1967), p. 225.

[14] Chevalier Louis de Jaucourt and Voltaire, entries s.v. "Goût" in Diderot and D'Alembert, *Encyclopédie*.

taste, and attain pleasure and satisfaction, so the cultured people taste the durable emotional states while they see them represented by an expression of the various emotional states with words, gestures, and derive pleasure and satisfaction."[15] The development of the meanings and uses of *rasa* over its long history is considerably more complex than the use of "taste" and its equivalents in European languages. But there are still noticeable similarities in the manipulation of a term of sense experience to refer to cultivated discrimination, to qualities of objects and of experiences and judgments, to the delight to be obtained in the particular and unique qualities of art. One hesitates to label the selection of taste as metaphor for aesthetic sensibility "natural," for this phenomenon is highly acculturated and is clearly variant across history and society. Nonetheless, taste certainly appears to be a concept that is ready to hand and suitable to express appreciative experience of art and other objects of aesthetic import. This very subjective bodily sense appears in a variety of traditions to offer a way of exploring elusive and otherwise nearly ineffable aesthetic values. This fact presents an irony to theories in which the sense hierarchy classifies literal taste as a lower sense, for it is this sense that readily furnishes a way to express experience and appreciation of the highest and most refined creations of culture.

Given the enthusiasm with which gustatory taste was exploited to analyze aesthetic discrimination, one might have expected it to develop a theoretical place of its own within philosophy. However, despite the power of the metaphor and the enthusiastic comparisons advanced by writers such as Dubos and Voltaire, modern European aesthetic theory eventually leaves literal taste behind altogether. The reason is partly that in the European context in which "Taste" develops as a theoretical term, the subjectivity of taste—the very quality of this sense that disposes it to aesthetic parallels—also poses a stubborn philosophical problem. Solutions to this problem permit aesthetic Taste to take its place in philosophical systems only because of the manner in which it differs from gustatory taste. To fail to note the differences between the two kinds of taste is to stop short of dealing with the pressing philosophical issue that faced eighteenth-century European philosophy: the threat of relativism to concepts of value and the consequent search for grounds to support claims of universal validity for value judgments. To understand why taste is a component of most aesthetic theory only in its metaphorical usage, we need to consider the problems faced by the theorists who developed analyses of beauty that became known as philosophies of Taste.

---

[15] Quoted in B. N. Goswamy, "*Rasa*: Delight of the Reason," in *Aesthetics in Perspective,* ed. Kathleen M. Higgins (Fort Worth: Harcourt Brace, 1996), p. 694. This essay is taken from Goswamy, *The Essence of Indian Art* (San Francisco: Asian Art Museum of San Francisco, 1986). See also Kanti Chandra Pandey, *Comparative Aesthetics,* vol. 1: *Indian Aesthetics* (Varanasi: Rameshwar Pathak, 1959); and Ananda K. Coomaraswamy, *Introduction to Indian Art* (Delhi: Munshiram Manoharlal, 1969).

The Problem of Taste

The so-called problem of Taste, briefly, is this: Aesthetic reactions are subjective because they constitutively involve pleasure. Yet judgments about beauty and about the values of art are more important than are mere reports of subjective states, and so they demand shared standards of assessment. How can a philosophy of Taste acknowledge the subjectivity of the aesthetic response and also accommodate the more than subjective importance of judgments of Taste? How, in other words, can a subjectivist position avoid relativism and give the object of appreciation its due? These questions had particular urgency in eighteenth-century debate because of changing analyses of the ontological status of beauty.

For some centuries before empiricism achieved dominance in seventeenth- and eighteenth-century European philosophy (especially anglophone philosophy), an eclectic brand of Platonism reigned in theoretical understandings of beauty. Such approaches are called "Platonist" because they assume that the faculty of the mind that apprehends beauty is a rational faculty, and because beauty is treated as an objective quality. The status of beauty had always been a bit mysterious because no uncontroversial objective quality could be correlated regularly with subjective feelings of appreciation. Discomfort about an objective correlate for beauty is revealed in the common French invocation of an elusive "je ne sais quoi" that makes objects beautiful, a phrase referring to some beauty-making property that resists articulate analysis. But under the growing influence of empiricism beauty was denied the status of objective quality altogether and analyzed as simply a species of pleasure. Because of other shifts in theories of perception and of value that were taking place in philosophy, the identification of beauty with pleasure raised a host of new problems that also affected the conception of Taste.

The early, influential British theory that formulated the problem of Taste derived many of its terms of analysis from John Locke.[16] Locke himself says little directly about beauty, but he offers an analysis of the operation of the mind that others modified into philosophies of Taste. In his *Essay Concerning Human Understanding* (1690), Locke argues that all "ideas"—an empiricist umbrella term used to refer to any contents of the mind—are derived ultimately from simple sense experience, that the contents of the mind are ultimately the result of contact by organs of perception with the external world.[17] Ideas may be of sensation—immediate sense experience—or of reflection—mental operations performed on other ideas; moreover,

---

[16] Dabney Townsend, "Lockean Aesthetics," *Journal of Aesthetics and Art Criticism* 49.4 (Fall 1991). Townsend argues, however, that few early aesthetic theories were really consistently empiricist. See also Carolyn Korsmeyer, "The Eclipse of Truth in the Rise of Aesthetics," *British Journal of Aesthetics* 29.4 (Autumn 1989).

[17] John Locke, *Essay Concerning Human Understanding* (1690), bk. 2, chap. 8, sec. 8, in *Collected Works* (Freeport, N.Y.: Books for Libraries Press, 1969), 1:243.

ideas may be simple or complex. Simple ideas are mental images of shapes, colors, texture, taste, and so on, and in combination they become components of complex ideas. The qualities perceived as belonging to bodies may be divided into two classes. Primary qualities (shape, size, solidity, states of motion and rest, etc.) belong to bodies as they are in themselves, considered in abstraction from their effects on human perceivers. Secondary qualities (color, sound, taste, etc.) are really just powers on the part of bodies to cause in us various simple ideas, ideas that in no way resemble or accurately depict their unknown physical causes. The mind, according to Locke, is able to operate on ideas but can add nothing of its own to them. It can abstract ideas from the various situations under which they were originally impressed; it can separate complex ideas into parts; and it can compose them again into new complex ideas. All mental processes involve such operations on ideas, but never can there be an idea the elements of which are not ultimately traceable to a sensible source.

Needless to say, beauty is denied objective existence. Locke speaks of beauty as a "mixed mode," which is a complex idea made up of simple ideas of different varieties, including pleasure and pain. Mixed modes, says Locke, are "compounded of simple ideas of several kinds, put together to make one complex one; v.g. beauty, consisting of a certain composition of colour and figure, causing delight in the beholder."[18] Beauty does not even have the obvious objective stimuli that ideas of secondary qualities do, and there is no universal agreement as to which objects prompt a perception of beauty. The variable in this phenomenon is one of the elements of the mixed mode: delight or pleasure. There is no guarantee that the color and figure that cause delight in one viewer will cause delight in another.

The danger of relativism incipient in this analysis of beauty is even clearer when we consider the understanding of pleasure that held sway in the seventeenth century. Pleasure was standardly regarded as a feeling that arises when some self-directed interest or desire is gratified. If pleasure is the crucial constituent of beauty, then beauty too partakes of the individual variability that characterizes pleasure. Thomas Hobbes, notorious for his egocentric and relativistic theory of value, presented an analysis of pleasure that, to many, spelled out the dangers of this approach. Hobbes's treatment of pleasure advances two basic tenets: that all action is motivated by desire or aversion, and that human beings, having both a selfish nature and insatiable appetites, always act in ways calculated to maximize their self-interest. Thus the pleasure that constitutes the beautiful is merely a signal of the self-interest that the observer might feel in response to the possible advantage that may appear in some object. Since not all people desire the same things, the use of these terms is relative to the user. "For these words of good, evil, contemptible, are ever

---

[18] Ibid., chap. 12, sec. 5, p. 281.

used with relation to the person that useth them: there being nothing simply and absolutely so; nor any common rule of good and evil, to be taken from the nature of the objects themselves."[19]

On Hobbes's account the assessment of value qualities is still a function of reason, which calculates the personal advantages and disadvantages of situations in the process of finding them beautiful or good. This analysis has ominous consequences for a theory of Taste: if beauty (the object of the judgment of Taste) is pleasure, and pleasure indicates appearance of the satisfaction of desire, and desire is directed toward the self, then judgments of Taste are not only subjective (referring to a feeling rather than a quality independently existing outside the mind) but also relative (differing from perceiver to perceiver as the governing self-interests do). This restricted catalog of pleasures, the role of rational calculation of personal advantage in the experience of beauty, and the connection of pleasure with the fulfillment of a self-interested desire were assailed in the subsequent flurry of aesthetic and moral theories refuting the egocentric core of Hobbes's philosophy.

Few philosophers of the period were happy with the idea that value judgments are merely manifestations of relative, selfish interests. (Unsettling enough for matters of Taste and judgments about beauty and art, this conclusion seemed catastrophic for moral theory and ideas about good and bad behavior.) The conclusion that beauty is a type of pleasure, however, was fairly well fixed. Most theorists of value, therefore, devoted considerable time to revising the understanding of pleasure. They sought to show that pleasures were neither always directed to the self nor relative to the individual. The variations on this theme are manifold.[20] The fundamental move, which early writers of the century such as Lord Shaftesbury and Francis Hutcheson pioneered and Kant later systematized in the *Critique of Judgment,* was to recognize and analyze a type of pleasure that is not the signal of a satisfaction of desire, a pleasure that thus must be completely free from selfish interest or personal concern. This exigency contributes centrally to the theoretical separation of literal taste from aesthetic Taste.

In his *Inquiry into the Original of Our Ideas of Beauty and Virtue* (1725) Francis Hutcheson built upon Locke's theory of ideas, reducing beauty and the various qualities of moral approval to pleasure. Unlike Locke, Hutcheson did not view beauty as

[19] Thomas Hobbes, *The English Works of Thomas Hobbes of Malmesbury,* ed. Sir William Molesworth, 11 vols. (London: J. Bohn, 1839–45), 3:40–41. Hobbes distinguishes between two kinds of pleasures: sensual pleasures—largely the gratification of the senses of taste and touch—and pleasures of the mind. The latter—which include both aesthetic pleasures and the bases of moral assessments—come about by the fulfillment of imaginative expectation. A useful discussion of these points is to be found in C. D. Thorpe, *The Aesthetic Theory of Thomas Hobbes* (Ann Arbor: University of Michigan Press, 1940).
[20] See Peter Kivy, "Recent Scholarship and the British Tradition: A Logic of Taste—The First Fifty Years," in *Aesthetics: A Critical Anthology,* ed. George Dickie and R. J. Sclafani (New York: St. Martin's Press, 1977).

a mixed mode that is assembled by the mind. For him, beauty is perceived directly and passively, like the ideas of sense experience.[21] Since pleasure is a sensation, it must have a sense organ to receive it. Hutcheson refers to this as an "inner sense," by which he means a capacity of human beings to enjoy, to receive pleasure of a certain sort: "the word *beauty* is taken for the *idea raised in us,* and a *sense* of beauty for *our power of receiving this idea.*"[22] The propensity to receive this idea is common to human nature, Hutcheson thought (a claim that will be explored over and over throughout the century), and the job of the philosopher is to discover the source of common approval and good Taste, and the causes of perversities of Taste that interrupt the proper functioning of the inner sense and bring about disagreements of aesthetic judgment. Common pleasure is possible, surmises Hutcheson, only if there is a species of pleasure that is not a response to the satisfaction of a desire or the advantage of self-interest.

The term that gradually comes to be used to designate this feeling is "disinterested pleasure," though writers use several descriptions to distinguish it from the sorts of pleasure that do follow from the satisfaction of desire or the gratification of self-interest.[23] The satisfaction of desire is only one sort of pleasure, a "rational" pleasure, according to Hutcheson. Rational pleasures are those discovered by the intellect as it ponders the possible effects of the possession of various objects and the amount of advantage they afford. But the object perceived as beautiful affords a sensible pleasure that is immediate, not dependent on desire, and not affected by the operations of reason. Hutcheson observes, "Hence it plainly appears that some objects are *immediately* the occasions of this pleasure of beauty, and that we have senses fitted for perceiving it, and that it is distinct from that *joy* which arises upon prospect of advantage."[24] Beauty—or what will later be termed more generally aesthetic value—is therefore noninstrumental or nonpractical. The absence of interest also distinguishes beauty from moral considerations and from scientific interests, since it sets beauty apart from desire and rational calculation. The judgment of Taste, as it comes to be known, is a judgment that an object is beautiful, which is to say, that

---

[21] Whether the idea of beauty that he envisages as the object of an inner sense is simple or complex is a muddy issue. See Peter Kivy, *The Seventh Sense* (New York: Burt Franklin, 1976).

[22] Francis Hutcheson, *Inquiry into the Original of Our Ideas of Beauty and Virtue* (1725), ed. Peter Kivy (The Hague: Martinus Nijhoff, 1973), p. 34. Hutcheson's explicit target is Bernard Mandeville, whose theory of value is also rationalist and egocentric. Hutcheson refers to it as the "rational interest theory."

[23] Disinterested pleasure plays a central role in aesthetics from the eighteenth century through the twentieth. But contrary to popular generalization, the concept of disinterested enjoyment of art was not new in the eighteenth century; it has much older forebears. See Summers, *Judgment of Sense,* pp. 63–65. Jerome Stolnitz traces the concept of disinterestedness from the eighteenth through the twentieth centuries in "On the Origin of 'Aesthetic Disinterestedness,'" *Journal of Aesthetics and Art Criticism* 20 (Winter 1961): 131–43.

[24] Hutcheson, *Inquiry,* p. 37.

it is suited to arouse aesthetic pleasure. The disinterested character of aesthetic pleasure by no means guarantees agreement about judgments of Taste. Rather, it is prerequisite for the possibility that judgments of Taste ideally converge and agree among those who develop refined aesthetic sensibility.

The central role played by this special, nonpractical aesthetic pleasure is one of the chief reasons why literal taste is left behind in the development of aesthetic theories, in spite of the analogy it continues to provide for aesthetic sensibility. Gustatory enjoyment is often invoked as an excellent example of an immediately sensed pleasure, and as such it remains comparable to aesthetic enjoyment. But at the same time it is typically presented as an example of preference that does involve satisfaction of interest—the appeasement of hunger and the satisfaction of a bodily appetite. Indeed, Hutcheson stipulates that the inner sense of beauty responds to ideas of only two of the five external senses: hearing and vision. As he says, "The ancients observe the peculiar dignity of the sense of seeing and hearing, that in their objects we discern the *kalon* [beautiful], which we don't ascribe to the objects of the other senses."[25] Though taste is invoked repeatedly as an analogy that explains the operations of Taste, it is ultimately marginalized in philosophical responses to the problem of Taste.

Exercise of gustatory taste does not qualify as a "judgment of Taste" partly because eating is quite evidently a practical activity bound up with intimate interests. Traditional thinking about bodily pleasures was not disposed to challenge the separation of the two sorts of taste. Gustatory pleasures were habitually conceived as clearly bodily and animal and thus were not taken seriously as candidates for higher aesthetic pleasure. (When Condillac examined sensory experience by imagining a statue with gradually awakening senses, it was taste to which he assigned the most immediate and distracting pleasures.)[26] Little seemed at stake in disagreements over taste preferences; absence of gourmet sentiments does not reflect badly on a person's character, and indeed a degree of asceticism may be viewed with favor. In short, insouciance regarding disagreement among taste preferences is congruent with the traditions that slight the importance of this kind of experience. Of even greater importance for the division of Taste from taste is the fact that the objects of literal taste were not suffering the same conceptual shifts that beauty was undergoing. Early modern aesthetic theory was developed in the process of responding to the problem of Taste and affirming some sort of stable foundation that provides shared standards for aesthetic judgments. Literal taste perceptions were already considered both subjective and relative; taste preferences had long served as confirmation of adages such as "There's no accounting for taste," "De gustibus non est disputandum," "Chacun a

---

[25] Ibid., p. 47.
[26] Abbé Etienne Bonnot de Condillac, *Treatise on the Sensations* (1754), trans. Geraldine Carr (Los Angeles: University of Southern California Press, 1930), pp. 55–56.

son goût," and the like. Philosophers might have made the opposite move and argued that there are commonalities for shared preferences in food and drink that are as reliable as for objects of beauty. Since literal taste qualities were already accepted as subjective and relative, however, they were left unexamined, assumed to raise no troublesome philosophical issues. But beauty had formerly been conceived as an objective quality, however puzzling. With the advent of empiricism, beauty was newly subjectivized and had to be rescued from the perils of skepticism. Both in formulating the problem of Taste and in establishing standards for Taste, philosophers saved beauty from relativism by showing how it must differ from literal taste qualities. The all-important problem of Taste was not conceived to pertain to sensory taste.

The separation of taste and Taste as subjects for aesthetic inquiry was gradual and not entirely clean. The analogies between the two remained in use, and literal taste continued to be employed to characterize the phenomenon of aesthetic discrimination. One of the most influential philosophers who pursue this line of thought is David Hume, who takes the analogy more seriously than those who follow him. Hume explicates his standard of Taste by means of a lengthy comparison with literal taste that remains controversial to this day.

The Key to Hume's Standard of Taste

One of the most famous analogical arguments in philosophies of Taste occurs in Hume's essay "Of the Standard of Taste" (1757). Hume begins by noting the apparently opposed extremes that a theory of Taste must deal with: on the one hand, Taste is individual and varies from person to person; on the other, everyone agrees that some judgments of Taste are better than others. How can these claims be reconciled, given the fact that aesthetic values are not objective qualities but phenomena of subjective response? Hume compares the subjectivity of beauty with the subjectivity of flavor: "To seek the real beauty, or real deformity, is as fruitless an enquiry, as to pretend to ascertain the real sweet or real bitter. According to the disposition of the organs, the same object may be both sweet and bitter; and the proverb has justly determined it to be fruitless to dispute concerning tastes. It is very natural, and even quite necessary, to extend this axiom to mental, as well as bodily taste."[27]

Hume's solution to the problem of Taste is to embrace the subjectivity of both kinds of taste, and to argue that human beings are constituted with sufficient similarity that we are disposed to enjoy—to have similar subjective pleasure responses to—the same qualities in objects. Unlike many of his contemporaries, he resists the

[27] David Hume, "Of the Standard of Taste," in *Essays Moral, Political, and Literary*, ed. T. H. Green and T. H. Grose, 2 vols. (London: Longmans, Green, 1898), 1:269.

urge to isolate particular qualities of objects that reliably and demonstrably make for beauty.[28] Rather, the "standard" of Taste is constituted by the judgments and the cultivated pleasures of experienced critics and appreciators of art who have developed an especially fine ability to discriminate subtle distinctions and nuance in works of art. These he refers to as men of "delicate [T]aste." Not everyone has delicate Taste, though implicitly anyone in fortunate enough circumstances can develop it through education and practice. Once Taste is developed, good critics enjoy more or less what other good critics do; a test of the delicacy of their Taste is the enjoyment of works that have already won the admiration of others—the canon of great works, so to speak.

Hume continues the analogy of critical Taste with literal taste throughout the essay. It serves to illustrate the conditions under which someone refrains from judgment, knowing that he is not in a good position to discern the quality of a work. Just as "a man in a fever would not insist on his palate as able to decide concerning flavours,"[29] so too does the critic of artworks need to be in good receptive and discriminatory tune, that condition designated delicacy of Taste.

Illustrating the characteristics of a delicate Taste, Hume adapts for his purposes two characters from Cervantes's *Don Quixote,* kinsmen of Sancho Panza, who engage in a remarkable wine-tasting contest. Each man sips from a hogshead of wine. One notes that the wine is very good except for a faint whiff of leather, and the other concurs but identifies the taint as a trace of metal. Their companions, oafs without delicate taste, hoot in derision, for they taste nothing but what is proper to wine. But when the hogshead is drained, at the bottom is discovered a key attached to a leather thong that has accidentally been dropped into the vat. Sancho's kinsmen are vindicated, and Hume rests his case for delicacy of Taste, which requires organs of perception "so fine as to allow nothing to escape them, and at the same time so exact as to perceive every ingredient in the composition." Concluding the anecdote about the key in the wine, Hume asserts that "the great resemblance between mental and bodily taste will easily teach us to apply this story."[30]

The parallels between the two sorts of taste confirm Hume's method for discovering a standard of Taste in the constitution of human nature. As Luc Ferry puts it:

---

[28] Hutcheson, for example, posited uniformity amidst variety as the stimulus for aesthetic pleasure. William Hogarth preferred the line of grace; see his *Analysis of Beauty* (1753) (New Haven: Yale University Press, 1997). Though Hume does not name objective qualities that trigger aesthetic pleasure, he does refer to principles that describe the object of Taste, complicating interpretations regarding what constitutes his standard of Taste.

[29] Hume, "Of the Standard of Taste," p. 271.

[30] Ibid., p. 273. This story and its place in Hume's theory has received much critical attention, and commentators are divided about its appropriateness. Some consider it to represent a criterion for delicate Taste distinct from the reference to the joint verdicts of critics. I discuss Roger Shiner's claim that the gustatory and aesthetic comparison is "deeply misleading" in Chapter 4.

The anecdote's meaning is twofold: it indicates first of all that Hume's aesthetic model is found, in conformity with the original meaning of the word "taste," in the culinary arts, and that the Beautiful is here reduced to the pleasant. But on the other hand, if the Beautiful is only that which pleases, that which suits the internal, quasi-biological structure of men, its criterion will be provided by the most essentially human constitution, that is by that of the best experts, which will possess, de jure anyway, a certain universality (in the sense that, in so far as it is essential, it should be that of all men).[31]

Collapsing the distinction between the pleasant and the beautiful was in fact an unusual move for the time, if indeed Ferry correctly characterizes Hume's line of argument. Philosophers from Aristotle onward commonly observe that we do not call the objects of any senses except hearing and sight "beautiful," since the bodily senses provide sensuous pleasure rather than the contemplative delight occasioned by beauty. We shall return to this issue shortly, but first let us chart the historical fate of the extension of the taste metaphor that Hume embraced. For Hume went as far as anyone in attempting to establish a standard of Taste upon the fact that human beings are morphologically and psychologically similar to one another. However, Hume's willingness to accept this sort of standard was not to prevail as aesthetic theory developed, nor was the parallel standing of gustatory and aesthetic appreciation sustained at the level that Hume supports.

Hume's criteria for a standard of Taste are somewhat looser than his critics would have liked. Not only was he nonspecific about the properties of beautiful objects and the principles underlying great art, he was content with a standard for Taste that achieves only a general agreement among experts.[32] He allowed for the possibility that not everyone will necessarily concur about the value of works of art—even among a group whose Taste is similarly honed to a condition of delicacy—no more, presumably, than all gourmets will agree about their favorite dishes. Various factors may account for residual disagreement, such as the differing ages of judges or different cultural affinities, and under such conditions "we seek in vain for a standard, by which we can reconcile the contrary sentiments."[33] Other philosophers were less content with a standard consisting of the practice of judges and their general agreement over time. They demanded firmer grounds for beauty and for Taste, and this required that the two kinds of taste be distinguished philosophically with greater

---

[31] Luc Ferry, *Homo Aestheticus*, p. 58.
[32] George Dickie argues that this is in fact a virtue of Hume's theory that makes it superior to others of his century: *The Century of Taste: The Philosophical Odyssey of Taste in the Eighteenth Century* (New York: Oxford University Press, 1996).
[33] Hume, "Of the Standard of Taste," p. 281.

rigor to head off any confusion between the beautiful and the pleasant. This difference becomes an indispensable claim for that attentive and appreciative critic of Hume and his empiricist brethren: Immanuel Kant.

Kant: The Agreeable vs. the Beautiful

Kant, who draws one of the strictest exclusionary zones around genuine aesthetic judgments, also adopts the literal sense of taste as the metaphor for aesthetic sensibility. Immediacy of subjective response, centrality of pleasure to evaluation, singularity of judgment—all these factors link literal and aesthetic taste. For Kant, however, taste remains a metaphor that keeps its distance from the operation of the aesthetic judgment. He will not sustain the parallel between aesthetic and gustatory taste the way Hume does, for only judgments of what he calls pure beauty permit Taste the kind of universality that his philosophy seeks.

Kant, rather like Hume, frames his aesthetic theory with reference to what he terms an antinomy of Taste: judgments about beauty seem on the one hand to be purely subjective, for they are judgments of pleasure. Differences among individual judgments are not reconcilable by appeal to shared concepts. On the other hand, judgments about what is beautiful are matters of importance that transcend the whims of individual perceivers and ought to be matters for adjudication by appeal to principle. Kant was not satisfied with an empirical generalization about what usually pleases men of delicate Taste. He set out to show how judgments of beauty are not only generally agreed upon in fact but, more important, achieve a kind of universality and necessity. In pronouncing a thing beautiful, one expresses one's own pleasure, takes that pleasure to be the sole "determining ground" of the judgment, yet implies that all other spectators can and should take pleasure in the object of perception as well. To make his case, Kant strengthened the sense hierarchy and the traditional divide between aesthetic judgments based on visual and auditory experiences on the one hand and pleasures of the bodily senses on the other. He does so first of all in his distinction between the "agreeable" and the "beautiful."

As regards the *agreeable* everyone acknowledges that his judgment, which he bases on a private feeling and by which he says that he likes some object, is by the same token confined to his own person. Hence, if he says that canary wine is agreeable he is quite content if someone else corrects his terms and reminds him to say instead: It is agreeable to *me*. This holds moreover not only for the taste of the tongue, palate, and throat, but also for what may be agreeable to any one's eyes and ears. To one person the color violet is gentle and lovely, to another lifeless and faded. . . . It would be foolish if we disputed about such differences with the intention of censuring another's judgment as incorrect if it differs from ours, as if the two were opposed logically. Hence about the agreeable the following principle holds: *Everyone has his own taste* (of sense).[34]

As is clear from this passage, all the senses offer experiences that may be agreeable, or "merely pleasant." This fact alone does not distinguish the proximal senses of taste, smell, and touch from the distal senses of sight and hearing. But it does distinguish the two sorts of judgments of taste / Taste. While we say "To each his own" regarding literal taste preferences, we also quarrel about differences of aesthetic judgments. Though there are no rules that one can appeal to in order to settle a dispute about Taste (hence Kant says that it is true there is no "disputing" about Taste), it is not the case that an aesthetic judgment is greeted with the same spirit of generous anarchy that meets judgments about what is agreeable to the senses.[35]

Kant requires a sharp distinction between the character of literal taste sensations and the experience of beauty. He stipulates the following conditions for a pure aesthetic judgment: First of all, a judgment of Taste—that is, a judgment that some object of perception is beautiful—involves a disinterested pleasure. That is to say, it is not an approval based on whether an object is morally good, practically useful, or sensuously pleasant; it is pure pleasure in the presentation (*Vorstellung*) of the object of perception. Second, although this feeling of pleasure that constitutes the judgment of Taste is subjective (as pleasures must be), it is also a judgment that commands a special sort of universal validity. Partly because aesthetic pleasure is disinterested, it is available to all on the same terms from the same objects. We expect judgments of Taste to be shared by others. Not only are aesthetic pleasures universal, Kant notes that judgments of Taste have a kind of exemplary necessity: because they are based on features of the mind that are universal, all perceivers ideally concur in the apprehension of the beautiful.

Earlier stages in Kant's Critical philosophy had already established the grounds for a priori elements of knowledge, experience, and morals: the structure of human rationality itself. That which obtains a priori for experience of any rational being must be both universal and necessary. While aesthetic judgments do not employ determinate concepts and hence do not directly call into operation the empirical application of the organizing categories of the understanding, the very presence of rational frameworks makes possible aesthetic pleasure that is universal and necessary. Devoid of all personal interest, the aesthetic situation is one in which the imagination plays freely within the formal structure of the understanding. When the form of

---

[34] Immanuel Kant, "Analytic of the Beautiful," I:7, *Critique of Judgment*, trans. Werner S. Pluhar (Indianapolis: Hackett, 1987), p. 55.

[35] Kant's acceptance of the saying that "there is no disputing about Taste" requires him to distinguish between disputing and quarreling: "über den Geschmack lässt sich streiten (obgleich nicht disputieren)" (*Kritik der Urteilskraft,* ed. Karl Vorländer [Hamburg: Felix Meiner, 1968], p. 196.

an object of perception appears to the mind without any particular function or purpose being invoked, it brings about an apprehension of "purposiveness without purpose" (*Zweckmässigkeit ohne allen Zweck*), which is signaled by the pleasure of a judgment of Taste. This concerns pure beauty only; that is to say, pleasure taken in a presentation without consideration of what its object is or how it compares with anything else.[36] As a result, this section is only secondarily a theory of art. But it is theoretically of the most central importance to Kant's philosophy of beauty, for it is pure pleasure in aesthetic form that provides the requisite universality and necessity for judgments of Taste.

To summarize, there are several reasons why the bodily sense of taste does not conform to the requirements of a pure aesthetic judgment. The involvement of the body makes the relation between subject and object a practical one and calls into play the determinate concepts that Kant outlaws from the pure judgment of Taste. Tasting and eating promote interest of the most urgent sort: Will this assuage my hunger? Will this taste be delicious or revolting? Will this substance nourish or poison me? Only a pleasure that is free from practical desires, including the appetites of hunger and thirst, can transcend individual whim and idiosyncrasy and lay claim to universal agreement. In the purgation of interest from beauty one recognizes the old wariness regarding appetites of the body, for the two kinds of desire that most interrupt aesthetic contemplation are hunger and sexual appetite—the lower sense again paired with the base, carnal drive.

Sexual pleasure has a related but rather different fate from taste in the formulation of theories of aesthetic Taste. Sexual attraction in fact appeared to some philosophers to be a close cousin to aesthetic appreciation, perhaps even a progenitor of the more refined, cultural sensibility. Edmund Burke claims that love of the beautiful begins with attraction of male to female, and Kant himself speculates that human sensibility for beauty has its origin in the sublimation of sexual desire. In his somewhat bizarre "Conjectural Beginning of Human History," Kant imagines the development of human beings from primitive to civilized, a process he sees as requiring the mastery of sense by reason: "Refusal was the feat which brought about the passage from merely sensual to spiritual attractions, from mere animal desire gradually to love, and along with this from the feeling of the merely agreeable, to a taste for beauty, at first only for beauty in man but at length for beauty in nature as well."[37]

---

[36] Many theorists of the time made a distinction similar to Kant's, whereby "free" beauty is pleasure taken in a perception itself, without comparison with anything else; "comparative" or "dependent" beauty is pleasure taken when an image is compared with some original of which it is a representation. The latter is the legacy of mimetic theories of art. Dependent beauty for Kant employs determinate concepts.

[37] Immanuel Kant, "Conjectural Beginning of Human History" (1786), trans. Emil L. Fackenheim, in *Kant on History*, ed. Lewis White Beck (Indianapolis: Bobbs-Merrill, 1963), p. 57. Central to the mastery of the senses was a control of sexual instinct, which also increased sexual attraction. "The fig leaf, then, was a far greater manifestation of reason than that shown in the earlier stages of development."

Innocent of the imaginative deceit that psychoanalysis has accustomed us to suspect in transactions from erotic to sublimated activity, eighteenth-century philosophers breezed happily from speculation about the sensual origin of beauty to stipulations about the purity of true aesthetic pleasure.[38] Certainly by the time Kant isolates pure beauty from other pleasures, it is free from any messy sexual origins. Detaching beauty from suspicion of such a source is one more route Kant follows to a conclusion already familiar: only vision and hearing qualify as aesthetic senses. While any sense experience may be merely pleasant, experiences employing vision or hearing may also deliver presentations for aesthetic judgments. Merely pleasant or agreeable sensations can never yield universally valid judgments, because sensuous pleasure and displeasure do not "belong to the cognitive faculty concerning objects; they are rather determinations of the subject."[39]

Kant also distinguishes taste and smell from the other senses because they are "subjective" senses. Since the judgment of Taste is subjective also, being an experience of pleasure, subjectivity may not appear to disqualify these senses from the realm of the aesthetic. This use of "subjective," however, precludes aesthetic pleasure. Because taste draws attention to the state of one's own individual body, the pleasures of taste are idiosyncratic and relative and the grounds for universality and necessity are absent.[40] Attention is not drawn to the object of contemplation, as is possible with sight and hearing, and in its cognitive mode touch. Touch can be grouped as "bodily" and "sensuous" when its pleasures are considered, but in its exploratory role, touch coordinates with vision more than any other sense, and in this case it provides information about objects. It is the latter aspect of the sense of touch that Kant has in mind when he remarks that three of the five senses are

> more objective than subjective, that is, they contribute . . . more to the cognition of the exterior object, than they arouse the consciousness of the affected organ. Two, however, are more subjective than objective, that is, the idea obtained from them is more an idea of enjoyment, rather than the cognition of

[38] The speculation about beauty and sexual attraction resurfaces in texts that purport to be theses about generic perceivers and human nature. Among the things that are naturally agreeable to human nature, for example, Hume lists music, good cheer, and "the fair sex." And as Kant puts it, "The man develops his own taste while the woman makes herself an object of everybody's taste." See David Hume, *Treatise of Human Nature*, ed. L. A. Selby-Bigge, 2d ed. (New York: Oxford University Press, 1978), p. 424; Immanuel Kant, *Anthropology from a Pragmatic Point of View*, trans. Victor Lyle Dowdell (Carbondale: Southern Illinois University Press, 1978), p. 222.

[39] Kant, *Anthropology*, p. 142. Kant's assiduous attempt to render aesthetic pleasure free from sensuous pleasure leads him to rule color out of the object of pure beauty. Of the absence of sensuous pleasures from Kant's aesthetic, Derrida remarks: "It will be, for (arbitrary) example, a colorless and scentless tulip (more surely than color, scent is lost to art and to the beautiful . . . just try to frame a perfume)": Jacques Derrida, *The Truth in Painting*, trans. Geoff Bennington and Ian McLeod (Chicago: University of Chicago Press, 1987), p. 82.

[40] See Kant's *Anthropology*, pp. 40–48, 141–43.

the external object. Consequently, we can easily agree with others in respect to the three objective senses. But with respect to the other two, the manner in which the subject responds can be quite different from whatever the external empirical perception and designation of the object might have been.[41]

Taste and smell are identified in this comment as "chemical" senses. The chemical senses are chiefly senses of pleasure that do not appreciably direct attention to the object of perception and are both cognitively and aesthetically empty. Kant has the least flattering assessment of smell, which he calls "taste at a distance." Smell is the least important, most dispensable sense, though it does serve a purpose in warning us to avoid noxious or poisonous things. Taste is next in terms of dispensability, though Kant grants it a role in the pleasant company of dinner (provided one's companions don't smell bad, one assumes). He rather grudgingly remembers that "the benefit of food is closely linked with a rather certain prediction of pleasure as long as luxury and indulgence have not overrefined the sense."[42] However, these thoughts about the pleasures of the chemical senses pertain only to sensuous pleasure; there is no scope for aesthetic sensibility in the discussion of smell or taste.

Let us grant for the moment the claim that taste and smell direct attention away from their objects and toward the perceiving body (a venerable if dubious claim that will be examined more critically in the next chapter). This description alone supposedly renders taste and smell not only less worthy but less theoretically interesting than the other senses. Preferences for their objects are (according to this line of thought) truly relative to the individual percipient; theories about them therefore do not tap elements of common human nature or universal truths about epistemic or aesthetic relations. This latter judgment is particularly questionable, for the greater phenomenal subjectivity of certain modes of sense ought only to direct and focus our interest in ways appropriate to the sense, not eliminate it altogether.

At the same time, advocating taste as a subject of philosophical importance requires that we heed what is sound in the observations about the operation of this sense, and along with smell and touch it does have a closer attachment to bodily sensation than is the case with vision and hearing. The literal distance between subject and object of perception again makes an appearance in connection with another aesthetic category explored in the eighteenth century: the sublime. "Sublime" refers

---

[41] Ibid., p. 41.

[42] Ibid., pp. 45, 46. Alain Corbin argues that the concern for bad smells manifest in Kant's writings is part of the phenomenon of the control of stench and miasma in the eighteenth and nineteenth centuries. Corbin's study interestingly illuminates the ambiguity of smell as a civilized sense, for the more refined members of society have sensitive noses and are particularly adept at smelling out dangerous stenches, whereas the lower orders merely stink and are less bothered by the odors they help to create. See *The Foul and the Fragrant: Odor and the French Social Imagination,* trans. M. Kochan, R. Porter, and C. Prendergast (Cambridge: Harvard University Press, 1986), esp. chaps. 7–9.

to extreme, awe-inspiring experience to be had from situations in art or nature (particularly the latter) that verge on the terrifying, in which the mighty forces of the world and the cosmos overwhelm the observer with their power and ineffability. The sublime is powerful, thrilling, and awesome, and the experience it occasions is profound and sufficiently terrible that labeling it pleasure strains at the limits of that concept. The relatively restricted tolerance for extremes of bodily sensations has been invoked to explain both the narrow range of expressiveness possible through the proximal senses and the limits on the abilities of any of the bodily senses to furnish a glimpse of sublimity.

Explicit discussion of the hierarchy of the senses arises infrequently with the sublime. Perhaps the bodily senses appear too obviously feeble to invite us to consider seriously the routes they may provide to sublimity. Only the imaginative faculty and the senses that are capable of comprehending a world utterly distinct from and alien to the puny human perceiver can aid in the experience of the sublime. What is more, it is probable that the strength and extremes of experience required by the sublime would not yield a desirable experience even if they could be translated into taste or smell. In his *Essay on the Sublime* (1747) John Baillie wrote that "the *Eyes* and *Ears* are the only *Inlets* to the Sublime. *Taste, Smell,* nor *Touch* convey nothing that is Great and Exalted." Edmund Burke saw it this way: "*Smells,* and *Tastes,* have some share too, in ideas of greatness; but it is a small one, weak in its nature, and confined in its operations. I shall only observe, that no smells or tastes can produce a grand sensation, except excessive bitters, and intolerable stenches."[43] Burke granted that *descriptions* of these sense excesses may contribute to the sublime in art, for the mediation of representation reduces the pain of foul tastes and smells. However, the difference between the representation of stench and the experience of stench itself is significant; the imagination may linger over the represented stench without obliging one to double over with nausea. The margins of tolerance for the experiences of touch, taste, and smell are narrower than for the distance senses. But the barriers to sublimity in taste are even more importantly conceptual. Sublime vistas stimulate the mind to contemplate its own limits and to reflect upon the limitless powers of nature or the ineffability of divinity. Since the bodily senses are purportedly feeble in their mental or intellectual registers, they do not provide inlets for the mental stimulation that prompts awe before the sublime. In Chapters 5 and 6 I shall challenge this presumption, but for now I note that with the expansion of philosophical interest to a wider ambit of aesthetic qualities that included the sublime, taste receded yet further from theoretical attention. What is more, the widening divide between taste

[43] Edmund Burke, *A Philosophical Enquiry into the Origin of Our Ideas of the Sublime and Beautiful* (1757), ed. James T. Boulton (Notre Dame: University of Notre Dame Press, 1986), p. 85. The quote from Baillie occurs in Boulton's introduction, p. liv.

and Taste is even more apparent when we consider the role of the senses in philosophies of art.

Aesthetic and Artistic Senses

According to the account of aesthetic pleasure developed by philosophers of Taste,
the way in which objects of gustatory taste are perceived prevents their being experienced with the kind of detachment that is necessary for a genuine aesthetic experience. When theorists turned their attention to the objects of taste—food and
drink—they found related inadequacies that disqualify these substances as media
for arts. Their reasons are often extensions of perceptual theories: since art is something that delivers aesthetic pleasure, the objects of the nonaesthetic senses have
characteristics that preclude the proper sort of enjoyment. The formalism that is
strong in modern theory is a major factor here, for (it is argued) foods and their
tastes do not have the organizational complexity of the objects of the distance senses
and hence their possibilities for compositional development are meager. Objects of
vision are easily assessed for their formal properties, as are objects of the sense of
hearing. Indeed, composition, balance, harmony are all aesthetic qualities that make
up standard critical vocabularies of the arts. By comparison, taste sensations are relatively unstructured. As a rule tastes and smells tend to blend and lose their discrete
components in the experience of a meal. They cannot, therefore, be made into
works of art.

One finds such attitudes among many writers on art, though even more commonly the exclusion of the bodily senses is simply implicit in the absence of the subject altogether from discussion. One philosopher who did develop reasons to ex-
clude taste and food from the important world of art was Hegel. Hegel is a salient
bridge from eighteenth-century to contemporary aesthetics, for not only is he a towering figure in European philosophy generally, the idealism of his system was, in
several varieties, a mainstay of aesthetics well into the twentieth century.

Hegel's metaphysics lends heft and passion to his brief for the traditional sense
hierarchy, and he posits differences between proximal and distal senses in a particularly dramatic way. Briefly put, Hegel states that works of art always make some sort
of presentation to the senses or to the imagination, which must be included to account for sense images arising in experience of the literary arts. But no art can be ad-
equately understood if one examines only its sensory dimension, and so again the
greater affinity of vision and hearing with the mind is centrally important in the assessment of the senses. Of essential importance is the concept art conveys. Hegel understands all of history and human life as the progress of living thought manifest in
the dynamism and change of human culture, which he sums up with the term "Absolute Spirit." Taken as a whole, art manifests the process of Absolute Spirit becoming conscious of itself. Hegel is not interested in beauties of nature because nature

simply *is*—it has no consciousness. But products of culture are the results of human consciousness. Spirit makes itself known through consciousness, and art is therefore essentially to be valued for its sensuous presentation of the Absolute. This is the source of Beauty.

Idealism of any sort requires a certain disregard for the physical body. Art is essentially spiritual, a working out of consciousness and self-consciousness of humanity. Art has a sensuous dimension as well, but its purpose is "not merely for *sensuous* apprehension; its standing is of such a kind that, though sensuous, it is essentially at the same time for *spiritual* apprehension; the spirit is meant to be affected by it and to find some satisfaction in it."[44] Sense perception is among the lowest and least satisfying ways to apprehend art objects, and the desire that one may feel for an object of perception is only one degree superior. The reasons are by now familiar, though cast in Hegel's distinctive language and justified by the terms of his elaborate system: sense perceptions and desire relate to things as individuals, not as instances of universal categories, which require the exercise of theoretical intelligence. The particular virtue of art is its ability to present in sensuous form something individual, which at the same time leads the mind to a universal truth. This result can come about only if the object is apprehended by a mode of perception that is free from desire or practical intervention. The bodily senses do not qualify. In Hegel's words:

> Consequently the sensuous aspect of art is related only to the two theoretical senses of sight and hearing, while smell, taste, and touch remain excluded from the enjoyment of art. For smell, taste, and touch have to do with matter as such and its immediately sensible qualities. . . . For this reason these senses cannot have to do with artistic objects, which are meant to maintain themselves in their real independence and allow of no *purely* sensuous relationship. What is agreeable for these senses is not the beauty of art.[45]

The senses of sight and hearing are "theoretical" not only because they need not involve the operation of desire but also because they can operate without touching their objects—the distance between the perceiver and the objects coming again into play. Thus Hegel introduces yet another way of observing the two levels of sensory operation, theoretical and practical: "The purely theoretical process is managed by the tools of the senses of seeing and hearing; what we see or hear we leave as it is. On the other hand, the organs of smell and taste are already the beginnings of a

---

[44] G. W. F. Hegel, *Aesthetics: Lectures on Fine Art*, trans. T. M. Knox, 2 vols. (Oxford: Clarendon, 1975), 1:35.
[45] Ibid. pp. 38–39.

practical relation. For we can smell only what is in the process of wasting away, and we can taste only by destroying."[46]

It is the nature of smell and taste to require the loss or transformation of their objects, which cannot therefore endure as lasting works of art. (Hegel has in mind the five proper fine arts—architecture, sculpture, painting, music, and poetry—which he ranks in ascending order according to their ability to manifest spirit.) For all these reasons, Hegel concludes that only two of the senses are "capable by their nature of being organs for the apprehension of works of art." Sight and hearing alone are not capable of apprehending all kinds of art, however, so Hegel adds the imagination, with its ability to call up images in the mind, to put together ideas by memory, and to relate objects according to their essential qualities. These three perceptual-cognitive modes let their objects persist independent of the perceiver and the act of perception; and they do not require the practical relation of desire to obtain between perceiver and object. None of the bodily senses qualifies for this role. Of taste, Hegel remarks: "A cultivation and refinement of taste is only possible and requisite in respect of foods and their preparation or of the chemical qualities of objects. But the *objet d'art* should be contemplated in its independent objectivity on its own account."[47]

Hegel's account of the differences between the distance senses and the bodily senses with regard to the aesthetic potential of their objects slides quickly into a distinction between the senses whose objects may be works of art and senses that do not develop art among their objects. The bodily senses are quite absent from the roster of senses relevant to the true arts, or the `"fine" arts, as they came to be called. They do not serve the mind sufficiently, so their "subjectivity" curtails their artistic possibilities. As we have seen, the concept of aesthetic value was formulated by means of its contrast with practical values, and the bodily senses are more difficult to abstract from practical functions than are the distance senses. Similarly, the notion of fine art emphasizes the creation of objects with no external purposes other than their own being.[48] This value, summed up in the notion of artistic autonomy, is a staple of the modern idea of fine art. And it is a criterion suited for neither food nor drink, which, even in the most refined and gratuitous dining and imbibing, carry nutritional and digestive perils that cannot be overlooked for long. For the most part, of course, eating and drinking must serve even more immediately instrumental ends. The concept of fine art more or less caps the long history of reasoning that

[46] Ibid., pp. 137–38.
[47] Ibid., 2:621–22.
[48] Martha Woodmansee, *The Author, Art, and the Market: Rereading the History of Aesthetics* (New York: Columbia University Press, 1994). Woodmansee notes that Coleridge, adapting Kant, explicitly distinguishes the pleasures of the palate and of art (pp. 123, 136).

distinguishes and ranks the different senses. The aesthetic senses come to be designated the artistic senses; and the nonaesthetic senses are not conceived to provide a sensory mode for the development of an art form in anything but a derivative sense.

Aesthetic Taste and Gustatory Taste Revisited

The eighteenth-century philosophers who refined the concept of the aesthetic considered themselves to be articulating a mode of perception that is "universal," that is, recognizable by any person of sensitivity. Their goal seemed to require the separation of aesthetic Taste, which warrants shared values, from gustatory taste, which does not carry with it the expectation that agreement is either forthcoming or important to secure. While the latter presumption has remained more or less unquestioned over the centuries, the goal of establishing a universal foundation for Taste has come in for considerable criticism. Today this Enlightenment project can be seen to manifest a set of social presumptions and exigencies peculiar to its time, and many contemporary critics have interpreted philosophies of Taste skeptically as components of the historical development of certain class interests.[49] By this analysis, philosophies of Taste posit the traits of universal human nature by generalizing about an ideal member of a privileged, educated class, who is held to represent the whole of human nature, or human nature at its "best." Insofar as these theories are guilty of such a move, philosophies of Taste obscure the differences among people of different classes, locations, genders. Moreover, they not only ignore Tastes of different peoples, they occlude the very possibility of their recognition by asserting as the norm the aesthetic refinement of an elite group. The philosophers of Taste of the early eighteenth century were aware that their project focused on an ideal critic of education and leisure who was in a position to develop Taste. But the stronger grounds for universality of Taste established by Kant in his requirement for a pure aesthetic judgment refer less to empirical social development than to the a priori grounds for a common sense of beauty that can be met by any rational being. However, the very disengaged, disinterested attitude that Kant requires for the pure judgment of Taste, it has been argued, represents a lofty remove that is indeed not a universal possibility but a privilege made easy only for someone who confidently occupies a socially privileged position within a dominant and respected group.[50]

---

[49] Terry Eagleton, *The Ideology of the Aesthetic* (Oxford: Blackwell, 1990), pp. 23, 25.
[50] Richard Shusterman, "Of the Scandal of Taste: Social Privilege as Nature in the Aesthetic Theories of Hume and Kant," *Philosophical Forum* 20 (Spring 1989), revised and reprinted in Mattick, *Eighteenth-Century Aesthetics*. Dabney Townsend, "Lockean Aesthetics," observes the difference between theories of Taste in the early and the late eighteenth century and their relative consciousness of the class expectations of the ideal person of Taste.

A strong version of this critique has been advanced by the sociologist Pierre Bourdieu, who moreover frames his critique of Taste in ways that favorably direct attention to literal gustatory taste. Indeed, one could read Bourdieu as returning to the old comparison of the two kinds of taste that launched so many early modern aesthetic theories. He opens *Distinction: A Social Critique of the Judgement of Taste* with this statement: "But one cannot fully understand cultural practices unless 'culture', in the restricted, normative sense of ordinary usage, is brought back into 'culture' in the anthropological sense, and the elaborated taste for the most refined objects is reconnected with the elementary taste for the flavours of food."[51]

While his intent is entirely different, some of Bourdieu's comments begin with the kinds of observations made by Dubos or Hume: "The dual meaning of the word 'taste' . . . must serve . . . to remind us that taste in the sense of the 'faculty of immediately and intuitively judging aesthetic values' is inseparable from taste in the sense of the capacity to discern the flavours of foods which implies a preference for some of them."[52]

Bourdieu argues that preferences of all kinds are closely related and are products of what he calls the "habitus" of different social classes. The habitus includes economic factors, education, and other social determinants that influence the way we understand and experience the world. The habitus, itself invisible, produces categories of perception and artistic appreciation.[53] Pressure to structure one's preferences according to the tastes of established elites is manifest, for example, in the prescriptions that pepper theories of Taste (he rightly observes that Kant makes heavy use of the imperative mood). Bourdieu assails eighteenth-century defenses of a uniform and universal standard of Taste as disguised class hegemony that regulates values of domination and submission in European societies. He particularly has it in for Kantian approaches, which most stringently purify aesthetic pleasures from their social roots. Rather than providing the grounds for universal aesthetic pleasures that transcend the differences of individuals, Bourdieu argues, Kant's disinterested pleasure is a product of history that prescribes a contemplative, detached attitude possible only among people wealthy enough for leisure. In asserting that aesthetic preferences need to be referred to the conditions of daily life and practice, Bourdieu debunks the distinction between high and popular arts, between contemplative aesthetic enjoyment and sensuous pleasure, between appreciation of art and relish of foods, and by implication between aesthetic and nonaesthetic senses.

---

[51] Pierre Bourdieu, *Distinction: A Social Critique of the Judgement of Taste,* trans. Richard Nice (Cambridge: Harvard University Press, 1984), p. 1.

[52] Ibid., p. 99.

[53] See, e.g., ibid., pp. 56, 170, 466. "The habitus is not only a structuring structure, which organizes practices and the perception of practices, but also a structured structure: the principle of division into logical classes which organizes the perception of the social world is itself the product of internalization of the division into social classes" (p. 170).

Bourdieu emphasizes the empirical correlation his research in France reveals between the artistically adept and those who eat haute cuisine, and between "vulgar" artistic Tastes and the eating habits of working men and women. "Social subjects . . . distinguish themselves by the distinctions they make, between the beautiful and the ugly, the distinguished and the vulgar, in which their position in the objective classifications is expressed or betrayed. And statistical analysis does indeed show that oppositions similar in structure to those found in cultural practices also appear in eating habits."[54] Bourdieu characterizes the eating habits of the leisured bourgeoisie as the "taste of liberty or luxury" and those of the working class as the "taste of necessity." The latter favors food that is nourishing and filling, bulky, gulpable, massy. The taste of luxury is for lighter fare, since it need not nourish a body engaged in hard labor. Luxurious taste also puts a premium on the presentation of dishes and the visual display of a table; it is tolerant of the fiddling necessary to consume dainty or elaborate dishes without dribbles and spills.

The links that Bourdieu draws between literal taste and aesthetic Taste contrast interestingly with the comparisons made by classic philosophies of Taste, for he has in a way turned the value hierarchy on its head. Unlike most philosophers of Taste, Bourdieu emphatically rejects the qualitative distinction between literal and aesthetic Taste. There is no universality of Taste untainted by class privilege, no pure judgment of aesthetic pleasure. And therefore there is no need to stipulate a particular sort of Taste to ground universal aesthetic standards. Both kinds of taste are part and parcel of the same social forces. In fact the oral pleasures of tasting, primitive and infantile, subtend the developed preferences of aesthetic Taste and remain their point of reference.[55] The philosophical superiority of aesthetic Taste is an illusion rooted in the attempt to make class distinctions irrelevant to contemplative ideals of aesthetics, but far from being irrelevant, they have been rendered only invisible. Bourdieu's energetic attack on the Kantian notion of Taste assails the very distinction that is responsible for the demotion of literal taste from philosophical importance. He rejects the pretense of universality for matters of Taste preference, and hence is led to collapse aesthetic Taste into the same category of relative liking and disliking in which we find gustatory taste.

Because this analysis undermines the conceptual tradition that neglects the literal sense of taste and restructures cultural values in a way that grants eating par value with art, Bourdieu's approach is in many respects congenial to my own reclamation

---

[54] Ibid., p. 6.

[55] "It is no accident that even the purest pleasures, those most purified of any trace of corporeality . . . contain an element which, as in the 'crudest' pleasures of the tastes of food, the archetype of all taste, refers directly back to the oldest and deepest experiences, those which determine and over-determine the primitive oppositions—bitter / sweet, flavourful / insipid, hot / cold, coarse / delicate, austere / bright— which are as essential to gastronomic commentary as to the refined appreciations of aesthetes": ibid., pp. 79–80.

project for taste, food, and eating. His challenge to Kantian or purist aesthetics, however, presumes a false dichotomy. He considers philosophical attempts to discover universal bases for value fruitless, but in so doing he seems to be assuming a correlation between universality and philosophical interest that need not be granted. He assumes either that literal taste has just as firm a claim to importance as aesthetic Taste (and is potentially universal in some sense) or that aesthetic Taste is just as idiosyncratic and socially bound as is literal taste. Since the former proposition is evidently false, it seems to follow that neither kind of taste deserves the attention that philosophers traditionally devote to the subjects in their bailiwick. In fact, he implies that philosophy in general is a groundless enterprise based on the fiction of pure, contemplative inquiry.[56] Philosophy, however, is hardly so restricted in its approach. I intend to argue on behalf of the aesthetic power of food and the discerning abilities of the sense of taste; but it is as big a mistake to collapse the fine arts and cuisine into a single category as it would be to elevate food to a fine art. The distinctive qualities of both are obscured in the service of what is apt to become a largely rhetorical gesture, and the complex prejudices against the sense of taste remain unexamined if it is reclaimed only to denigrate the ideas of aesthetic discrimination, fine art, and high culture.

As we have seen, multiple factors conspire to shunt the sense of taste and its objects away from the sorts of philosophical treatments bestowed upon Taste and the arts. At first glance these factors purport to make evident the reasons why taste is simply not of any special interest, yet that is clearly not the case. Sense experience of all sorts, the human body and its pleasures, and food and drink are the subjects of sufficient studies, art forms, and obsessions to belie any thoughts that they have no intrinsic appeal or interest. The question is, What kind of philosophical treatment do they admit, permit, or invite? Answers to this question turn out to be remarkably difficult to capture and examine. The very language we use makes the answers elusive. The neglect of the sense of taste (and smell) is perpetuated both by theoretical exigencies and by the language of theory itself, which makes revision of philosophical issues surrounding the sense hierarchy somewhat complicated. This returns us to the subject with which this chapter opened: the use of taste as a metaphor for aesthetic appreciation and the understanding of the sense experience that the metaphor of Taste presumes.

The addition of taste and food to the domain of established aesthetic theory presents problems: both inevitably come off distinctly second rate, trailing the distance senses and fine art. It is not necessarily that they are intrinsically of less interest or importance, but rather that their particular interests and importance are not directly illuminated by the traditional concerns of aesthetic appreciation. Yet at the same time, the parallels of taste and Taste mean that the gustatory experience is kin of sorts to

---

[56] Ibid., p. 496.

aesthetic experience, and that food is not utterly different from familiar examples of aesthetic or artistic objects. It is this combination of kinship and difference between the two kinds of taste that leads me to reject Bourdieu's wholesale flattening of the territories of taste into the sociology of eating. The investigation of literal taste must proceed right on the margin of established theory: staying close to the well-trodden paths of the tradition, but also departing from them into investigations that ignore the expectations of theory and root out the distinctive elements of eating and tasting.

The reason that analogies, comparisons—metaphors generally—are so useful in philosophy is that abstract, opaque concepts can be brought to clarity by apt comparison with a concrete, particular, and familiar thing. The disadvantage of analogies and metaphors is that when the comparison is dubious, the very elusiveness of the targeted concept makes it liable to distortion in the process of comparison. (As George Eliot remarks of one of her characters, "We all of us, grave or light, get our thoughts entangled in metaphors, and act fatally on the strength of them.")[57] In the case of Taste, we have proceeded on the assumption that the readily accessible and familiar phenomenon of literal taste can clarify and indeed articulate the more obscure phenomenon of aesthetic appreciation. But what if the descriptions of literal taste that seem to make it an appropriate analog to aesthetic Taste are themselves questionable?

Certain aspects of the way the literal, gustatory sense of taste was understood predisposed it to appropriation as the metaphor for aesthetic discernment and appreciation. Taste is classically understood as a "natural" sense, one that operates directly, that is unmediated by rational deliberation, that does not depend on the application of general concepts, that is intimately acquainted with incorrigible pleasure. These presumed attributes have been—and continue to be—exploited in theories that stress the immediacy of aesthetic pleasure and its independence from rational deliberation. However, this characterization of the sense of taste also emphasizes its unruly, idiosyncratic side, components of its notorious subjectivity that require tailoring if aesthetic Taste is to achieve standards. Hence we have a situation in which the sense provides the analogy for aesthetic sensibility yet is not itself admitted into philosophical deliberations. Before pursuing a philosophy of taste for its own sake, we first should learn something about how this sense actually functions and investigate how much of the traditional understanding of this sense is accurate. We shall then have grounds for further considering the appropriateness of taste as a metaphor for aesthetic appreciation. In the next chapter I shall present reasons to suspect that some of the traditional assumptions about this sense exaggerate both the degree to which it is a natural disposition to respond with pleasure or displeasure and its stubbornly subjective character. Unraveling the philosophical prejudices in regard to taste appropriately takes a turn here in the direction of scientific studies of this sense.

---

[57] George Eliot, *Middlemarch* (1871–72) (London: Penguin, 1965), p. 111.

The Science of Taste

The features of the sense of taste that by tradition have resulted in its low esteem traverse several of the major branches of philosophy. As we have just seen, the character of taste sensations and the nature of food and drink disqualify both from aesthetics and philosophy of art. In the moral sphere, the temptation of bodily pleasure and the vice of gluttony—in Christian categories one of the seven deadly sins—caution against the enjoyments of eating and drinking. Epistemically speaking, taste and its kin, smell, are not considered senses that deliver a high degree of perceptual information to the mind. These general castigations of taste can be summed up in the ambiguous and complex claim that runs through the history of philosophy: taste is a *subjective* sense that directs attention to one's bodily state rather than to the world around, that provides information only about the perceiver, and the preferences for which are not cogently debatable.

Here I look more closely at the classifications by which taste is traditionally understood in order to sketch a clearer picture of the operation of this sense and to begin to detail the grounds upon which certain prejudices may be overturned. For almost certainly many of the claims disparaging taste are in fact false. In this chapter I skirt the moral and aesthetic questions, to which I shall return later, and focus on how the sense actually functions. The declaration that taste is a subjective sense turns out to be a highly complex claim that requires detailed unpacking before one can decide upon its validity. To prepare the way for this determination, the facts of the operation of taste need to be established. To this end, I undertake a brief review of research on the science of taste, which will take us through consideration of some additional points often advanced against the sensitivity of taste before ending with a proposed analysis of the phenomenology of taste experience.

My approach mixes scientific review with meditation on the sense of taste, and the richness of the latter endeavor necessarily varies with the depth of experience of those engaging in reflection. As an ally in my own considerations, I invoke the insight of a taste enthusiast of scientific bent, the gastronomer Jean-Anselme Brillat-Savarin. Brillat-Savarin represents a type of writing about taste and food that so far I have given short shrift. Against all the negative assessments of taste and eating that I have reviewed, one must balance another vast literature on gastronomy and cuisine. From cookbooks to treatises on the art of eating, gourmands from ancient times to the present and all over the globe have recorded the feasts and daily repasts of kings and courtiers, peasants, farmers, and clergy; and the gluttons, ascetics, sybarites, cooks, and consumers among them.[1] The more articulate and enthusiastic of these works describe in loving detail particular gastronomic delights, favorite recipes, travel experiences, and variant traditions of cooking and eating. What is more, food and eating occupy a large area of anthropological and sociological studies, a reflection of the fact that, philosophical considerations aside, eating is an activity that occupies all people at least some of the time and is an indispensable aspect of individual and social life.

The bulk of this material alone could serve as a counterweight to the denigrators of taste, whether philosophical or scientific. In fact, one might think of the disparate scholarly and meditative literature on tasting, eating, cooking, and food as constituting one pole of what we might call after Kant a "meta-antinomy of taste," reconstituting on a theoretical level the kinds of considerations that philosophers sought to resolve in treatises on standards of taste. This antinomy observes that there is a body of ideas about the sense of taste and its relative unimportance that is so established it has entered common parlance and conceptual frameworks; and at the same time another body of literature takes food so seriously it is clear that its poor standing in general schemes of value is contested. Brillat-Savarin is an enthusiast in the latter category. His approach is wholeheartedly scientific as well as sensuous, and he himself is situated firmly within the philosophical tradition that frames this investigation. Brillat-Savarin compiled the research, speculations, and opinions that went into his *Physiologie du goût* over almost three decades, publishing it at his own expense in 1825, just a few months before his death. The book immediately captured attention, and it remains a worthy model of a study of taste that is serious yet lighthearted, moderate without moralism, speculative yet sensible. It is also a monument of its kind to what can be accomplished through amateur research and thoughtful introspection. While the bulk of this chapter will present more recent research on the physiology and psychology of taste, discussing the tongue and its receptors, the chemistry that causes taste sensations, and research on taste differences and preferences, I begin with Brillat-Savarin's work and refer to it repeatedly. It will prove a useful point of comparison both for contemporary scientific studies of taste and smell and for attempts to include taste in aesthetics and food in philosophies of art, which are discussed in the next chapter.

[1] A survey of literature on cuisine in ancient Egypt, China, India, the Arab world, and Europe may be found in Jack Goody, *Cooking, Cuisine and Class* (Cambridge: Cambridge University Press, 1982). See esp. chap. 4, "The High and the Low: Culinary Culture in Asia and Europe."

Un Homme de Goût

Born in 1755, Brillat-Savarin lived at a time when taste—both aesthetic and gustatory—was of foremost intellectual and social interest.[2] He pursued a career in the law, becoming a judge in the latter part of his life. He was a royalist of a mild sort, but at that time such politics were dangerous in any degree, and he spent some years abroad as a result, including two in New York.[3] Perhaps both his politics and his historical time shaped his development as an *homme de goût*, though his pursuit of the literal aspects of that sobriquet may have been more assiduous than a Voltaire would have recommended. *The Physiology of Taste, or Meditations on Transcendental Gastronomy* is a series of aphorisms, dialogues, essays, and ruminations about the sense of taste, food, appetite, drink, sex, and pleasure. The book blends science, theory, history, and practice, and to the latter end includes some recipes and tips for food preparation.

Brillat-Savarin begins with a discussion of the senses, and to them he often returns. In addition to the standard five, he adds a special sense for sexual desire. That sex should rank as a distinct sense is consistent with the two preoccupations that shape his study, pleasure and the perpetuation of human health and prosperity. As Brillat-Savarin puts it, "If *taste,* whose purpose is to enable a man to exist, is indisputably one of his senses, then how much more reasonable it is to call a sense that part of him destined to make mankind itself survive."[4] While this reasoning contains the lingering influence of Enlightenment optimism, the belief that the universe is constituted according to a pattern that ensures the health of the whole and its parts, it also presages more recent science that appeals to evolutionary selection to explain the development of the senses. Throughout his discussions, Brillat-Savarin mingles consideration of the operation, the useful purpose, and the pleasures of the various senses.

As befits his enthusiasm for the table, a number of his famous "aphorisms" depart from the ascetic elements of philosophy common to both Greek and Judeo-Christian traditions. While writers who worry about the baseness of appetites tend to treat their satisfaction as a matter of nutritional necessity at best, Brillat-Savarin focuses on the manner of pursuing that satisfaction to distinguish crude nourishment from refined gastronomy: "Good living is an act of intelligence, by which we choose things which have an agreeable taste rather than those which do not." One of the standard reasons for classing the bodily senses as lower than the intellectual

---

[2] In this chapter and hereafter I drop the practice of distinguishing orthographically between taste and Taste.

[3] In a sense his loyalty to the Bourbons contributed to his death anyway, for he died from complications of a cold he caught while attending services for the beheaded Louis XVI in a drafty chapel.

[4] Jean-Anthelme Brillat-Savarin, *The Physiology of Taste, or Meditations on Transcendental Gastronomy,* trans. M. F. K. Fisher (New York: Heritage Press, 1949), p. 25.

or distance senses is that the former are fully shared with nonhuman animals. Appetite and sexual pleasure are even referred to as "animal passions." Brillat-Savarin acknowledges this undeniable commonality but calls attention to an equally evident difference in quality when he says, "Animals feed themselves; men eat; but only wise men know the art of eating." He also anticipates Feuerbach with the assertion "Tell me what you eat, and I shall tell you what you are."[5] Absent from these aphorisms is worry about any real danger in pleasure, largely because an Aristotelian mean of sorts governs genuine pleasures, for "men who stuff themselves and grow tipsy know neither how to eat nor how to drink." He wastes no time worrying that taste is a sense unworthy of his attention and believes it a faculty of extraordinary acuity, referring to the (perhaps apocryphal) gourmands of Rome, who "could tell by the flavor whether fish was caught between the city bridges or lower down the river." And despite potential excesses, gastronomy, the science of tasting, eating, and food preparation, is a civilizing force that brings people together. "It is gastronomy which so studies men and things that everything worth being known is carried from one country to another, so that an intelligently planned feast is like a summing-up of the whole world, where each part is represented by its envoys."[6]

Brillat-Savarin's encomia to the pleasures of the table begin with discussion of the mechanics of eating and the senses relevant to this process. Taste had long been classified as a "chemical" sense, though the exact chemistry that produces different taste sensations was not known in his time, and indeed retains some of its mysteries to this day. Taste and smell are chemical senses because they operate by detecting molecules of dissolved or vaporous substances that come into contact with the organs of sense and react chemically within their membranes, stimulating neurotransmitters that send messages to the brain and produce sensations. Brillat-Savarin formulated his own analysis in terms that refer to simple, unenhanced observation: "This sensation is a chemical operation which is accomplished . . . by moisture. That is to say, the sapid molecules must be dissolved in no matter what kind of fluid, so that they may then be absorbed by the sensitive projections, buds, or suckers which line the interior of the apparatus for tasting."[7] Though the invocation of chemistry is modern, this description by itself takes us little beyond the observations of ancient science, which also noted the requirements of solubility and contact in order for sapid substances to be perceived. The tiny but observable "projections, buds, or suckers" of the tongue have long been targeted as the likely taste-sensitive tissue, though how this sensitivity is accomplished has been discovered only recently.

---

[5] Brillat-Savarin's English translator, M. F. K. Fisher, points out the comparison between this statement and Ludwig Feuerbach's more familiar "Der Mensch ist was er isst."
[6] Brillat-Savarin, *Physiology of Taste*, pp. 45, 53. The aphorisms appear at the start of the work, on pp. 1–3.
[7] Ibid., pp. 35–36.

The Anatomy of the Tongue and the Chemistry of Taste

The tongue is a rough-surfaced muscle that churns and moves food during the process of mastication and swallowing. Its surface is dotted with small bumps, which indeed look rather like buds. The little bumps observable to the naked eye, however, are not themselves the receptors for tastes. The actual taste buds—too small to be seen unmagnified—were discovered in 1867 in the walls of the observable bumps, or papillae.[8]

The tongue can be mapped according to both the papillae that dot its surface and the relative sensitivities to different tastes that characterize its zones (see Figure 3.1). Along the sides toward the back are stripy projections known as foliate papillae; the large circular protrusions on the back of the tongue before the slide down the throat are the circumvallate papillae. Sprinkled on the surface are large fungiform papillae (which resemble mushrooms when magnified) and smaller filiform papillae. The fungiform papillae are dispersed over the surface but are more numerous toward the

[8] Edwin G. Boring, *Sensation and Perception in the History of Experimental Psychology* (New York: Appleton-Century-Crofts, 1942), p. 450.

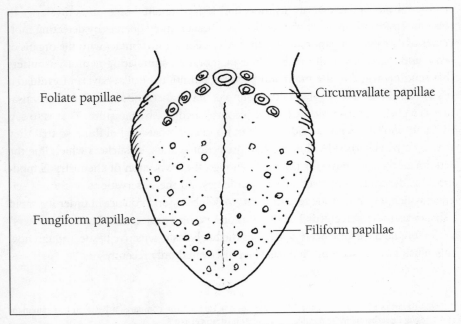

3.1. *The papillae of the tongue. (After Frank Arthur Geldard,* The Human Senses, *2d ed. [New York: Wiley, 1972], p. 488; and A. W. Logue,* The Psychology of Eating and Drinking *[New York: W. H. Freeman, 1986], p. 52.)*

front. As a rule taste buds reside singly at the center of fungiform papillae, in multiples in the walls of foliate and circumvallate papillae and in the valleys between them; filiform papillae contain no taste buds in mammals. Incidental taste buds can also appear elsewhere in the mouth, such as the palate or pharynx.

Taste buds themselves are clusters of between 50 and 150 taste receptor cells. They are globular with an opening called a taste pore at the top (see Figure 3.2). Molecules of dissolved substances—"tastants"—enter the taste pore and interact with microvilli, stringy projections from interior taste cells that surround the pore. In the microvilli, chemical reactions between the tastants and receptor molecules in the taste cells cause reactions that produce further chemicals, which act as neurotransmitters

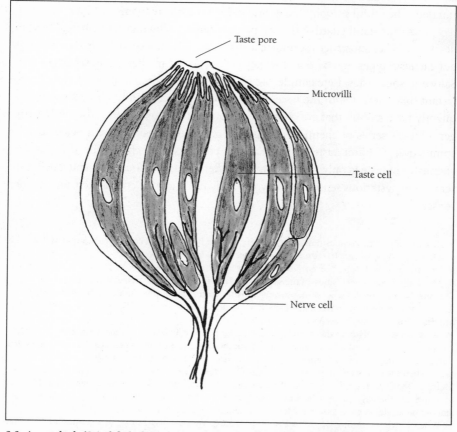

3.2. *A taste bud. (Simplified after Susan McLaughlin and Robert F. Margolskee, "The Sense of Taste," American Scientist 82 [November–December 1994]: 541.)*

and stimulate neurons that extend into the taste bud. The neurotransmitters convey information along one of several cranial nerves to the brain, and then the taste sensation itself occurs to consciousness.[9] Four nerves run into the tongue and mouth region and are variously responsible for providing conduits of information back to the brain. Most of the taste information travels the *chorda tympani* branch of the facial nerve along a loopy path from tongue to medulla via the region of the ear, and from the medulla through the optic thalamus to the cortex. There are various types of cells in the walls of the taste buds, and they are renewed frequently, every ten days to two weeks in adult humans.

While receptors for all tastes are distributed over the tongue, sensitivity for the individual four basic tastes—sweet, sour, salt, bitter—is particularly acute at various positions on the tongue. The tip is most sensitive to sweetness. Sourness is most acute along the sides. Reception for saltiness occurs along the front and sides, and bitterness is relegated to the back of the tongue, just before the throat. It is speculated that this distribution constitutes a safety factor, for tentative licks of sweetness can detect healthful carbohydrates, and many poisons are intensely bitter. The bitter receptors thus stand guard at the last point where swallowing can be halted, and indeed very bitter substances stimulate a gag reflex.[10] Taste experiments have to single out the taste types one by one, for they do not all act in chemically similar ways.[11] Salty and sour tastes, for example, are generally responses to ionized particles in the tastant that interact with the taste-cell membrane. Sweet and bitter tastes more frequently have stimuli that are complex molecules that do not ionize but rather trigger a longer series of chemical changes before neurotransmitters are released. The stimulation of bitter tastes is particularly complex and chemically diverse. The chemistry of taste is only now becoming understood, and thus taste and smell have remained mysterious senses well beyond fairly full scientific comprehension of other senses.[12]

[9] This account of the composition and chemistry of taste buds is taken chiefly from Susan McLaughlin and Robert F. Margolskee, "The Sense of Taste," *American Scientist* 82 (November–December 1994). I have also relied on A. W. Logue, *The Psychology of Eating and Drinking* (New York: W. H. Freeman, 1986), and on Frank Geldard's general study of the senses, *The Human Senses*, 2d ed. (New York: Wiley, 1972).

[10] It fits the functionalist analysis of sensitivity distribution that humans can detect bitter tastants in solutions far more dilute than those in which they can detect the other tastes. See Diane Ackerman, *A Natural History of the Senses* (New York: Vintage Books, 1991), p. 139.

[11] Several researchers note the stunning coincidence between information that is emerging about the chemistry of taste and smell and speculations from the Epicurean atomist Lucretius. Lucretius hazarded that sweet tastes occur when sapid substances are made up of smooth, rounded atoms, harsh or bitter tastes when the atoms are irregular and jagged (*On Nature*, trans. Russel M. Geer [Indianapolis: Bobbs-Merrill, 1965], bk. 4, pp. 133–35). If one draws models of the molecules of tastants, something like this is confirmed: the large, sharp-edged molecules of bitter substances look rough in comparison with the smooth molecules of sweet tastants (McLaughlin and Margolskee, "Sense of Taste," p. 538).

[12] When Edwin G. Boring wrote his history of the experimental psychology of sensation in 1942, he noted that the chemical senses had a sparse history. While he ceded some credit to the view that these senses are simply not so important to human beings as vision, hearing, and touch, he targeted as the real

The Disparagement of Taste

Even given the gaps in knowledge that have characterized the study of taste, many of the comments researchers have made about it appear gratuitously denigrating. Consider this opening statement from the chapter on taste in Frank Geldard's *Human Senses:* "Taste is the 'poor relation' of the family of senses. It is poor in having only a restricted set of qualities to contribute to the sum of human experience. It is also relatively poor as an object of productive scientific inquiry. The two things are not unrelated. Gustatory phenomena do not loom large in the world of human affairs, not so large as the number of gourmets and gourmands in it would seem to imply."[13]

Negative assessments of the sense of taste cluster around three sorts of assertions, two of which are implicit in Geldard's comment: (a) there are really only four tastes—sweet, salt, sour, and bitter—so the range of tastes is boringly limited; (b) taste is "poor" because most flavor is contributed by smell; and (c) both taste and smell are somehow "primitive" senses. Though these claims are often uttered dismissively or in passing, they call for consideration of a number of issues relevant to the assessment of claims about taste and food preferences. These particular remarks about taste are not exclusively "scientific," for they are commonly heard in conversation as well. But they are particularly powerful when they come dressed in the legitimacy of empirical studies. My goal is hardly to dispute the findings of laboratory research but to examine the justice of the values sometimes derived from its findings.

Tracking the Basic Flavors: The Alleged Poverty of Taste

A standard reason advanced for the claim that taste is a sense of limited scope is that there are really only four tastes: sweet, sour, bitter, and salt. Combinations of these basic components deliver more complex flavors, but the rest is supplied by the nose. What should we make of this widespread and implicitly derogatory claim?

The attempt to separate tastes into primary or fundamental categories has been a perennial aspect of studies of this sense since antiquity. The categories of sweet, salt, acid (or sour), and bitter were present in speculations about taste by the ancient Greeks as well as by theorists of other intellectual traditions. The number of tastes

---

reason for the scanty scientific study of taste and smell the fact that their operation had yet to be understood (*Sensation and Perception*, p. 438). In 1994 McLaughlin and Margolskee also noted the number of unknowns still remaining to be discovered about taste ("Sense of Taste").

[13] Geldard, *Human Senses*, p. 480. This is not a recent study, but it has served as an important general work on the senses for years, appearing in references as diverse as the philosopher Monroe Beardsley's *Aesthetics: Problems in the Philosophy of Criticism* (Indianapolis: Hackett, 1981) (the first editions of both Geldard's and Beardsley's books appeared in the 1950s), and Logue, *Psychology of Eating and Drinking*.

selected as "basic" has declined over the years. At the end of the sixteenth century, nine basic tastes were recognized: sweet, sour, sharp, pungent, harsh, fatty, bitter, insipid, and salty. In the next century Linnaeus added astringent, viscous, aqueous, and nauseous, but omitted pungent and harsh; Albrecht von Haller added to the original list spirituous, aromatic, urinous, and putrid, but dropped fatty.[14] Some current researchers consider adding metallic, alkaline, and savory or *umani* tastes, but these remain controversial and the four basics prevail in most discussions.[15]

Any introspection of the taste of a meal will suggest that the sensations of tasting and eating overflow these basic taste types. ("The number of tastes is infinite, since every soluble body has a special flavor which does not wholly resemble any other," notes Brillat-Savarin.)[16] But analytic categories are developed to formulate answers to questions, and the modern scientific questions about the basic components of taste do not address experience alone. These lists were gradually pruned in the process of scientific experimentation to rule out the confusion of taste with sensations that blend the sensitivities of more than one kind of receptor. Astringent, for example, has too much of a cutaneous dimension to qualify as a pure taste; that is, it relies on the prickling or burning sensations received by the skin of the mouth. Physiologists interested in the taste receptors must isolate what is received by taste alone. The four tastes are what remain when the contributions from cutaneous sensation and from olfaction are eliminated from consideration by the controls of experimentation. These controls include plugging the nose of the subject and applying solutions of tastants with a well-aimed pipette or swab to keep the test substances away from the nasal passages near the throat, so that no texture or scent or visual clue can contribute to the identification. Under such strict controls, it is generally agreed, taste receptors alone regularly identify only sweet, salt, sour, and bitter.

In what sense are these four taste types "basic?" Do they compare, for example, with the primary colors, mixtures of which produce all the visible colors in all their subtle varieties? They do not, despite frequent misstatements to the contrary.[17]

---

[14] Geldard, *Human Senses*, p. 504. Smell researchers have also tried to identify a basic set of smells, but their results have not been very successful despite some creative and interesting lists. In the nineteenth century, for example, Zwaardemaker arrived at nine basic scents: ethereal (supplied by fruits, for instance), aromatic (spices), fragrant (flowers), ambrosiac (sandalwood, musk), alliaceous (garlic), empyreumatic (coffee), hircine (goat), foul (bedbugs), and nauseous (feces) (ibid., p. 455.) But the incredible sensitivity of the nose seems to resist smell classifications. It is also noteworthy that Zwaardemaker's list refers to actual odorous substances—such as goats—rather than simply scent types. This also makes the classification of odors different from the categories of tastes.

[15] Valerie B. Duffy and Linda M. Bartoshuk, "Sensory Factors in Feeding," in *Why We Eat What We Eat,* ed. Elizabeth Capaldi (Washington, D.C.: American Psychological Association, 1996), p. 146.

[16] Brillat-Savarin, *Physiology of Taste*, p. 36.

[17] McLaughlin and Margolskee open "Sense of Taste" by noting that the four tastes "can be blended and combined to create the many shades and hues of flavor," but they must mean something other than physical mixing, for the reasons given above.

These four represent categories of taste, not substances to be mixed; indeed, physical mixing of the four basic tastes is conceptually incoherent.

Certainly flavors mix, and some mix in such a way that the taste sensations of their original components are retained. In lemonade, for example, the sourness of lemons and the sweetness of sugar blend to create a lemonade taste, yet the introspective taster can still discern the components that went into the drink. Other substances interact chemically with each other to produce something qualitatively different. For example, salt usually enhances sweetness but may decrease it, depending on the substances in question; sugars reduce the sourness of acids, but acids do not reduce sugar tastes. Caffeine, rather than blending its bitterness with sour substances, increases their sourness.[18] The alchemy in the mouth is unpredictable.

That the "blending" of the four basic tastes into all other possible tastes cannot be a matter of simple mixture is also evident. If one sips lemonade and is asked to identify its basic taste types, it is easy to come up with sour and sweet. But not just any sour and sweet add up to lemonade. A blend of vinegar and honey, a solution of which may be similar in its intensities of sourness and sweetness, does not add up to lemonade. Here we see that the blends of the basic tastes are not conceptually equivalent to the blends of primary colors. Red pigment of any shade and blue pigment of any shade result in violet of some shade or other. The lack of equivalence between the behavior of primary colors and that of basic tastes is partly due to the fact that the basic tastes are really taste *types,* whereas primary colors are either pigments or light waves, depending on one's domain of reference. (Both mix to produce the range of colors, though the primaries are different: red, blue, and yellow for pigments; red, blue-violet, and green for light.) One can mix pigments, blend light waves; one cannot blend types, but must choose instances of a type—sugar, honey, fructose. To claim that the four basic taste types mix to make all the tastable flavors is to commit a category mistake. Though types are not physically blendable, however, they can serve as reference points to describe taste sensations. As A. W. Logue notes, "It is important to keep in mind that the primaries for gustation and olfaction would not be those tastes or odors with which all tastes and odors could be made chemically, but those with which all tastes and odors could be *described.*"[19] Perhaps we can therefore translate "basic" to mean that given these four categories, any taste can be analyzed in these terms by the subject who is asked to do so.

This type of identification is one of the purposes of a three-dimensional map of tastes advanced by Hans Henning in 1916, when he proposed that tastes could be related by being arranged on a tetrahedron (Figure 3.3). The apex of each angle of the tetrahedron represents a pure primary taste. Combinations of any two tastes are

[18] Geldard, *Human Senses,* pp. 507–10.
[19] Logue, *Psychology of Eating and Drinking,* p. 50.

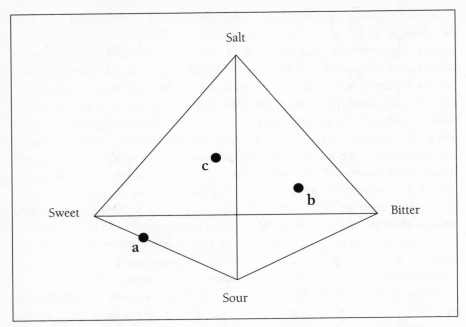

3.3. *Henning's taste tetrahedron. (Adapted from A. W. Logue,* The Psychology of Eating and Drinking *[New York: W. H. Freeman, 1986], p. 51.)*

represented as points sitting on one of the edges of the figure. Lemonade, for example, might sit at about point *a*, between sour and sweet. Combinations of three of the primaries would be located on one of the planes of the tetrahedron. Romaine lettuce—especially the muscular type available in winter—might be located at *b*. If a substance combines all four tastes, the described sensation floats somewhere inside the figure. Perhaps beef cabbage soup would hover in the interior around point *c*. (These references to actual foods raise a further complexity of identification and categorization: with the exception of that which is simply harvested and eaten, food is prepared, and preparation is culturally variant. It is likely that not all possible subjects will be able to place beef cabbage soup on the tetrahedron at all if they taste it only under laboratory conditions, because identifying the flavors depends in part on identifying the substance. Some of the cognitive factors that contribute to taste are discussed below.)

A problem of labeling is built into this description of tastes. It invites a rather contrived exercise, since in ordinary circumstances when asked how something tastes—say, rattlesnake—one is more likely to say "Like chicken" than "A cautious blend of sweet and salt." Our words for the sensations of taste and smell are often hard to come by, and this perhaps is another reason we succumb rather passively to the idea that there are "only" four basic tastes. Brillat-Savarin complains that "there is not a single circumstance in which a given taste has been analyzed with stern ex-actitude, so that we have been forced to depend on a small number of generaliza-tions such as *sweet, sugary, sour, bitter*."[20] Relatedly, Logue notes that the ability to recognize and identify smells is limited in spite of this sense's incredible acuity, in part because of the poverty of the linguistic labels we ordinarily apply to odors.

Nonetheless, understood in terms of the descriptive perameters of the taste tetra-hedron, the claim that there are four basic taste types hardly invites the conclusion that the sense of taste is impoverished. A multitude of tastes swarm on and within its four planes. One suspects that the readiness with which taste is dismissed as im-poverished or limited by its four basic types manifests the old sense hierarchy in sci-entific disguise.

The Nose and the Tongue

Ironically, the second charge to be considered against the sense of taste boosts that kindred chemical sense also often neglected: smell. The sense of smell has been the subject of research both in the laboratory and in the field,[21] and I shall argue shortly that the sensitivity of smell ought to support rather than undermine the claims of taste. First, however, let us consider a common complaint: taste is a poor (and rela-tively unimportant) sense because much of what we think we taste is really an ol-factory contribution of the nose. As Geldard comments, "olfaction . . . furnishes the most elaborate of experiences connected with food, for it is the receptor system sit-uated high in the nostrils that supplies the overtones for the fundamental tastes, that adds 'aroma,' that transforms sheer acceptance of food into appreciation of flavor. Were there no sense of smell there would be no gourmets, only consumers of nutri-ments."[22]

Often accompanying this observation is another regarding sense acuity: the aver-age human taster has a far higher threshold for the detection of tastes than for smells. In fact, of the three senses that are called into play while one eats—touch, taste, and smell—smell is by far the most acute. This can be demonstrated by ex-posing the relevant tissues to ethyl alcohol: the taste threshold (the point at which a taste sensation is aroused) is reached with only one-third the concentration needed to arouse a cutaneous sensation of burning, but smell requires stunningly less: only

[20] Brillat-Savarin, *Physiology of Taste*, pp. 37–38.
[21] The anthropologists Constance Classen, David Howes, and Anthony Synnott explore cross-cultural studies of smell in *Aroma: The Cultural History of Smell* (New York: Routledge, 1994). See also Classen's *Worlds of Sense: Exploring the Senses in History and Across Cultures* (London: Routledge, 1993). Research on the physiology of smell is reviewed in Natalie Angier, "Powerhouse of Senses, Smell, at Last Gets Its Due," *New York Times*, Feb.14, 1995, pp. C1–C6.
[22] Geldard, *Human Senses*, p. 438. This comment is made frequently also by the researchers on smell; e.g., Alain Corbin, *The Foul and the Fragrant: Odor and the French Social Imagination* (Cambridge: Harvard University Press, 1986), p. 235.

1/60,000 of the concentration needed for cutaneous stimulation.[23] Observers since Aristotle have noted the acuity of the sense of smell, sometimes marveling that a human being, who seems to need this sense so little in comparison with creatures such as dogs, should be capable of such discrimination. (Dogs of course are much more sensitive smellers than humans; rats are even better.)

If much of what we think we taste is actually supplied by smell, one might conclude that taste is merely the clumsy and crude companion to a sharper, subtler sense. However, the charge that taste is impoverished, and that credit for gustatory sensation belongs to smell, is actually dispensed with rather easily by drawing attention to the connotations of "taste" in different contexts.

First of all, the mutual action of taste and smell is hardly an arcane scientific discovery. It is perfectly obvious from ordinary experience and is recorded in studies of the senses since ancient times. (Indeed, as we saw earlier, the dullness of the sense of taste that accompanies a head cold served Hume as a comparison for a person with limited aesthetic sensibilities.) But the fact that the nose plays an important role in both the discernment of taste qualities and the pleasures of eating in no way justifies the conclusion that claims made by gourmets and other enthusiasts on behalf of taste are overblown and scientifically unsupportable. Rather, it points up yet another ambiguity in the term "taste."

The physiology of taste, strictly and scientifically speaking, comprises a narrower band of interests than that studied by one such as Brillat-Savarin. Understanding the anatomy, chemistry, and neurological setup of the receptors of the mouth demands that those functions be isolated from their neighbors and thus requires that sensations from these sites be clearly distinguished from olfactory and cutaneous sensations. But none of the encomia on behalf of taste issuing from Brillat-Savarin or any other gastrophile requires such restrictions. Brillat-Savarin is an enthusiast for taste experiences at their fullest, which include not only the savory odors of food but the accompaniments supplied by other senses in the full pleasure of the table. Never one to delimit pleasures needlessly, he invokes all the senses in the following passage (which reveals him to be an *homme* de goût indeed): "Any man who has enjoyed a sumptuous meal, in a room decorated with mirrors and paintings, sculptures and flowers, a room drenched with perfumes, enriched with lovely women, filled with the strains of soft music . . . that man, we say, will not need to make too great an effort to convince himself that every science has taken part in the scheme to heighten and enhance properly for him the pleasures of taste."[24]

---

[23] Geldard, *Human Senses,* p. 439.
[24] Brillat-Savarin, *Physiology of Taste,* p. 30. Brillat-Savarin believes the pleasures of the table are as appropriate for ladies as for gentlemen. Nevertheless, his description of the fair gourmande makes her out to be as delicious as what she eats. This line of thought is continued in Chapter 5.

In a less sybaritic and more scientific mood, Brillat-Savarin not only acknowledges but embraces the cooperation of smell and taste: "I am not only convinced that there is no full act of tasting without the participation of the sense of smell, but I am also tempted to believe that smell and taste form a single sense, of which the mouth is the laboratory and the nose is the chimney; or, to speak more exactly, of which one serves for the tasting of actual bodies and the other for the savoring of their gases."[25]

Brillat-Savarin is not alone in this observation; all writers on similar subjects mingle comments about tongue and nose in their discussions of foods and drinks. (Experts even refer to the "nose" of a particular wine or scotch.) Thus any attempt to discredit taste by pointing out that the tongue alone is a limited sense for those experiences trades on an ambiguity between the experience of taste, which clearly exceeds the stimulation of the receptors of the tongue, and the sensory apparatus that, for purposes of analysis of the different avenues of information of the world via different sensory receptors, is also labeled "taste." Until now this ambiguity has not appeared important; philosophies of taste that compare literal and metaphoric or aesthetic taste were concerned not with the sensory experience of the tongue alone but with what Brillat-Savarin would call gastronomic pleasures. But now that we consider the science of taste, it is important to note that such experiences (whether pleasurable or not) depend on both the sense of taste (on the tongue) and the sense of smell.

Indeed, we can do the boosters of smell one better and observe that the sensations of eating also depend on touch, that sense which the ancients placed as the closest companion to taste. The surface of the tongue, it should be remembered, has touch receptors as well as taste buds. As anyone returning from the dentist knows, loss of sensation in the tongue reduces not only taste sensation but also the sensitivity of touch that allows chewing and swallowing without leakage. Eating with a numbed tongue is hardly worth the effort, no matter how nice the food smells—an observation that may serve to balance the claims about the privileged role that olfaction plays in flavor. Moreover, many of the piquant sensations of eating are cutaneous; that is, sensations of the skin of the tongue and mouth. Hot spices, chili peppers, garlic, and onions inspire not only tastes but also tingling or burning sensations. A judge of food is interested in its texture as well as its other properties—another instance in which "taste" in the larger sense relies on the sense of touch. (Many people reject okra on the grounds that, unusual among vegetables, it has a slimy texture.) To distinguish between taste in its narrow and expanded senses, from now on I shall refer to the sensation delivered by the taste buds alone

[25] Ibid., p. 38.

as "taste sensation," and label the fuller sense of taste that includes smell and touch "taste experience."

Even granting the above, it should also be noted that the role of the nose in taste is more intimately connected with the mouth than at first it might appear. The first sniff of food or drink occurs while the substance to be ingested is still outside the body, vapors wafting toward the nostrils, and with inhalation the substance is smelled in a typical act of olfaction. But the business of the olfactory sense is not complete, for more nasal passages lie in wait at the back of the throat to deliver a finishing kick to the full taste experience. (They are the culprits when nose drops or eye drops seep into the throat and taste bad.) While it is accurate to note that the retronasal passages at the throat deliver olfactory sensations to the experience of taste, it is also not idiomatic to call this an experience of "smell." It certainly does not involve sniffing a gaseous substance, and in fact sniffing at that point in the eating process makes one likely to choke.

The assertion that a large part of flavor is provided by olfaction is often delivered as an accusation mixed with condescension for the poor sense of taste. "Without smell, there are hardly any tastes" may have the same taunting quality as "If you didn't see the label on the bottle, you couldn't tell Château Lafitte Rothschild from wino red." But the two claims are quite different. The latter exposes either pretension on the part of the drinker or the absence of quality in the wine to justify its price. The former is a claim about the operation of the senses that contribute to the experience of taste. It is true that the full experience of taste requires sensations both olfactory and gustatory, as well as haptic. But this is not an embarrassing disclosure that requires a demotion for the sense of taste, only an observation that has been recognized by anyone who thinks about the matter, whether on the basis of a bad cold and boredom at mealtime or more enthusiastic inquisitiveness about the pleasures of the table.

The purview of taste that is subject to laboratory test is limited to what Brillat-Savarin calls "direct" sensation. Eliminated are "complete" sensation, which employs the nasal passages, and "reflective" sensation, the evaluation arrived at after pensive swallowing. These three occur one after another, and full taste is complete only after the last lingering sensation has diminished. It is this series that gives tasting its sequential quality and lends it subtlety, richness, and depth.[26] (Roland Barthes makes note of "certain multiple and successive apprehensions: entrances, returns, overlappings, a whole counterpoint to sensation: to *perspective* in vision [in the great panoramic pleasures] corresponds *sequence* in taste.")[27] Some scientific researchers also make this point, especially if they are critical of isolated approaches to the study

---

[26] Ibid., p. 391.
[27] Roland Barthes, "Reading Brillat-Savarin," in *The Rustle of Language*, trans. Richard Howard (New York: Hill & Wang, 1986), p. 250.

of the senses. James J. Gibson, who prefers to analyze what he calls "perceptual systems" rather than isolated types of sense receptors, is not inclined to disparage taste.

> Smelling and tasting, however, need not be defined by receptors and nerves. They can be defined by their functions in use, smell being an accompaniment of breathing and taste of eating. . . . Sniffing the air has one function, chewing another. The different receptors for the volatile and the soluble components of food, located in the connected cavities of the head, can be incorporated in the same perceptual system. Conversely, the same olfactory membrane can be incorporated in a different perceptual system when sniffing occurs than it is when eating occurs.[28]

Other researchers speak of a "mouth sense" that combines taste, olfaction, chemical sensitivity, temperature, and touch.[29] This synthetic attitude would surely be embraced by Brillat-Savarin, as this vigorous rendition of the senses called into action while eating demonstrates:

> As soon as an edible body has been put into the mouth, it is seized upon, gases, moisture, and all, without possibility of retreat.
> Lips stop whatever might try to escape; the teeth bite and break it; saliva drenches it; the tongue mashes and churns it; a breathlike sucking pushes it toward the gullet; the tongue lifts up to make it slide and slip; the sense of smell appreciates it as it passes the nasal channel, and it is pulled down into the stomach to be submitted to sundry baser transformations without, in this whole metamorphosis, a single atom or drop or particle having been missed by the powers of appreciation of the taste sense.
> It is, then, because of this perfection that the real enjoyment of eating is a special prerogative of man.[30]

Rather than pit the chemical senses against each other as rivals, we should consider the two to be complementary players in taste experience.[31] If the separate contribution from the receptors on the tongue is somewhat limited, then the incredible sensitivity of olfaction fills in the gaps and supplies subtlety and range to taste experience. Even this does not fully account for taste, for the texture and temperature of

---

[28] James J. Gibson, *The Senses Considered as Perceptual Systems* (Boston: Houghton Mifflin, 1966), pp. 136–37.
[29] Duffy and Bartoshuk, "Sensory Factors in Feeding," pp. 147–50.
[30] Brillat-Savarin, *Physiology of Taste*, pp. 44–45.
[31] Despite their intimacy, taste and smell do not report to the same area of the brain. Smell is embedded in the limbic system, which is also the seat of sexual arousal. Perhaps this accounts for one of the few universals of food: its common association with sex. Another explanation for this linkage points to the sim-

food and drink and the cutaneous sensations of different substances are supplied by touch. One can add, as Brillat-Savarin does above, that the visual presentation of food and the audible surroundings are part of the full pleasure of the table, though this perhaps goes further than an analysis of taste experience needs to go. But the taste of even something fairly simple, such as a dill pickle, cannot even be described without reference to the sensations of taste, smell, and touch. In short, the argument for the poverty of taste can be turned on its head, and the richness of smell and the added dimensions provided by the haptic sense support the assertion of the gastronomer that taste experience is lively, quick, and refined.

Primitive Senses and Savage Appetites

The third claim sometimes made to disparage the sense of taste and its objects is that taste is somehow a "primitive" sense. Smell is often also classified this way. "Primitive" of course can mean many things. Consider these comments:

> To the epicure, nothing represents the height of refinement better than the diverse tastes of a fine meal. To the biologist, nothing could be more basic than the molecular mechanisms underlying taste. The chemical senses—taste and smell—are the most primitive of the sensory modalities. Before warning labels were invented, people had to rely on their sense of taste to distinguish nutritionally useful substances, which taste good, from potentially toxic substances, which taste bad.[32]

> The sense of taste has a simple function. It acts as a gatekeeper for the organism's digestive system in that it provides information about the substances that may or may not be ingested.[33]

These sorts of comments invoke two possible meanings of "primitive": (1) that the senses of taste and smell developed early in the creatures that eventually evolved into the animals that exist today, including human beings; and (2) that they evolved for protective purposes necessary for life and to some extent still function that way. Both claims are widely agreed upon among scientists, for chemical sensitivities are observable in simple, even single-celled creatures that have no auditory or visual receptors of even rudimentary form. (Moreover, the organ that evolves earliest in sim-

---

ilarity of neural receptors called Krause's end bulbs in the lips, tongue, and genitals (Ackerman, *Natural History of the Senses,* p. 132).

[32] McLaughlin and Margolskee, "Sense of Taste," p. 538.

[33] Henry Gleitman, *Basic Psychology* (New York: Norton, 1983), p. 116.

ple organisms is the mouth.)[34] We humans use our senses of taste and smell routinely to learn about the safety of food, for we can sniff decay before it is visible and taste that something is "off" in a dish that looks delectable. These two meanings of "primitive" both appear to be accurate with regard to taste and smell, but also they carry with them no necessarily negative value judgment. That is, senses that are "primitive" insofar as they evolved early and provide safety and health need not on those grounds be disparaged as somehow low or base.

Yet the term "primitive" is hard to separate from the more pejorative connotations it carries. Other writers explicitly add such meanings, construing "primitive" to mean also (3) a sense that developed early in evolution and has not progressed beyond what it was needed for in those early stages. Therefore, a primitive sense might be (4) one that is shared by lower life forms and employed in activities that differ little from similar activities in humans. From here it is a short step to reading "primitive" as also implying (5) a sense that is unworthy of extended attention.

We need go no further than one of the giants of the theory of evolution to find some of these implications. Charles Darwin wrote, "Those who believe in the principle of gradual evolution will not readily admit that the sense of smell in its present state was originally required by man, as he now exists. He inherits the power in an enfeebled and so far rudimentary condition, from some early progenitor, to whom it was highly serviceable and by whom it was continually used."[35] By this sort of analysis, smell would function in the human creature rather like the appendix. Everyone has one, but its once necessary function has atrophied. (Of course, Darwin had not heard of pheromones, those hormonal emanations that apparently affect creatures from moths to possibly even humans, though this type of "smelling" cannot qualify as a sensation since it operates below the threshold of consciousness.)

Again, we face problems that arise when an aspect of the chemical senses that is both true and unexceptionable is expressed with a term of ambiguous valence. The danger of the term "primitive" when applied to taste and smell is that it is very easy to slide from the sense of "early, basic" to the sense of "uncivilized." At that point, we are back in the territory of the theorists who classify the bodily senses as less worthy than the higher ones on moral grounds. Perhaps they worry that if we were to credit the chemical senses for what is best in their operations, we might encourage humans to engage in unseemly behavior, perhaps to investigate one another with doglike sniffing. But if the chemical senses still participate in primitive dispositions, we might preferably try to appreciate the common threads of life in the manner of Diane

[34] Ackerman, *Natural History of the Senses,* p. 143.
[35] Charles Darwin, *The Descent of Man* (1871), quoted in Warren Gorman, *Flavor, Taste, and the Psychology of Smell* (Springfield, Ill.: Charles C. Thomas, 1964), p. 48. See Corbin, *Foul and the Fragrant,* for an analysis of the social context of Darwin's judgment.

Ackerman: "If smell is a relic, it's of a time of great intensity, need, instinct, and delirium, a time when we moved among the cycles of Nature as one of its promising protégés."[36]

There is a final sense of "primitive" that needs to be singled out, not because any of our authors necessarily intended it but because it lurks as a possible rider to the term. A sense that functions primitively, it could seem, operates by instinct, little framed by culture, a vestige of wild nature breaking through the veneers of civilized living. As Condillac put it in his *Treatise on the Sensations* (1754): "The sense of taste is so self-taught that its need for teaching is hardly perceptible. The reason no doubt is that it is necessary for our preservation from the moment of birth."[37] Clearly this connotation of "primitive" cannot correctly be applied to taste. Indeed, it collides with another common statement, that taste preferences are inescapably relative to individuals and to cultures. If such were the case, taste (and smell) behaviors could not be primitive in the sense of instinctive, for their nature would resist cultural molding. These questions take us back to the subject of the relativity of taste and of taste preferences, and to what is entailed by the alleged subjectivity of taste.

De Gustibus Redux

Reflection about sense experience prompts some of the most accessible philosophical questions: What does the world look like to someone else? When I say "green" and he says "green," are our sensations the same, or could our visual experiences differ systematically? A person with all five senses functioning puzzles what it would be like to be blind or deaf. One to whom music is mere sound wonders what he is missing when he sees the rapt faces of a concert audience. What would it be like to see like a fly, what is it like to be a bat? These sorts of questions permit relativistic answers, and relativism is nowhere more tempting than with the sense of taste. How similar are the taste sensations of different individuals? Is there anything about the pleasures of taste that can be counted as "universal," or are all such preferences variable? In the last chapter we saw that philosophical treatments of the problem of taste have relegated literal taste to the sidelines of analysis because it is assumed that such tastes are indeed relative both to individuals and to cultures. Such relativity is standardly held to disqualify a subject from philosophical treatment for three reasons: (1) Individual tastes are recalcitrant to change, since they cannot be swayed by argument. Likes and dislikes are products of individual physiology, whim, and associations resulting from experience, all of which render taste

---

[36] Ackerman, *Natural History of the Senses,* pp. 54–55.
[37] Abbé Etienne Bonnot de Condillac, *Treatise on the Sensations* (1754), trans. Geraldine Carr (Los Angeles: University of Southern California Press, 1930), p. 188.

idiosyncratic. (2) Cultural differences are interesting insofar as they inform about the many ways human societies live. But their interest is descriptive and hence of only sociological, historical, or anthropological interest. Important as these areas of research may be, no philosophical issues arise with the detailing of cultural taste preferences. And finally, (3) taste preferences are not about anything important enough to demand universality anyway. While these reasons are beginning to recede as standard assumptions about what makes for a philosophical issue (for increasingly philosophical concepts are analyzed in terms of the historical determinants that influence their development), the continued assumption that this sense falls outside philosophical purviews indicates lingering acceptance of these considerations. It is now time to confront the competing claims about difference, relativity, culture, and taste.

Physical Differences and Tastes

Research into the physiology and psychology of taste typically includes a component that is absent from studies of the other senses: the pleasure or displeasure subjects take in different taste sensations. That different people have different likes and dislikes among the foods they eat is obvious, and when one person relishes a dish that is revolting to another, we may ask if the actual taste sensations they are having can possibly be similar. Sometimes there are reasons to doubt that they are.

The numbers of papillae on the tongue and the numbers of taste receptors among the papillae can vary tremendously from person to person. Brillat-Savarin noted the variation in the visible papillae and invoked it to explain why one person's sumptuous feast is another's boring meal. Contemporary research sustains his observation: the taste researcher Linda Bartoshuk estimates that about 20 percent of the population are what she calls "supertasters," people with densely packed papillae who are especially sensitive to flavors (especially to sweet and sour). Another 20 percent have comparatively few taste buds and dull taste perception. Most of us fall in between.[38] Papillae vary in number, as Brillat-Savarin could see with the naked eye. But so too do the numbers of taste receptors within the papillae. On average about 200 taste receptors open into the moats around the circumvallate papillae, but as many as 865 have been counted on one papilla, and as few as 100 on another.[39] (Alas, in old age the number of taste buds steadily declines.) The taste sensations of people vary accordingly, and the taste sensations of an individual change over the years as the number of receptors residing on his or her tongue declines.

[38] Bartoshuk's research is summarized in Thomas Levenson, "Accounting for Taste," *The Sciences* 35 (January–February 1995).
[39] Geldard, *Human Senses*, p. 489.

What is more, genetic factors determine whether a person can taste certain substances at all. There are several bitter tastants for which the thresholds of discernibility are either very low or very high. The one tested most often is phenylthiocarbamide (or PTC). Persons who can taste PTC find it intensely bitter; others hardly notice it at all. A related chemical is found in broccoli, a vegetable of particularly uneven appreciation, and other substances of similar chemical composition, such as saccharin, exhibit like patterns of discernibility.[40]

Evidence of a physiological basis for variations in taste sensations must be balanced with other factors that appear to offer some universals, not only for what can be tasted but for taste preferences. Why do we eat? Partly because we are hungry, because our bodies need nutriments, because we desire to taste something for the pleasure it delivers.[41] The desire for the pleasure of tasting is the reason most likely to vary from person to person, but all these factors are subject to both genetic and environmental influences.

There appears to be a universal, genetically based preference for the taste of sweet things. This preference is functional from an evolutionary point of view, for in nature "sweet" signals "ripe fruit," a good source of nutrition. A liking for sweetness is apparently not learned, though *which* sweet substances one is inclined to select is another question. The same holds true for salt—another substance that is necessary for the body. Liking for salt is universal in humans and other species as well. Sour and bitter are not so easily liked, but newborn babies display typical facial expressions when exposed to these tastes, evidence of some kind of reaction that is common among humans.[42]

Genetic factors also figure in the development of the diets customary in different societies. Not all people can digest cow's milk and dairy products after infancy, for example, so globally these foods exhibit an uneven consumption pattern. Members of large populations in Asia and Africa stop secreting lactase, the enzyme that digests the lactose in milk, by late childhood. This has influenced the basic components of the cuisines of many areas and hence the acculturated taste preferences as well. (Agricultural resources and animal use are other important influences over the development of eating patterns and hence the taste preferences that emerge in different regions.)

The features of human physiology reviewed above are causal factors for the tastes we experience and for a certain range of variation both in taste preferences and in the intensity of the taste sensations that individuals can have. The number of papil-

---

[40] Logue, *Psychology of Eating and Drinking,* p. 56. The presence of PTC in cruciferous vegetables is mentioned in the *University of California at Berkeley Wellness Letter* 13.5 (February 1997): 3.

[41] Logue explains theories of hunger and thirst in pt. 2 of *Psychology of Eating and Drinking.*

[42] "In nature, poisons are bitter; sour fruit is not ripe; sweet fruit is ripe; and a preference for salt will produce ingestion of many needed materials. Beyond these simple genetically mediated preferences, however, food choice is learned": Elizabeth Capaldi, *Why We Eat What We Eat,* p. 6.

lae on one's tongue, one's genetic makeup, the enzymes supplied to one's system are not alterable features of the experiencing body. They are to that degree recalcitrant and brute, aspects of taste ability that are not subject to education or the refinement of connoisseurship. To the extent that they contribute to variations of taste experiences, they are certainly not open to dispute if by that is meant persuasion of their incorrectness. Certain physiological features thus make taste intractably conservative. Moreover, all of us have physical limits to tolerance, only some of which can be overcome by education. Allergies, for example, are common for foods (but incoherent for music, a relevant distinction between foods and arts). An iodine-intolerant person, who incidentally may still like the taste of shellfish, cannot eat it without becoming ill. No course in lobster appreciation will change that. Allergies are idiosyncratic and not as a rule culturally bound (with the exception of genetically based intolerances common to groups). Taste is not the only sense that admits of acuity and defect, of course. Vision and hearing clearly do so as well. But for many sufferers from myopia and hearing impairment, the intervention of technologies can adjust deficiencies to a standard of "normalcy." There is no technology to assist taste; the causal factors of this variation discovered by science simply confirm that such differences exist as stubborn fact.

Culture and Taste: The Edible and the Inedible

Basic biological needs and the taste preferences that accommodate them are rudimentary in comparison with other influences on the things people actually eat. While it is easy to grant that everyone needs salt, the way salt is delivered into the diet can vary hugely. All persons may like sweet, but there are still vast differences in preferences for honey or sugar, chocolate candy, praline, maple syrup, fruit, or shredded coconut. The cultural factors that frame food preferences seem by far the greater influence on eating habits. Tastes for particular foods are to a large degree inculcated by culture and learned by experience, as well as chosen according to individual predilection.

Cultural differences have occasioned much research, documentation, and analysis on the part of anthropologists, who have provided evidence for the variation that human diet displays. In the summative words of Peter Farb and George Armelagos:

Humans will swallow almost anything that does not swallow them first. The animals they relish range in size from termites to whales; the Chinese of Hunan Province eat shrimp that are still wriggling, while North Americans and Europeans eat live oysters; some Asians prefer food so putrefied that the stench carries for dozens of yards. At various times and places, strong preferences have been shown for the fetuses of rodents, the tongues of larks, the eyes of sheep, the spawn of eels, the stomach contents of whales, and the windpipes of pigs. . . .

People in every society regard their own preferences as sensible and all deviations from these as perverse or even loathsome.[43]

This passage details what can be regarded as the conflict points of eating habits, the exotic aspects of cuisine—those foods that are relished within one group and greeted with nauseated disgust by another. In all likelihood some of the foods eaten in all societies will be palatable to (if not preferred by) almost anyone, and Farb and Armelagos go on to argue that there are nutritional reasons supporting even the most seemingly peculiar of food choices.

At this point an apologist for taste might object that variety and conflict among eating preferences have been given undue weight, as if disparity of taste were singular among human cultural differences. Physiological bases for eating preference account for a tiny fraction of the disparities that can be accounted for by culture. And cultural differences are as evident with preferences for painting, sculpture, and music as they are for food. Is there any reason therefore to count taste disagreements more profound or theoretically limiting than the variation of preferences for music, theater, dance, or design? Furthermore, other cultures or groups or historical times need not remain strange. Just as studying different traditions of music sorts unfamiliar janglings into patterns of harmony and rhythm, so acquaintance with other cuisines accustoms one to try, to tolerate, and even to like foods that were once dubious and unfamiliar.

The comparison of food preferences with accepted styles of arts brings out an aspect of tasting that is obscured by the scientific search for determinants of taste. The laboratory conditions under which taste reception is tested typically use unidentifiable substances as tastants. The purpose is to blunt the expectations of the subjects so that they can neither guess at what is being tasted nor have their imagination interfere with the report of sensations. But these are obviously not the conditions under which we normally make taste choices. We usually identify what we are about to eat (or taste) before we ingest it. Indeed, knowing what one is eating—or smelling—can be indispensable not only for enjoying the object of experience but even for having the "correct" experience—that is, the experience of the substance in question. Some examples illustrate this point: A fluffy yellow mound swallowed under the expectation that it is lemon sherbet undergoes a period of consternated unpleasantness before it is rightly interpreted as whipped butter. The intervening sensation is without clear quality at all, just confusion and dismay. The temperature is wrong, the texture is wrong, the taste is wrong. There are panicky thoughts of poi-

[43] Peter Farb and George Armelagos, *Consuming Passions: The Anthropology of Eating* (Boston: Houghton Mifflin, 1980), p. 165.

son. But then, when butter is identified, the experience rights itself; the quantity in-gested is recognized as entirely too much to be appropriate to the substance, but the overall flavor becomes quite correct as butter, if terrible as sherbet. In such cases, there is no initial sensation possessing clear qualities that is subsequently and op-tionally interpreted and reflected upon. The interpretation—the recognition of the substance to be ingested—precedes or coincides with the taste enjoyment. In other words, the taste properties exemplified in a food must be rightly categorized in order to take shape, in order to be experienced as the things they are. The same is true of smell: the odor of an overflowing litter box transforms into the pungency of ripen-ing Raclette cheese when its source is correctly identified.

One may object that this statement is unscientific, that it violates the conditions that permit determination of how the tongue functions without benefit of extra-sense information. This may be true if the investigation concerns the neurochem-istry of the sense. But if one is also interested in examining the experience of taste, then ruling out identification of the substance tasted is artificial and distorting. In fact, it is a version of a formalist fallacy that one can find in certain philosophies of visual art. Theorists interested in the purity of aesthetic experience have proposed that the object of true, unmixed aesthetic attention is just the form of an object without regard for its content—for what it represents or is otherwise "about."[44] But not only is it impossible to hold form alone in conscious perception, it is distorting to what is seen. Alexander Calder's large stabile at the Museum of Modern Art, for example, is made up of several black metal segments arching over each other. From a distance it appears delicate and playful. The label naming the piece is mounted in-side, so the viewer must enter under the arches to read it. Once within, the arches all encircling, one reads: "Black Widow." Immediately what was delicate and playful becomes menacing, and because one was inveigled into experiencing it that way, it becomes also witty and teasing. Is this only the effect of incidental imagination pro-jecting onto the sculpture aesthetic qualities that it does not "really have"? Ab-solutely not, even though those qualities do not come into focus until the subject of representation is identified. The interpretation clarifies what one is looking at and permits the emergence of the visual aesthetic qualities.

Depriving taste experience of information about the tastant may have scientific purpose, but once that purpose is served, it only distorts the taste experience in much the same way that removing the label from the Calder sculpture would de-prive the viewer of access to the aesthetic qualities of the piece. What we know we are about to eat legitimately affects how it tastes. Not just whether or not we enjoy it, but actually how it is experienced, including whether we find it even palatable. As

---

[44] Clive Bell is the formalist favored by philosophers because of the rigorous and extreme consistency of his theory (*Art* [London: Chatto & Windus, 1914]).

Arthur Danto observes, the importance of correct identification of the object of experience extends to multiple pleasures, including artworks, sex, and food.

> The knowledge that [a work of art] is an imitation must then be presupposed by the pleasure in question, or, correlatively, the knowledge that it is not real. So the pleasure in question has a certain cognitive dimension, not unlike a great many even of the most intense pleasures. Part of sexual pleasure, surely, is the belief that one is having it with the right partner or at least the right sort of partner, and it is not clear that the pleasure would survive recognition that the beliefs taken for true are false. Similarly, I should think, there are beliefs presupposed by the pleasure one derives from eating certain things, namely that they *are* the sorts of things one believes one is eating: the food may turn to ashes in one's mouth the moment one discovers the belief to be false, say that it is pork if one is an Orthodox Jew, or beef if one is a practicing Hindu, or human if one is like most of us (however good we might in fact taste). It is not required that we should be able to taste the difference for there to be a difference, since the pleasure in eating is commonly more complex, at least in humans, than the pleasures in tasting and . . . knowledge that it *is* different may in the end make a difference in the way something tastes.[45]

When one knows that the food before one is in a dubious or prohibited category, surely the taste experience changes as well; for certain physical experiences are rooted in culture and its interpretations, including the somatic reaction of disgust.[46] Even long after a meal is over, if an individual discovers he has unknowingly eaten, perhaps even enjoyed, a prohibited food, he may vomit at the discovery. Mr. Weller, in Charles Dickens's *Pickwick Papers,* soliloquizing on his fondness for veal pie, muses, "Wery good thing is weal-pie when you know that lady as made it, and is quite sure it an't kittens; and arter all, though, where's the odds when they're so like weal that the wery piemen themselves don't know the difference?"[47] Mr. Weller's hypothetical kittens taste like veal pie only so long as they are interpreted as veal pie. (Jack Goody recounts how prohibitions persist even under conditions of privation. As a prisoner of war in World War II, he was induced to eat cat stew thinking it was rabbit. He found it acceptable, but his fellow prisoners could not be persuaded to

---

[45] Arthur Danto, *The Transfiguration of the Commonplace* (Cambridge: Harvard University Press, 1981), p. 14.

[46] Claude Lévi-Strauss notes that a standard division of foods among the peoples of South America he studied is not between what tastes good and tastes bad but between food that is "good to think" and "bad to think": *The Raw and the Cooked*, trans. John and Doreen Weightman (New York: Harper & Row, 1969).

[47] Charles Dickens, *Pickwick Papers* (1847) (New York: New American Library, 1964), p. 289.

find a cat for Christmas dinner, or to allow the common cooking pot to be used for that purpose.)[48]

In short, the fact that food is taken into the body contributes a certain conservatism to taste. It can be hard to educate both the palate and the digestive system away from disgusts and prohibitions that are inculcated early in life. (Perhaps the stomach should be considered that site philosophers have long sought for the interaction between mind and body.) Revulsion is, moreover, a largely involuntary reaction, powerful and overwhelming. Both the conservatism of taste and the reactive feature of revulsion probably contribute to the idea that tastes are brute facts and thus not disputable.

It is a serious mistake, however, to focus exclusively on the disjunction between relish and disgust. Not only does it exoticize food preferences and fortify the alien nature of Others, it distorts the way tastes are actually educated and are subject to change and refinement both within a society and between cultures. While it is true that humans eat radically different foods, of equal interest is the ability to craft one's taste preferences away from the habitual. We can and often do expand our tastes, and we learn to make subtle discriminations among foods that once seemed all alike.[49] What at first is below the threshold of notice can, with experience and attention, emerge on one's own tongue.

The ability to educate one's palate is an almost uniquely human trait. "Animals feed themselves; men eat; but only wise men know the art of eating," says Brillat-Savarin. Humans are distinctive in their cultivation of taste sensations that on first experience are unpleasant or irritating, such as those delivered by chili peppers.[50] Not only can taste be cultivated, but this course is positively recommended: we are urged to try a wine our host has discovered and to try a dish we have not encountered before. This phenomenon is an effective rejoinder to those who continue to classify food, eating, nutrition, and taste in a merely functional category that sustains our "animal" nature. While it is true that all animals eat, only human animals develop what can be called cuisines.

Jack Goody recounts the development of culinary traditions in those societies with both strong class hierarchies and written records that pass along modes of preparation, serving, and eating and that develop distinctions between "high" and

---

[48] Goody, *Cooking, Cuisine and Class,* pp. 84–85.
[49] Richard Watson writes of the subtle distinctions among the foods of Holland in "On the Zeedijk," *Georgia Review* 42.1 (Spring 1989): 19–32. He discusses cheese, licorice, gingerbread, sugar cookies, yellow cakes, breads, puddings, and porridges. While he claims not to be able to tell the differences among the many varieties of some of these items, he never doubts that there are such differences and that others can distinguish them.
[50] Paul Rozin, "Sociocultural Influences on Human Food Selections," in Capaldi, *Why We Eat What We Eat,* pp. 238–40; and Elisabeth Rozin and Paul Rozin, "Some Surprisingly Unique Characteristics of Human Food Preference," in *Food in Perspective,* ed. Alexander Fenton and Trefor M. Owen (Edinburgh: John Donald, 1981).

"low" cuisine. The presence of food writing in a literary tradition makes food a subject for reflection and may demonstrate connections with philosophical systems. Culinary writings that prescribe foods for medicine and as appropriate for particular walks of life, that see eating as a reflection of cosmological principles, that prescribe certain foods for the higher classes and others for the lower are found across the globe—in Egypt, China, and India since ancient times; in the classical Arab world; and in medieval and modern Europe, whose cuisine derives ultimately from the Persian Empire.[51] (They are absent in most regions of Africa, according to Goody, where all peoples tend to eat the same foods regardless of social rank.) Because haute cuisine is a product of class hierarchies and separates the luxury of the rich from the relative scarcity of the poor, it is accompanied frequently by the development of sumptuary laws and attendant disapproval of excess. In some traditions, such as the Hindu and Christian, ethics may incorporate ascetic values, thus linking eating practices and moral philosophies.

Written traditions regarding foods and their preparation permit the articulation of shared critical vocabularies to refer to tastes. Food writing also becomes a genre of its own that may be playful, poetic, sensuous, and satiric as well as informative.[52] It is commonly asserted that the linguistic resources available to describe and analyze taste experience are relatively scanty in comparison with the resources to describe the experiences of other senses, especially vision. But this is not strictly accurate if one considers the vocabularies developed by culinary experts and oenologists. There are rich critical lexicons referring to food and drink, preparing and tasting, which are understood by initiates, if baffling to outsiders. The bewilderment a novice feels reading the reports of wine tasters has given rise to jokes that spoof the language of the connoisseur. Once a taste is labeled *and experienced,* however, what seems overblown and preposterous language to discriminate between white and red expands both one's vocabulary and one's ability to communicate with mutually comprehensible exactitude. Having discriminating distinctions available in words also aids the refinement of the experience of subtly different tastes. Certainly writing about taste, food, and drink fosters meditation and reflection on food, and the introspective analysis of the literary tradition of a Brillat-Savarin.

The Phenomenology of Taste

I shall now attempt to map out the "structure" of taste and to put in schematic form the various elements that contribute to the complex phenomenon of a taste experi-

---

[51] Goody, *Cooking, Cuisine and Class,* esp. chap. 4.
[52] Of a cookery book from sixteenth-century England, Goody remarks: "The result is less a guide to understanding than a display of esoteric verbal ingenuity of a kind that is dependent not only on specialist activity associated with the leisure class but in some degree upon the use of the written and especially the printed word" (ibid., p. 138).

ence. Once these components are identified and arranged, the hoary description of taste as a subjective sense may be assessed more clearly. Because I am interested in analyzing how taste functions in practice, much of the structure of the phenomenology of taste must concern consumption: eating and drinking the substances that are the objects of taste.

Several contexts or background conditions contribute to taste experience. One is the condition of the body and its senses, including the physiological factors that furnish and restrict the ability to taste. These factors are as it were hard-wired in the individual and not subject to alteration. They consist of certain basic universal taste dispositions as well as unchangeable individual differences. We can think of them as causal conditions of the body and label them B factors. B factors may have aspects that can be present to consciousness: if one is supersensitive to bitter flavors, this is an item of conscious awareness. Other B elements are not the objects of awareness. One cannot be aware of one's genetic makeup, in the sense of being aware of one's genes as objects of sensation, though of course one can know that one possesses a certain gene configuration.

There are other bodily factors as well. Tasting varies somewhat according to the disposition to eat, which fluctuates according to the state of hunger or satiation of the taster. Detection of this state is a kind of proprioception, wherein the object of awareness is the state of one's body (I am hungry, thirsty, stuffed, nauseated . . .). Proprioceptive conditions vary over time with a single individual in a rhythmic and predictable manner. I shall label them H factors (after hunger). There is variability to taste brought about by H factors, but this variability is manipulable (if one isn't hungry at the moment, one has only to wait.) It is not mysterious, and most persons readily recognize when their bodies are disposed to eat or drink. If one is sick, appetite may be almost entirely absent. If one has just eaten, foods taste rather different (and not so pleasant) than if one is hungry. If one is ravenous, almost anything tastes good and gobbling is intensely enjoyable. If one is close to starvation, foods must be ingested carefully and slowly to avoid illness or even death; in such circumstances obtaining nourishment may be a painful necessity and tasting more or less beside the point.

Because of basic bodily needs for nutrition, hunger and thirst are often classified as "drives." The notion of a drive connotes an uncontrollable, physically generated urgency, and it signals another way in which taste may be associated with "primitive" forces. Hunger or the desire to taste or eat is seen as a disposition of the individual that cannot be helped, perhaps a residue of instinctual force interfering with the civilized veneer of rationality. Again, I think that reflection easily reveals this to be a crude generalization about a complex phenomenon. Sometimes hunger and thirst are general and have no particular intentional object. If one is very hungry, it may hardly matter if one blunts that hunger with foods that taste one way or another. At other times one may be hungry or thirsty for a particular type of food or drink (a craving for chocolate, a desire for something sharp-tasting such as a pickle). The degrees of specificity that H factors admit are seldom noticed when hunger is characterized as a "drive" and thereby an aspect of the irrational natural forces that induce certain feelings and behaviors. For one thing, hunger may be a very general drive that presumably is powered by body chemistry that takes over when the flesh demands. (I must eat or I will faint!) The desire to eat may not be so primitive, however; wanting a specific taste experience that has as its object a special type of food may be a highly developed disposition. Tasting, insofar as it is embedded in H factors, serves a bodily need. To that degree it partakes of a kind of urgency that sometimes amounts to a drive. But urgency does not characterize the exercise of the sense in general. Tasting, like eating, spans the range from satisfaction of brute hunger (and salvaging a body from death by starvation) to the most frivolous, chosen experimentation. The particular circumstances under which one eats are not incidental but become significant in the meanings of foods and tastes, as we shall explore later.

Taste experience is partially dependent on both the invariant B factors and the changeable H factors. There are other contexts that embed taste as well, including the culturally informed acceptance of certain foods as edible or inedible, good to eat or bad to eat. These cultural factors, designated C, vary by society. They are broadly manipulable by education, experience, and practice, but may have some stubborn, bedrock resistances that individuals cannot and perhaps should not try to overcome. Examples would be religious and ethical prohibitions, such as the refusal of pork or of human flesh, or of animal products of any kind, that manifest themselves as a reaction of disgust. B, H, and C are conditions that contribute to the character of taste experiences. B and H may be considered causal conditions; C represents a cultural context in which the root causes for taste operate, and which shapes their phenomenal character.

Tasting is an intentional activity, which is to say, it is a conscious event that is directed to some object or other. The intentionality of taste is rather complicated, for there are several ways to construe its objects. Some formulations emphasize the subjectivity of taste but others accommodate the use of taste as a means of assessing the object of attention. Tradition holds that taste directs attention "inward" to the state of one's own body. When one tastes a flavor, such as curry, that flavor is positioned phenomenologically in one's mouth, nose, and throat; the sensation is perceived to be an alteration of the body. Taste is unlike vision in this regard, for the intentional objects of sight are never one's own eyeballs (unless one is looking in a mirror and examining them as physical objects). Hearing is typically more like vision, for sounds appear to occupy the space from which they emanate. Certain sounds, such as deep bass tones, however, may be perceived as vibrations in the body. Touch is in certain respects like taste, for the sensation of touch occurs on the skin; but the fingers can explore the object and direct attention to the object itself, and so touch is conceived traditionally as a sense that obtains objective information. Smell is ambiguous in its phenomenal placement. Like taste, the smell sensation is "in" the body; but the smell qualities are perceived as belonging to the object of smell in such a way that one perceives a greater distance between the site of sensation and the producer of sensation than one does in the case of taste. While more senses than taste and smell may have phenomenally subjective aspects, clearly one of the intentional objects of taste is the state of one's own mouth and tongue, which I call in shorthand T factors (for tongue).

Many analysts of taste stop here, guaranteeing that taste will be considered only subjective, by which they mean attention is directed to the state of one's own body. Another aspect of the intentional object of taste, however, clearly directs attention *outward* to the *object* that one is tasting. An intentional object of taste is also the substance tasted. A cook samples a stew to assess its progress, not to check on the state of his or her tongue. By means of attention to T, the mixture on the stove is assayed. When a professional wine taster evaluates a wine, he or she is interested in T only to the extent that it helps determine the properties of the wine itself. (When Sancho's kinsmen tasted iron and leather, they attended to properties of the wine that were later confirmed by the discovery of the object that possessed ferrous and leather qualities, and that therefore produced ferrous and leather tastes.) This confirms that taste attention is also directed "outward" to the object in question, and this element of the intentional object I call O (for object). T and O are probably aspects of the same thing, an intentional object approached from two directions, so to speak. But I separate them here to emphasize that taste experience has an objective element. The clear attention to the object tasted is underscored when we recall one of the cultural aspects of taste: the recognition of a food as edible or inedible. Discovery that a mouthful is a prohibited food directs attention so emphatically to the object that it may be spat out and expelled from the body, thereby reestablishing its "outside" object status. T becomes revolting because O's identity is recognized as unacceptable within C.

The double aspect of taste's intentional objects represented by T and O makes taste (and its smell component, for remember that taste experience involves both sensory systems) rather more like touch than it at first appeared. Earlier I repeated the common observation that touch is a sense that delivers objective information, because the fingers explore objects and obtain information about their dimension, shape, and texture. The purpose of such exercises is not sensuous enjoyment of one's own body, so touch in its cognitive role is thereby excused from the indulgences attributed to it when it is involved in the exercise of the pleasures of the bodily senses. Taste clearly has a similar role to play in discovering the qualities of its objects—the flavor, texture, and even identity of a substance that is taken into the mouth in an effort to determine its traits. *Savoring* flavor probably focuses more on T; one directs attention to what is in the mouth if the pleasure of the experience is attended to. Touch also has a pleasurable indulgence, in which case it has its own version of T. We can see, however, that the description of taste as a sense that directs attention inward and not outward betrays a fixation with the pleasure of the sense and ignores its epistemic role in discovery and diagnosis of objects in the world—foods and drinks as a rule, though other substances are sometimes assayed by their taste as well.[53] This distinction calls attention to another feature of taste, and that is the frequency with which it is colored by pleasure, which factor I shall call P. It may also be colored by pain or distaste, or indifference, though the former two usually induce us to stop eating.

In summary, taste experience may be analyzed formally as comprising these components:

B: Bodily causal factors that are unchangeable. They can be universal (such as a liking for sweet) or relative (such as the ability to taste PTC).

H: Bodily conditions at the time of ingestion. Perceived by proprioception, they vary in individuals in a regular and understandable manner. They may be timed so that they coincide in groups; one may plan a meal, for example, so that everyone who sits down to dinner is hungry and ready to eat.

C: Cultural factors that enter into the selection of food and drink as palatable, good, edible, tasty. They vary from group to group, and many variations are overcome with experience and what was considered inedible may come to be enjoyed. They also contain prohibitions that may be impossible or undesirable to overcome. C factors are a source of disagreement about taste, but certainly not of the kind of disagreement about which there is no disputing (as B factors can be).

T: The intentional object of taste that directs attention to the state of one's body, including the tongue and mouth, the nose, the throat, and elements of the digestive system.

O: The intentional object considered as the item tasted, the object in the external world that one takes into one's mouth.

P: The pleasure or displeasure taken in tasting. It may be an adjectival attribute of T or of C, and when attended to for its own sake it can become an intentional object in itself.

The Subjectivity of Taste

We can reassess the nature of gustatory taste by looking closely at the term often used to describe this sensory experience: "subjective." The alleged subjectivity of

---

[53] Tentative identification of a drug, for example. A geologist may taste a mineral to identify it. Smell clearly functions with both T and O parallels. Consider the difference between relishing a perfume (with T equivalents the focus of attention) and sniffing for a gas leak (when the intentional object is almost wholly O).

taste disposes this sense to comparison with the intimate discovery of beauty and other aesthetic qualities by means of one's own felt pleasure, as we have seen. "Subjectivity" has a multitude of meanings, however, and some of them have also served to disqualify gustatory taste from serious philosophical theorizing. How warranted is the claim that taste is a subjective sense? Referring to B, H, C, T, O, and P, we may now examine this claim.

It is often noted that the nature of taste is such that it is experienced as a state of the body. Since one experiences sensations of one's own body and no one else's, taste is subjective, meaning that it is apprehended as a state of the subject. Hence judgments of gustatory taste are reports of how one's body reacts or feels when certain substances are taken into the mouth. This claim refers to the fact that taste qualities are phenomenally subjective. While yellow, loud, and square are qualities perceived to be in the objects to which such adjectives are predicated, sweet, lemony, and spicy are qualities perceived to be on the tongue of the taster. This claim is true. But several others that it may seem to entail are not true, nor are they necessitated by the phenomenal subjectivity of taste.

Another claim about the subjectivity of taste, one that we saw repeated by philosophers such as Kant and Hegel, is that taste tells us something only about the subject doing the tasting. It yields no information about objects in the world. This widely repeated claim is certainly false. It confounds the phenomenal locale of taste sensations with the intentional objects of the experience. Sometimes tasting, particularly when the object of sensation is being enjoyed and savored, does indeed focus attention on the sensation taking place in the region of the mouth and throat. But not always; it is equally common to focus attention on the object that is being tasted. This claim for subjectivity focuses almost exclusively on the sensations that are an intentional object of taste, but taste also relays information about objects in the world, and attention to taste need not be locked on to subjective feelings. True, we rarely inquire about the external world by licking the objects around us, but only because taste is not a convenient means to explore most objects. When we do taste, however, we also learn about the world. Minimally, we discover *what* we are tasting. We might also find out whether it combines with other tastants to make a pleasant meal, whether it is sickening, and so forth. The description of taste as a sense that directs attention inward and not outward betrays a fixation with the pleasure of the sense and ignores its cognitive dimensions and its roles in discovery and identification of objects.

Sometimes it is also claimed that taste is unusually private. Its character is known only to the taster, since no one can have anyone else's sensations. This is an ultimately trivial claim that fails if it is intended to single out taste from the other senses. It is a version of the problem of other minds, which can be applied to any of the senses. Taste does have a unique feature, in that its objects are actually ingested and consumed, and only one mouth can chew and swallow the same portion of food.

Foods are easily and commonly shared, however, and unless the dish is variable in its tastes in different places (as in fact it can be—meat may be gristly in one part and tender in another), there is no reason to believe that there is a significant difference in the object of taste in question.

Finally, probably the most common claim about taste is that it is not only subjective but also relative. It depends on factors idiosyncratic to the taster. Preference for anchovies or goat cheese just depends on who you are. This is an aspect of the de gustibus argument that assumes tastes to be caused by factors that vary among perceivers but are constant within the individual subject. This claim focuses on T and P, and usually on the B factors influencing both T and P. There are clearly circumstances under which this claim is a sound observation, and preferences for goat cheese and anchovies, both of which are rottenly strong to those who dislike them and mild or piquant to those who like them, are good examples. Perhaps someday taste chemists will discover some substance sensitivity that will explain the extremes of likes and dislikes for such foods. Even though some preferences are rooted in physiology, however, they do not form a foundation for a wholesale argument about tastes in general. The assertion of this brand of subjective relativity for taste usually takes the extreme cases of likes and dislikes and sets them up as norms for taste experiences. This claim is not borne out by experience. It ignores the B factors that locate common dispositions to like certain tastes, singling out only those that produce variation of preference. It also overlooks the ability to develop and change one's taste preferences. The claim of relative preferences, while valid enough in some instances, is too extreme to serve as a generalization about taste. Interestingly enough, proponents of subjectivity rarely invoke cultural factors, even though C factors are demonstrably the largest contributors to variations of taste preferences. This is significant, for C factors militate *against* the privacy and idiosyncrasy of taste, demonstrating the extent to which it is a social and hence in some respects a public phenomenon.

I should like now to convert these responses to the putative subjectivity of taste into several observations. The first takes us back to matters covered in the last chapter: the employment of the metaphor of taste for aesthetic discrimination. Certain aspects of the way the gustatory sense has traditionally been understood predisposed it to appropriation as the metaphor for aesthetic discernment and appreciation. But as I have just argued, some of the assumptions about this sense exaggerated the degree to which it is a natural disposition to respond with pleasure to an object. These exaggerations and misunderstandings led to an overemphasis on the indisputability of taste reactions, which in turn contributed to the separation of the gustatory sense from aesthetic sensibility in theories that were intent on distinguishing the pleasant from the beautiful. Since taste does not actually operate in the way it was said to do by the founders of philosophies of taste, one wonders if certain influential aesthetic theories were formulated with the use of a metaphor that was too imperfectly understood to serve the purpose of clarifying the obscure by means of the familiar. Ironically, had the more complex and cognitive elements of taste been paid greater heed, the parallel between literal and aesthetic taste would have been stronger. Aesthetic responses might not have become so emptied of cognitive significance as they were at the height of formalist aesthetic theory, because the literal taste comparison might not have seemed so much a matter of sentiment over reason. The cognitive dimensions of taste and their parallels with art are pursued in the following chapter.

Moreover, the subjective aspects of taste that both predispose it to aesthetic analogy and traditionally serve as a barrier to its serious philosophical consideration demonstrate unique features of this sense. Taste points inward and outward simultaneously, as is schematized with T and O. This makes it, I believe, a profoundly *intimate* sense. Its mode of operation requires that its objects become part of oneself. Its exercise involves risk and trust, and for these reasons it is especially suited for development into a cultural bond in rites of eating. These are among the most important of C factors. In less ritualized forms, the subjectivity of taste is acknowledged in the sharing of pleasurable experiences. The phenomenal quality of taste is accessible immediately only to the taster. This experience, however, is no more private than any other sense experience when it is discussed or exercised in groups of people tasting similar things. Why else would one press a delicious mouthful on a friend? Or try to cultivate a taste for something exotic, unusual, or promising?

Taste also has its objective side. I noted above the simplest of O elements: the ability to identify and characterize and evaluate the foods and drinks one pays attention to. The fact that taste is directed outward into the world gives it a referential ability. One can manipulate the taste of foods so that they *mean,* so that they have significance. Consider the use many cultures make of sweet flavors to signify good luck or divine favor—for example, the practice of eating honey at the New Year among Jews. The sweet taste signifies the hope of a sweet season ahead. The taste sensation alone is just a sensation, but the taste experience in the constellation of events at Rosh Hashanah imparts meaning to that taste experience that includes a reference to an idea of well-being and prosperity and hope. The meaning of tastes and of food and drink is explored further in the next chapter, where the referential potential of tastes is elaborated.

A study of the sciences that have investigated taste and eating preferences lays to rest certain prejudices against this sense and its objects. That preference is a matter of intractable disposition or of rigid acculturation is clearly false. That there are no common grounds for preferences is dubious. An entire dimension to food and eating that has yet to be explored, moreover, challenges the assumption that the objects of taste are not sufficiently important to warrant philosophical attention. It is a premature assessment, and the next chapter addresses the various ways to consider what tasting and eating are "about." Little has been made of the expressive and symbolic elements of food in this discussion, though anthropologists have documented this phenomenon extensively. It is possible that the usefulness of their findings has been actually undermined by gourmet enthusiasms, which by and large stress the complex *pleasures* of taste. The science of the sense of taste, as we have seen, confirms the opinion of gastronomers that this sense is discriminating and refined, that it can be quickened and developed to a point of great sophistication. Moreover, the fact that taste is not "merely subjective" makes possible a lucid comparison between foods—the objects of taste—and works of art. Whether these reassessments qualify taste as a mode of aesthetic discrimination is a question to be addressed next.

CHAPTER 4

The Meaning of Taste
and the Taste of Meaning

Taste turns out to be a sense that is more complex, subtle, and worthy of interest than its placement in the history of philosophy would suggest. The sense of taste is an educable faculty, as the dizzying variety of eating preferences displayed across the globe testify. At the same time, as physiologists and psychologists have demonstrated, there are a number of inborn, universal preferences, such as attraction to sweet and salt and aversion to bitter. These responses not only account for common likes and dislikes but seem to be the foundation for common meanings assigned to flavors. A question that remains to be addressed is whether the educability and discrimination of taste permit a defense of its aesthetic importance. Can taste experiences be legitimately considered genuine aesthetic experiences?

This question needs to be paired with a related and equally important one concerning the status of food as art. This is not a simple question about linguistic habits, for terms such as "culinary art" are both widely used and perfectly clear. But the question persists: Is the artistic potential for food comparable in its own domain to the artistic potential for sound to be transformed into music, for pigments to become paintings, words to form poems? Opinion leans heavily to the negative, as we have already seen, and the distinction between aesthetic and nonaesthetic senses goes hand in hand with a distinction between artistic and nonartistic senses.

Taste and food have had their advocates, however. A few brave theorists have defended the aesthetic potential for the enjoyment of taste, and yet others have gone on to argue on behalf of the artistic possibilities of food and drink. Although to my mind these are not very robust defenses, they serve as a starting point for my exploration of the aesthetic dimensions of eating, drinking, and taste. Advocates of food as an art form employ several grounds on behalf of their position, but virtually all of them take as a model for artistic foods especially fine cuisine that affords the highest sort of taste pleasures. My own position is rather different: I claim that despite some insights and useful observations, defense of food and drink on the grounds that they afford aesthetic pleasure is ultimately incomplete. It fails to address the most important objections both to the classification of taste as an aesthetic faculty and to the artistic capacities of food. Missing from the account is recognition that much of the importance of food is cognitive; that is to say, it has a symbolic function that extends beyond even the most sophisticated savoring. Both foods and recognized art forms qualify as symbol systems within which common aesthetic features may be found. I do not argue that food ought to be classified as an art—or at least, certainly not as a fine art standardly understood. That would be a pointless advocacy in any case, since arts do not arise out of philosophical insistence. Foods and artworks nevertheless have a number of similar features, and I believe that comparison of foods with arts is instructive at least about the former, and perhaps about both.

Taste and Aesthetic Enjoyment

Arguments on behalf of an aesthetic dimension for taste must contend with two types of objection: that the nature of the experience and enjoyment of taste is simply not of the sort that qualifies as aesthetic, and that what might be called the "logic" of taste differs from the logic of genuine aesthetic judgments.[1] Although the second claim is the harder one to counter, most advocates have overlooked it and have chosen instead to defend taste by reflecting on the character of the experience, examining the phenomenal quality of that kind of sensory pleasure. In the early part of the twentieth century the American philosopher David Prall defended the aesthetic enjoyment of tastes, even though he continued to maintain their artistic weakness. Prall claims that taste, smell, and touch can in fact deliver elementary aesthetic pleasures, but the development of a genuine art of any of these senses is impossible because they lack any principles of order. Hence although we cannot distinguish between aesthetic and nonaesthetic senses, we can distinguish between artistic and nonartistic senses in terms of the potential for order and complexity of the objects of sense.

A widely read aesthetic theory at the time Prall wrote was that of George Santayana, who claims that bodily pleasures hardly resemble aesthetic pleasures at all. They call attention to a part of our own bodies rather than to an external object. Beauty, by contrast, appears outside ourselves as pleasure objectified. "The soul is glad . . . to forget its connexion with the body and to fancy that it can travel over the world with the liberty with which it changes the objects of its thoughts."[2] Prall defends taste against the familiar charge that it is too rooted in the body to deliver aesthetic experience. He begins by rejecting the idea that visual and auditory experiences are less intimately connected to our bodies than are experiences of the other three senses. As he puts it, "The palate is no more internal than the ear, and the taste

---

[1] As this book was nearing completion I learned that Frank Sibley had left a manuscript on taste and smell among his unpublished papers. I am grateful to Professor John Benson for making this manuscript available to me. Sibley analyzes the aesthetic status of taste and smell in detail, including a discussion of vocabularies to describe sensations and a brief for the cognitive merits of these senses. He concludes that tastes and smells have aesthetic stature, albeit of a relatively minor variety. Sibley's "Tastes and Smells and Aesthetics" will appear in a volume of his papers on aesthetics edited by John Benson, Jeremy Roxbee-Cox, and Betty Redfern, forthcoming from Oxford University Press.
[2] George Santayana, *The Sense of Beauty* (1896) (New York: Dover, 1955), p. 24.

of strawberries is no more a function of the human body than their color or their shape." Rather than stressing the sensuous dimension of visual and auditory appreciation, however, Prall unexpectedly and somewhat perversely detaches taste appreciation from much of the bodily activity involved in the exercise of the sense. The perception of the qualities of taste and smell, he remarks, is only accidentally connected to our actually taking them into our bodies; we may savor the taste of wine and food without going on to swallow the substance. As he puts it, "we devour the substance not the quality."[3] To a limited extent this is true, though this back-door defense of the aesthetic dimensions of taste is an acceptance of the sense hierarchy at its most basic. Because the objects of taste can be spat out at the last minute, this sense can behave (sort of) like the distal senses of vision and hearing. It is a very grudging defense, to say the least; one saves the aesthetic qualities of taste on grounds that one doesn't really have to *eat* what is tasted.

The model of deliberate tasting without swallowing is the professional wine taster. Faced with dozens of wines to evaluate, the taster sloshes wine around in his mouth, getting it as far back in the throat as possible in order to call into play the retronasal passages, and then spits the contents out and assesses the overall experience. The spitting is required because the substance under evaluation is intoxicating. It is hardly a recommendation for the best appreciation of wine or of any other substance. This line of defense, if pursued, would improbably sever the pleasures of tasting from the pleasures of eating. Tasting would be what makes food aesthetically valuable, swallowing an incidental matter of nutrition. Why would one want to draw these conceptual lines were it not for the hold that the sense hierarchy possesses over the terms of evaluation employed?

Prall seems to think that the imposition of such unnatural conditions upon taste is required in order to demonstrate the aesthetic possibilities of taste. Sufficiently detached from their instrumental values, the delights to be had from taste, smell, and touch may incline us to contemplate and savor their qualities in the same way we aesthetically contemplate and savor sounds and visual objects. A cup of coffee, for example, affords not only nourishment, warmth, and a salutary jolt of caffeine but also a measure of aesthetic satisfaction. "If we do not contemplate our cup of coffee for hours in complete absorption, we do really dwell on it a little in an act of attention directed to its qualitative nature alone, not as means but as end. . . . If it is not the highest sort of aesthetic satisfaction, it is at least a simple, clear example of disinterested sense pleasure on the very surface of experience directly had."[4]

It is interesting that Prall is willing to apply the term "disinterested" to tastes, since so many writers in aesthetics insist that the objects of the proximal senses are

[3] David Prall, *Aesthetic Judgment* (New York: Crowell, 1929), pp. 60, 61.
[4] Ibid., p. 39.

by their very nature interested. Evidently the fact that we can savor without think-ing about nutrition qualifies this taste pleasure as disinterested.[5] However, he strikes a note of agreement with the traditional sense hierarchy when he adds the proviso that tastes are not appreciated for their beauty. "But the fact remains that we do not say of the taste of even the most subtly blended salad or the most delicately flavored ice that it is beautiful. Hence it is clear that smells and tastes and vital feelings are not the materials of beauty in the sense that colors are, or sounds or forms, or even tex-tures, for they are obviously not the contents of typical aesthetic judgments."[6]

That smells and tastes are not the contents of "typical" aesthetic judgments is in-disputable, indeed overdetermined, for the sense hierarchy pervades our conceptual frameworks. At issue is not whether tastes can be defended as beautiful or ugly, however, but whether their proper terms of praise qualify as aesthetic discourse. And indeed, with appropriate adjustment to accommodate the sense modality, it seems they can be.

A crude account would understand the pleasure of eating as simply the satisfac-tion of a craving, the pleasure of feeling one's insides fill to capacity and beyond. Prall is correct to reject this description, which does not accurately characterize even rather ordinary experiences of tasting. Careful, alert tasting also directs attention to the object of sensation. It need not be even a complex or sophisticated experience; it might be something such as M. F. K. Fisher describes in her account of a frigid Strasbourg winter, when her "secret eating" was devoted to heating segments of tan-gerine on a hotel radiator, then freezing them quickly on the window ledge. The fla-vor thus produced could occupy her much of an afternoon and took her three pages to describe. It was, in her words, "subtle and voluptuous and quite inexplicable. . . . Perhaps it is that little shell, thin as one layer of enamel on a Chinese bowl, that cracks so tinily, so ultimately under your teeth. Or the rush of cold pulp just after it. Or the perfume. I cannot tell."[7]

Fisher's tasting of these tangerine segments required no fancy preparation or ar-cane gastronomic education—only a tangerine, a radiator, a cold winter, and a little patience. The description is an excellent account of aesthetic attention and enjoy-ment, even according to the strict version (now receding from fashion) that stipu-lates it be disconnected from moral or social or practical values. It is not that it is ut-

---

[5] The divide between the aesthetic and the practical often figures in the attempt to qualify taste as aes-thetic. Thomas Munro strikes a similar note when he asserts, "It is an obvious and recognized fact that lower-sense stimuli *can* be enjoyed for their own sake, and not as instrumental values": *The Arts and Their Interrelations* (1949) (Cleveland: Press of Case Western Reserve University, 1969), p. 137. Munro blames neglect of the lower senses on the dominance of "ascetic Christian morality" in Western culture.

[6] Prall, *Aesthetic Judgment,* p. 61. Philosophers often make this pronouncement, though as a generaliza-tion about conversational practice it is disputable. Writers on food such as M. F. K. Fisher do not hesitate to praise as "beautiful" a particularly luscious flavor.

[7] M. F. K. Fisher, *Serve It Forth* (1937) (San Francisco: North Point Press, 1989), pp. 31–32.

terly disinterested or nonfunctional (for she was avowedly interested in her tangerines and they were full of vitamin C). Rather, this experience is classically "aesthetic" because it is pleasurably reflective and gratuitous. Fisher's is an account of the savorability of perceptual experience in a version that is appropriate to the sense of taste. If it remains more "bodily" than the savoring of shape and color for vision or of melody and harmony for music, then that is just the inescapable way taste sensations occur: they require the object to be taken into the mouth. One could of course continue to insist that the bodily entry point for taste is reason enough to disqualify such experience as aesthetic, but this sort of stubbornness is immune to argument and simply stipulates sensory limits to aesthetic experience.

Elizabeth Telfer agrees with Prall that responses to foods sometimes can be aesthetic, by which she means "non-neutral, non-instrumental, having a certain intensity and often accompanied by judgments for which the judgers claim a kind of objectivity." By "objectivity" Telfer means that the aesthetic response is warranted by the qualities of the object, such that others could also appreciate it in the same way. Good food invites what she calls "aesthetic eating," which is "eating with attention and discernment food which repays attention and discernment."[8]

The case for an aesthetic dimension to tasting and eating appears strong, especially if we abandon the criterion popular in an earlier age that aesthetic experience release us from our corporeal existence. Santayana's view of beauty, for example, would disqualify tasting from the realm of the aesthetic unless we acquiesce in the unnatural contortions that Prall recommends and imagine that there would be sufficient pleasure in tasting without swallowing to warrant the theoretical gain. But tastes of food and drink may be savored for their own presentational qualities regardless of nutritional value (though not regardless of their toxicity, which is a reminder of the greater "bodily" nature of this sense. One can see appalling things without dying from them.) The discriminative capacities of tasters may be developed in ways similar to the capacities of eye or ear for the connoisseur of painting or music. And certainly tastes afford intense pleasures that induce the enjoyer to urge others to share the food. In fact, Brillat-Savarin's enthusiasm for these experiences led him to posit a tenth muse, Gasteria, who "presides over all the pleasures of taste."[9]

How far does this recognition of the possibilities for taste and for "aesthetic eating" actually take us, however? It seems insufficient to raise the experience of taste to a level of aesthetic response comparable in significance to the possibilities of the experiences from the eye and the ear. Does this simply warrant acknowledgment that taste's potential is more limited than that of these two senses? That taste, while

---

[8] Elizabeth Telfer, *Food for Thought: Philosophy and Food* (London: Routledge, 1996), pp. 43, 57.
[9] Jean-Anthelme Brillat-Savarin, *The Physiology of Taste, or Meditations on Transcendental Gastronomy,* trans. M. F. K. Fisher (New York: Heritage Press, 1949), p. 353.

it may admit an aesthetic dimension, has a comparatively impoverished scope? In fact, this has been the majority conclusion even among advocates for taste. We can see why when we turn to the question of food as a form of art. And once we discover the barriers conceived to keep food from qualifying fully as an art, we shall be in a position to investigate the aesthetic elements missing from the account thus far.

Prall observes that the absence of discoverable intrinsic order in the worlds of taste and smell entails that these experiences remain elementary, uncomplex. Therefore they cannot be constructed into works of art.[10] Such formalist reasons to account for the artistic poverty of taste and smell dominate what scant discussions there are of this subject in aesthetics of this century.[11] They fit together with the other values of art that emerge from the concept of aesthetic value: that art's value is intrinsic, for its own sake alone, and not dependent upon functional or practical values. The functional value of food as one of life's necessities has seemed to disqualify foods of even the most elaborate preparation from the company of fine arts.[12] Because food is to be eaten, because it fuels the body, even a meal prepared for the delectation of an expert, with wines so complex they require a vintner's thesaurus to describe, cannot escape the practical, functional dimension altogether.

Elizabeth Telfer does make a case for food as an art form, though decidedly not a major one. The concept of art she employs considers the defining feature of an artwork to be its status as an object for aesthetic consideration. Carefully planned and presented meals organize eating sequentially, harmonizing the flavors and textures to be experienced. This kind of cooking, she believes, qualifies as the making of food as art, an art that is appreciated through aesthetic eating. The kind of art that food represents, however, is simple compared to symphonies, buildings, poems, or paintings. The medium of food has four limitations that preclude its development into a proper fine art. First of all, as Prall also notes, the formal arrangements and expressive range possible are far more restricted in food than in the fine art media.[13] Moreover, Telfer argues, food is a transient medium. While recipes may linger, actual meals are consumed and their remnants disposed of. Foods therefore cannot garner the studied appreciation over time that elevates especially fine products of more durable media such as paintings and poetry into canonicity. Third, she claims that unlike other arts, foods do not have meaning.

---

[10] Prall, *Aesthetic Judgment*, p. 62. See also Prall's *Aesthetic Analysis* (New York: Crowell, 1936), p. 18.

[11] See, for example, Monroe Beardsley, *Aesthetics: Problems in the Philosophy of Criticism*, 2d ed. (Indianapolis: Hackett, 1981), pp. 98–111; Arnold Berleant, "The Sensuous and the Sensual in Aesthetics," *Journal of Aesthetics and Art Criticism* 23 (Winter 1964).

[12] Marienne L. Quinet defends food against this presumption in "Food as Art: The Problem of Function," *British Journal of Aesthetics* 21.2 (Spring 1981).

[13] See also Carolyn Korsmeyer, "On the Aesthetic Senses and the Origin of Fine Art," *Journal of Aesthetics and Art Criticism* 34.1 (Fall 1975).

To begin with, food does not represent anything else, as most literature and much visual art does. We can see the representational arts—painting and literature—as telling us something about the world and ourselves, and we can see the world and ourselves in the light of ways in which they have been depicted in the representational arts. But we cannot do either of these things with food. This is an important way in which some of the arts have meanings which food cannot have.[14]

Finally, food cannot express emotion (though a cook may "express herself" and feelings such as love for friends in the act of cooking). Nor can it move us in the way great art can. Its aesthetic and artistic limitations lead Telfer to conclude that while food affords aesthetic enjoyment and can be considered a simple art, it is also a *minor* art. This is not intended to be a criticism of food, just a recognition of its nature: "we must not be so heedless as to waste a satisfying kind of aesthetic experience, but not so precious as to expect more of it than it can give."[15] A similar sentiment is expressed by Frank Sibley: "Perfumes, and flavours, natural or artificial, are necessarily limited: unlike the major arts, they have no expressive connections with emotions, love or hate, death, grief, joy, terror, suffering, yearning, pity, or sorrow, or plot or character development. But this need not put them out of court."[16] This conclusion may be found as well in other defenses of food as an art form—but not a major art form—including that of the anthropologist Mary Douglas. Douglas believes the display function of food and its occasional dissociation from nourishment is reason to class certain types of foods with the *decorative* arts.[17] It seems that whatever pleasures food can deliver and however refined cuisine may become, it is in the end just pleasure, after all, and offers less to our minds and imaginations than do more important art forms.

Given the concept of the aesthetic Telfer employs, she has articulated a cogent and sympathetic defense of food as art. Yet it is a pallid victory if there is nothing more to be said. Gustatory delectation is a positive pleasure, and a discriminating palate is perhaps as hard to come by as a musical ear. But the suspicion lingers that the aesthetic experience of tasting is still not as *important* as the experience of seeing or hearing, which is confirmed by the above claims about the expressive limits of food and the classification of food as a minor or a decorative art. Advocates for taste may be tempted at this point to examine taste experiences even more closely and to boost their status in comparison with the enjoyments afforded through vision or

[14] Telfer, *Food for Thought,* p. 59.
[15] Ibid., p. 60.
[16] Frank Sibley, "Tastes and Smells and Aesthetics," unpublished manuscript. See n. 1.
[17] Mary Douglas, "Food as an Art Form," in *In the Active Voice* (London: Routledge & Kegan Paul, 1982), p. 107.

hearing. However, praise for the pleasures of tasting will still not take us further than we have already traveled if the second type of objection to taste is not addressed, namely, that the structure or logic of taste experience is not parallel to aesthetic appreciation. This objection returns us briefly to the alleged subjectivity of taste and to the use of taste as a metaphor for aesthetic discrimination.

Roger Scruton has reinforced the old aesthetic hierarchy with his observation that aesthetic pleasure is essentially directed to its object. Savoring harmony or line, for example, directs the attention of the percipient outward to the object and its phenomenally objective qualities. Scruton remarks that

> We should note here how different are the eye and the ear from the other senses. There is no such thing as savouring a visual impression while remaining incurious about its object. Visual experience is so essentially cognitive, so 'opened out', as it were, on to the objective world, that our attention passes through it and seizes on its object to the exclusion of all impressions of sense. Here is one explanation of a fact that has often been commented on by philosophers, the fact that aesthetic experience is the prerogative of the eye and the ear.[18]

The relative "objective direction" of aesthetic attention means that the experiences of art require more "reflective thought." But gustatory enjoyment stops short of the reflection about the world that aesthetic enjoyment prompts.

Much of this argument is a reprise of familiar ideas certain aspects of which have been addressed already, and it demonstrates the fact that the barrier to the aesthetic dimension of taste is not only the phenomenal character of taste experience but the structure of that experience represented by the intentional direction of taste. Scruton—like Hegel—aptly welds aesthetic pleasure and cognitive activity together. This illuminates the difficulty of elevating taste pleasures to aesthetic pleasures such as those afforded by the distance senses. They don't seem to be *about* anything other than how things taste. Therefore, they remain less important than genuine arts and more standard aesthetic apprehension. The defense of the aesthetic quality of the sensory enjoyment of tastes presented by Prall and Telfer does not challenge this view. They too assume that enjoyment of tastes is for itself alone and that foods do not refer outward to any subject beyond themselves. Food therefore does not *mean*

---

[18] Roger Scruton, "Architectural Taste," *British Journal of Aesthetics* 15.4 (Autumn 1975): 303. For a criticism of Scruton's point, see Barbara Savedoff, "Intellectual and Sensuous Pleasure," *Journal of Aesthetics and Art Criticism* 43.3 (Spring 1985).

anything. This dead end is a consequence of accepting the idea that taste is subjective, a complex claim that was unraveled in the last chapter. But before I employ the argument advanced there on behalf of taste, another aspect to the "logic" of taste presents an even greater challenge to the aesthetic legitimacy of taste.

We saw in Chapter 2 how philosophies of the aesthetic concept of taste develop through employing comparisons with literal, gustatory taste, both embracing similarities and insisting upon differences. The intimate acquaintance with the aesthetic object and the pleasure aroused in appreciation appear to parallel the pleasure response of gustatory taste. (As Luc Ferry put it, taste seems to be "the very essence of subjectivity; the most subjective within the subject.")[19] Yet at the same time the subjectivity of gustatory taste appears to entail a degree of relativity inappropriate for comparison with judgments of beauty, and the classic problem of taste requires solution only for aesthetic taste. No matter how entrenched taste now is in both philosophical and conversational vocabulary, questions persist about this basic sensory term. Roger Shiner challenges the original metaphor, which he believes obscures an essential difference between gustatory and aesthetic judgments, namely, that the former are products of *causal* factors that result in taste sensations, whereas the latter are *criterial* judgments that assess properties of works of art that may be examined and debated. Shiner argues that the very first move taken in the adoption of the taste metaphor is inappropriate and misleading. [20]

On the one hand, Shiner notes (with both Hume and Kant, though Hume is the target of his study) that the properties to which the judgment of taste refers are elusive; beauty and other aesthetic qualities do not appear to name objective properties. Rather, the use of aesthetic terms seems constitutively to include reference to the response of the percipient making the aesthetic judgment. If I praise a piece of music as "powerful" and "moving," a component of that judgment is my own emotive state (plus reference to certain rhythmic, tonal, and volume properties of the music). Even more, if I praise it as "beautiful," my judgment appears to be entirely an expression of my pleasure. Shiner labels this view of aesthetic judgments "internalism." It focuses on the subjective nature of the taste judgments construed as pleasures.

On the other hand, another common-sense observation notes that aesthetic preferences of people with similar sophistication and experience often converge. They converge because there are recognizably good reasons for judging one work better than another, and therefore some aesthetic judgments are better than others. This species of common sense is suspicious that the domain of aesthetic judgments can

[19] Luc Ferry, *Homo Aestheticus: The Invention of Taste in the Democratic Age,* trans. Robert de Loaiza (Chicago: University of Chicago Press, 1993), p. 19.
[20] Roger Shiner, "Hume and the Causal Theory of Taste," *Journal of Aesthetics and Art Criticism* 54.3 (Summer 1996).

possibly be purely "internal" to percipients, who are responding to qualities of art-works and other objects. The reason one judge of art may be more accomplished than another includes the fact that he or she is better able to discern aesthetically relevant features of the *object*. Shiner labels this species of common sense the "criterial theory," for he construes the ground for aesthetic judgments to be criteria for assessing qualities of art that are *not* grounded in the pleasure responses of percipients. Shiner believes that these two approaches are so incompatible that they cannot be reconciled under the organizing rubric of taste. The reason concerns the different "logic" of the two kinds of judgment, a difference occluded by the analogy between gustatory taste and aesthetic assessment. Gustatory taste, unlike aesthetic taste, is accounted for solely by reference to the factors that *cause* the sensation. For example, "What is this odd taste?" can be answered in causal terms, such as "I added asparagus to the soup." (The chemical properties of asparagus cause an unexpected taste in the mouth of the eater, who was anticipating broccoli.) Aesthetic judgments, Shiner argues, are criterial. They appeal to features of the object that qualify as reasons why one judges a book to be lyrically written or too long and wordy. Such reasons are references not to the causes of one's subjective responses but to standards for judgment that one invokes in the act of aesthetic assessment.

Because the analogy with taste is so entrenched, the actual differences between the two sorts of judgment have been habitually obscured, according to Shiner. Hume's famous exposition of delicate taste by invocation of the wine tasters who discern metallic and leather flavors from a dropped key is a "deeply misleading analogy—that between aesthetic taste and gustatory taste."[21] The aesthetic judgment is a criterial judgment about the reasons one responds one way or another, not a search for the causes of one's response. Criteria are accessible to introspection, analysis, and revision. Causes are governed by physical laws of chemistry and human physiology; they may operate successfully and never be known. When an aesthetic judge refers to rhythm and movement, he is referring to properties of the artwork, properties possession of which are criteria for the aesthetic judgment that music is powerful or moving or well played. The use of "taste" to refer to phenomena both of food and drink and of art permits the mistaken implication that a causal theory for aesthetic response is plausible. It is not plausible for art, but because it is the only theory available to account for gustatory taste, the metaphor of taste for aesthetics is intractably unsuitable.

Shiner's target of argument is the causal theory of taste that he believes is presumed by the major modern taste philosophies, but by extension his reasoning offers strong grounds for questioning the aesthetic nature of taste enjoyment. If gusta-

---

[21] Ibid., p. 240.

tory judgments are "internalist," as he claims, and if they are accounted for solely by reference to causal factors, then no matter how enjoyable and refined they may be, they are going to occupy a category different from judgments appropriate for artworks. In drawing the cause–criterion distinction, Shiner makes the traditional assumption that the bodily senses are more subjective than the intellectual senses and that judgments of literal taste are chiefly reports of one's own felt responses. Therefore, he concludes, the gustatory analogy is inadequate to capture the nature of aesthetic judgments, especially when those judgments concern complex public objects such as works of art. Not only does this objection undermine the metaphor of taste, but it is a more sophisticated version of the claim that taste experience is disqualified from genuine aesthetic experience—not so much because the quality of the experience is phenomenally inappropriate, but because the grounds for judgments of aesthetic experiences and taste sensations are logically of different types.

We may readily grant that causal reasoning is generally more appropriate to deal with gustatory taste than with aesthetic judgments. Accounts can be given in considerable detail of the chemical properties of substances that, because of the physical makeup of human taste receptors, cause specific taste sensations. As we saw in the last chapter, however, when the several factors that contribute to taste experience are identified, it is clear that the determinants of taste are not exhausted by reference to physical causes. The language of causation, combined with the assertion that causes operate whether or not one is aware of them (as in the chemical composition of foods), suggests that taste sensations are more or less fixed and unmalleable. This is obviously not the case; it is demonstrably true that the palate can be educated. One can cultivate a taste for foods for which one has an initial revulsion, such as cheeses in an advanced stage of ripening.[22] Of course, if there are physical impairments to the complex of factors that make taste sensation possible, this education will fail. What Hume would call delicacy of taste requires a certain basic fortune in the anatomy; but it is equally dependent upon development that occurs through practice. Physiological and chemical factors are rudimentary in comparison with other influences on taste preferences and eating practices, as we have seen; and once we acknowledge this, the degree to which taste is governed only by causal factors becomes debatable. The arguments presented earlier regarding the alleged subjectivity of taste lay to rest the prejudice that would maintain that taste cannot refer to the world beyond the phenomenal experience of the taster—that is, that it is a solely "internalist" judgment. Whether taste is therefore "criterial" in the same way as aesthetic judgments is unclear, and indeed causal factors would certainly seem to

---

[22] In his strenuous criticism of both brands of taste, Tolstoy compares decadent taste for high art with degenerate preferences for rotting cheeses. See Leo Tolstoy, *What Is Art?* (1898), trans. Aylmer Maude (New York: Bobbs-Merrill / Liberal Arts Press, 1960), chap. 10.

play a much larger role in the appreciation of food and drink than in the appreciation of works of art.[23] The challenge of Shiner's argument that must be met before the comparability of gustatory and aesthetic judgments can be finally assessed, however, is the same as the challenge outlined by philosophers preoccupied with the meager potential of food to be considered an art—namely, that taste is chiefly an *inwardly directed* experience. The key point of intervention in the traditional characterization of tasting and eating experiences concerns the claim that food does not have *meaning,* that it does not refer to a world beyond itself. This approach locks our understanding of the aesthetic significance of food into its sensory enjoyment, an approach that will not be able to muster much defense against Shiner's reasoning and that, in addition, cannot avoid the conclusion that food is of minor artistic import in comparison with the classic fine arts.

The ways in which taste qualifies as a cognitive sense that directs attention to objects and events in the world may now be elaborated, for any brief for foods that focuses on the enjoyment of the sensation of tasting alone is going to reach a limit very quickly. Without question good food is enjoyable, and a discrimination that is difficult and educable pays dividends in taste pleasures. The case that the perceptual discrimination and enjoyment of taste are at least close cousins, phenomenally speaking, to aesthetic discrimination and enjoyment is fairly easy to make. We can travel down this road to gourmet land and the haute cuisine that marks the dining possibilities of an elite, but the deeper kinds of significance granted works of art will not appear so long as refined enjoyment is the highest end of eating. Discriminating and relishing fine distinctions are only one part of aesthetic apprehension. Omitted are the insight, emotion, and deepened understanding that are expected from encounters with important aesthetic objects. Since among the latter are works of art, this merges into consideration of the status of food as art and a comparison of foods and drink with artworks. A case for comparability in this domain is harder to make, not because the grounds for comparison are absent but because of the tendency to continue attention to gourmet eating and fine dining when one seeks to understand the aesthetic qualities of food. Therefore, if we want to pursue the parallels between food and standard art forms beyond pleasant savoring and cultivated discrimina-

---

[23] Shiner assumes the incompatibility of internalism and criterial judgments, because he construes criteria to be independent of the sentiment response of the perceiver. However, the chief reason that taste was selected as a metaphor for aesthetic sensibility in the first place is that criteria alone *never* yield an aesthetic judgment. If they did, then one could reduce art criticism to a series of applications of principles to particular works, and there would be no problem of taste to begin with. I develop this argument in more detail in "Taste as Sense and as Sensibility," *Philosophical Topics* 27.1 (Spring 1997). See also two discussion pieces of Shiner's article: Mary Mothersill, "In Defense of 'Hume and the Causal Theory of Taste,'" which also points out that aesthetic responses do not proceed from the application of criteria; and John W. Bender and Richard N. Manning, "On Shiner's 'Hume and the Causal Theory of Taste,'" which argues that gustatory judgments may be criterial; both in *Journal of Aesthetics and Art Criticism* 55.3 (Summer 1997).

tion, we need to inquire about the possibilities for the cognitive dimensions of taste and food.

Tasting Symbols

Of the multitude of philosophies of art in circulation, one in particular provides a useful resource in efforts to understand the nature of foods and of eating: the cognitivist theory of art formulated by Nelson Goodman. When Goodman's *Languages of Art* was first published in 1968, it commanded immediate attention for its unsettling interruption of what had been standard debates in aesthetics.[24] Goodman bypassed customary attention to aesthetic perception and artistic value in favor of an analysis of symbol systems, of which artworks are among the most interesting examples. Symbols come in a variety of forms in Goodman's broad construal of the concept, and in the course of his argument he compares artworks with diagrams, maps, models, gauges—a collection of systems of meaning that have obvious cognitive functions (though perhaps not obvious aesthetic ones). He does not mention food, but his treatment of symbols and their aesthetic characteristics offers insights that are applicable to food and will extend our grasp of its aesthetic dimensions well beyond the range of sensuous pleasure.

Goodman's starting point is an analysis of representation, and the standard example of representation is a picture. A picture represents something, he argues, only and simply if it *denotes* it. Thus he circumvents all worries about resemblance, depiction, portrayal—about the way a picture looks, in short— by calling attention to the relation of reference between a picture and its subject. In his terse summary, "Denotation is the core of representation and is independent of resemblance."[25] That the picture at the center of a U.S. $1 bill is of George Washington, for example, has nothing to do with the degree of resemblance between the first president and a small green head; the dollar's picture is of George Washington because it denotes him. (In the same way the Stars and Stripes represent the United States while in no sense resembling it.)

This reasoning works, however, only if there is (or was) a George Washington to denote; fictions are not covered by this analysis. A picture of a unicorn cannot denote unicorns, for there are none to refer to. Goodman analyzes fictional pictures not as representations at all, strictly speaking, but as types of pictures. A picture of a

---

[24] Nelson Goodman, *Languages of Art* (Indianapolis: Bobbs-Merrill, 1968). Citations are from the revised second edition (Indianapolis: Hackett, 1976). Francis Sparshott remarks on the dramatic influence Goodman has had on subsequent aesthetics in "Reconsiderations I," *Journal of Aesthetics and Art Criticism* 49.1 (Fall 1980): 82.

[25] Goodman, *Languages of Art*, p. 5.

unicorn is a unicorn-picture, or more generally a mythological beast–picture.[26] Of course, a unicorn-picture may be used to denote something real, whether an individual, a collection, or an abstract concept.[27] An allegory in which purity is symbolized by a unicorn is an example of "representation-as"; it is a mythological beast–picture denoting purity, which is to say, representing purity as a unicorn.

Representation is but one of the multiple symbolic functions of art. Another, equally important, is exemplification. An apple, for example, is typically red. It *possesses* the property red (or, as Goodman would say, it is denoted by the predicate red). It is an example of a red thing, and for that reason it may be used to *exemplify* red. It also may exemplify crispness, tartness, or being a Winesap. When it takes on the function of exemplification, the apple is presented in a way that calls attention to these qualities. (It might possess but not exemplify other properties, such as weighing 5 ounces or having been sprayed with a pesticide.) Savoring the redness of an apple—whether painted or actual—is an aesthetic activity that requires color properties to be especially present to awareness. Savoring the tart flavor is directing attention to the exemplified taste properties, often with the expectation that certain properties but not others will emerge in the experience. If properties that should be there are missing—if the apple is bland and grainy rather than tart and crisp, for instance—then the judgment is negative on the grounds that properties that should be exemplified by Winesap apples are missing.

Artworks are commonly noted for their expression of some idea, mood, or emotion. Goodman compares the *expressive* properties of art with the literal *possession* of properties. The apple literally has the properties red and tart, and because red and tart are important qualities of apples that enter into their evaluation (for which they are enjoyed), the apple exemplifies as well as possesses redness and tartness. But objects may also express properties both simple and complex that they do not literally possess. Goodman categorizes expression as "metaphorical exemplification," or reference to a metaphorical property that is possessed by the object. The apple given to Snow White by the evil queen, for example, is not only red and round but also *sinister,* a metaphorical property when applied to apples. The wicked intent of the queen to do away with her stepdaughter is implicit in the sinister quality of the apple, so with the exemplification of the sinister quality comes the expression of a proposition: that the queen is a wicked woman who wants to kill Snow White. An apple in the hand of Eve expresses or metaphorically exemplifies a complex proposition about the fall of man and original sin. Noticing the biblical significance of an

---

[26] A fictional picture (or "x-picture") is analyzed as an unbreakable one-place predicate rather than the two-place predicate of denotation.

[27] Goodman is a nominalist and permits only individuals and predicates into his system. It is permissible, however, to use his system without abiding by his metaphysical restrictions, as he himself allows. In this discussion I am ignoring Goodman's nominalism.

apple in the hand of a woman produces an emotive valence because of the recognition of the apple's symbolic function. Mom's apple pie is not baked with apples from Eden. Their emotive force is different because the properties they metaphorically exemplify are different. Noticing their different emotive tenor requires the perceiver to become aware of their exemplifications—an awareness both cognitive and emotive. It is also *aesthetic:* a merger of discovery and emotional response in the appreciation of qualities presented to experience. Registering these qualities requires more than mere identification. It invites savoring, lingering experience, bringing into play all the perceptive and emotive sensitivity at one's disposal. Aesthetic attention, in short—or the kind of perception and judgment that an earlier age termed the exercise of taste. This kind of appreciation is enjoyable, and it may possess a sensuous dimension. But Goodman's analysis also reveals that aesthetic appreciation is constitutively cognitive, for it requires awareness, recognition, and affective response in the apprehension of the varieties of symbolic activity. As he puts it, in aesthetic appreciation of art, the "emotions function cognitively."[28] This view does not seek to reduce aesthetic to intellectual experience, but seeks to recognize that cognition takes many forms and delivers many psychological effects. As he says, "In contending that aesthetic experience is cognitive, I am emphatically not identifying it with the conceptual, the discursive, the linguistic. Under 'cognitive' I include all aspects of knowing and understanding, from perceptual discrimination through pattern recognition and emotive insight to logical inference."[29]

Goodman's recommended classifications of different types of symbolic relations are cast in technical language (much of which I have omitted) that does not promise to become widely employed. But it has several indispensable features: He locates the sites of aesthetic sensitivity at just the places where symbols function with greatest subtlety, so that aesthetic reactions and discerning assessments are involved with the apprehension of meaning. The aesthetic is cognitive; the sensuous and emotional layers of response have meaning. This concept of the aesthetic is far more robust than either post-Kantian formalist renderings that stress disinterested attention to presented qualities or the more general analysis of pleasures appropriately detached from gratification of appetite that Prall and Telfer defend. (Despite stylistic differences, Goodman has more in common with theorists such as Alexander Baumgarten and Hegel.) The cognitive elements embedded in the various symbolic relationships extend the concept of aesthetic appreciation considerably beyond pleasure to the insight and emotional depth for which art is valued.[30] Not all art manifests

---

[28] Goodman, *Languages of Art*, p. 248.

[29] Nelson Goodman, "Reply to Beardsley," *Erkenntnis* 12.1 (January 1978): 173.

[30] Narrower analyses of the aesthetic do not pretend to do justice to all the values of art. Cognitive concepts of the aesthetic more easily accommodate the range of values for which art is noted, including moral insight and expressive power of ideas.

every type of symbol, and these symbolic relations are features of non-art objects as well. Therefore rather than presenting necessary and sufficient conditions to define the aesthetic, Goodman identifies five "symptoms" of the aesthetic, including exemplification and what he terms "relative repleteness," a condition in which "comparatively many aspects of a symbol are significant."[31] It now must be determined if these symbolic relations aptly characterize food and drink.

In addition to its illumination of artworks, Goodman's symbol system provides a set of categories that fit food quite well and will help to deepen our grasp of its aesthetic significance. I have resisted the urge to argue that food is an art, but one can still reserve judgment on that issue and note that food may satisfy all of Goodman's symbol types: representation, expression, and exemplification. I turn now to an application of these symbolic concepts to foods and the circumstances of their consumption. There are so many examples to choose from that this demonstration can be no more than indicative. It should be evident from just this sampling, however, that symbolic function pervades all types of eating, from the humblest meal to elaborate ceremonies.

Representational Food

Many philosophers, including Telfer and Scruton, have concurred that food does not represent anything outside itself and thus fails in one of the standard tasks of art, to deliver understanding and insight about life and the world. The disclosure of the symbolic functions of food will dispel that misunderstanding. The most obvious example of symbolic food, what would be classified as representational food, is food that is crafted to look like something other than itself. The examples I offer may appear at first to be incidental, perhaps even frivolous, but they direct attention to the pervasiveness of meaning in foods. In fact, representational foods are quite common. Consider the following very limited list:

Gummy bears, candy canes, sugar skulls, cinnamon hearts, candy corn, the metaphorical chocolate kiss

Gingerbread men, hamentaschen, hot cross buns, pretzels, croissants, braided breads, chocolate Yule logs

Radish roses, goldfish crackers, melon boats, vegetables cut and assembled into bouquets of flowers

---

[31] Nelson Goodman, *Ways of Worldmaking* (Indianapolis: Hackett, 1978), p. 68. See also *Languages of Art*, pp. 230, 252–55. Other symptoms of the aesthetic that I do not employ here are semantic and syntactic density and multiple and complex reference (for which an argument can be made on behalf of certain foods, though I do not do so here).

Easter eggs, butter lambs, molded gelatins shaped like stars, tequila sunrises,
    birthday cakes in the shape of basketballs, wedding cakes that look like
    temples, carved ice sculptures flanking a buffet table
The bread and wine of the Christian Eucharist

These few examples are hardly all comparable in the significance that their representations possess. Most of them appear to be more or less sui generis cases of
nondenoting representations, shaped foods that are fun or witty or pleasant or decorative. (The bread and wine of the Eucharist are a striking exception and possibly
appear shocking lined up with the other cases.) But they illustrate the intriguing fact
that an enormous amount of what we put into our mouths represents (in some sense
or other) something else. Many such instances derive from actual representations of
things or events, though if their popularity persists long enough, that function may
be lost to awareness and they may lose their original significance.

Consider the pretzel (Figure 4.1). In Italy, where pretzels are said to have been invented, the word denominating this food is *bracciatelli*, which translates into English
as "folded arms." In the early seventeenth century, an inventive monk twisted a string
of dough and baked it into the curved outline of the arms of a brother at prayer to dis-
pense as a reward for his pupils who recited their catechism correctly.[32] In some parts
of Europe pretzels are a Lenten food, and presumably there the curls of the snack are
recognized to denote the folded arms of a monk. (Coincidentally, the curves that
make up the arms and hands of a monkish St. Matthew in an illumination from the
Echternach Gospel also describe those of a pretzel [Figure 4.2]).[33] When the monk
representation is pointed out, the experience of eating a pretzel is transformed very
slightly and perhaps achieves the aesthetic predicate "witty." The food takes on a new,
expressive dimension, and the aesthetic apprehension of the pretzel expands.

Another familiar food that began its life as a symbol is the croissant. Croissants
were invented in Vienna in 1683. In celebration of the successful defense of the city
against the Ottoman Turks, Viennese bakers crafted little buns in the shape of the
crescent moon on the flag of their enemies. In this case, not only is the crescent
shape recognized as denoting the foreign enemy, but the fact that one *devours* the
crescent reenacts the defeat of the invaders, and perhaps also represents Christianity conquering Islam. How long such references continue to function will vary
greatly with time and place, and in this case the representational function of croissants is only a historical curiosity. But it is a curiosity with a lesson that cautions
against any easy dismissal of the representational possibilities of food. The fact that

---

[32] Martin Elkort, *The Secret Life of Food* (Los Angeles: Jeremy P. Tarcher, 1991), p. 100.
[33] Susan Feagin points out the coincidence of form between the loopy pretzel shape and the strapwork
that borders the St. Matthew illumination in Figure 4.2.

4.1. *A pretzel*
4.2. *Symbol of the evangelist Matthew, Echternach Gospels, mid–eighth century. (Bibliothèque Nationale, Paris; Foto Marburg / Art Resource, New York.)*

crafting an item of daily bread was so readily turned to triumphant commemoration should indicate the easy commerce between food and shared social significance, a significance manifest in the symbolic use of foods.

Some of the most famous food representations have been intended to deceive, and hence qualify as a type of illusionism. Such is the case with items of the meal satirized by Petronius in his account of Trimalchio's feast in the *Satyricon,* during which apparent live boars turn out to be skins filled with birds, cooked fish seem to swim in their sauces, a hare sprouts wings, and dishes that look like piglets are really sweet cakes. But we need not rely only on such legendary excesses; a visit to a Japanese restaurant will provide plenty of examples: carrots trimmed into small turtles and fish, or radishes and onions mimicking bunches of tiny flowers. Here there are also deceptive possibilities, such as the pale-green leaf shapes that appear to the uninitiated to be bland substances such as mashed avocado but are actually puréed horseradish. Employing Goodman's idiom, we could say that these are leaf-representations that metaphorically exemplify coolness but possess furious hotness. The combination might be described as ironic.

The most extravagant examples of this type of food preparation on historical record are furnished by one of the great master chefs of French cuisine, who himself has been promoted as an artist of the culinary sort. The historian of food Jean-François Revel has defended cuisine as an art on the grounds that at the point of its highest development, cuisine requires a professional touch possible only after years of training and education in food preparation and meal composition.[34] In other words, the sheer difficulty of rendering foods in certain special, complex ways—both their taste and their presentation—qualifies cooking as a genuine culinary art and its products as works of art. If any chef deserves to be accounted an artist on these grounds, it is the great Marie-Antoine (Antonin) Carême (1784–1833), chef to many noble households in the early nineteenth century. Carême is credited with revolutionizing the use of spices, which by long practice were used heavy-handedly in virtually all dishes. As Revel puts it, flavors were "mixed" rather than "combined," and it took a Carême to point the way to a more judicious marriage of herbs, spices, and the natural flavors of foods. Carême's stature as an artist and the elevation of his preparations as works of art were vigorously promoted in his own day as well. (Brillat-Savarin enjoyed his dishes when a guest of Talleyrand.) A few years after the death of the great chef, his pheasant paté was praised by extravagant—though admittedly somewhat tongue-in-cheek—comparison with the monuments of French literature: "It is *Le Cid,* it is the *Horace* of Pierre Corneille, it is the *Tartuffe* of Molière," raved Jules Janin.[35]

Carême himself wrote copiously on cuisine, and a memorable comment of his is often repeated: "The fine arts are five in number, namely: painting, sculpture, poetry, music, and architecture, the principal branch of the latter being pastry."[36] He was exaggerating only slightly. In addition to the elaborate decoration with which he

---

[34] Jean-François Revel, *Culture and Cuisine,* trans. Helen R. Lane (New York: Da Capo, 1984).

[35] Prefatory notice to Antonin Carême, *Le Cuisinier parisien, ou L'Art de la cuisine française au dix-neuvième siècle,* 3d ed. (Paris, 1842), p. xiii.

[36] Quoted in Revel, *Culture and Cuisine,* p. 222.

4.3. *Carême's decorated boar's head and suckling pig. (From Antonin Carême,* Le Cuisinier parisien, ou L'Art de la cuisine française au dix-neuvième siècle *[1842]. Courtesy, the Lilly Library, Indiana University, Bloomington, Indiana.)*

served his banquets (Fig. 4.3), he created legendary display pieces, or *pièces montées*. These architectural wonders were made from foods disguised as building and land-scape materials, though not so well disguised that the artistry of rendering a scene in these unusual media could not be recognized and admired. They were formed from spun sugar, almond paste, and other malleable purées and patés (Fig. 4.4). The *pièces montées* were prepared for the elaborate parties of his noble patrons and were designed with the occasion and its attendants in mind. A guest might admire a sug-ary confection adorning his table, and thereby discover his own name inscribed on the base. Here is M. F. K. Fisher's description of one titled "A Culinary Fantasy: The Cautious Carp":

> A froth of green foliage forms its base—leaves of mashed potato as delicate as ever grew from pastry tube. From that a Doric column, garlanded with pale full-blown flowers of lobster meat, diminishes twice.
> At the top, on a pedestal edged with little shells and shrimpy rosebuds, is a pool of the clearest blue-green sugar, crystallized. And from it, with only the ankles of his tail held in the crystal, curves a fresh plump fish, every scale

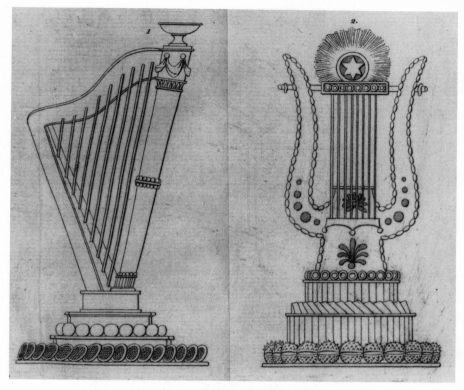

4.4. *Carême's sugar harps. (From Antonin Carême,* Le Pâtissier royal parisien *[1815]. Courtesy, the Lilly Library, Indiana University, Bloomington, Indiana.)*

gleaming, his eyes popping with satiric amusement, and a beautiful umbrella of spun sugar held over his head by one sturdy fin![37]

Carême was particularly fond of architectural pieces featuring ruins, temples, churches, and pavilions, and many such appear in his books. He describes his "Grand Chinese Pavilion" (Fig. 4.5) in great detail for the instruction of others who might try to imitate his accomplishment:

The bridge ought to be formed of white almond paste, on which one sketches, with a small paintbrush coated with mahogany color, some nodes as the de-

[37] Fisher, *Serve It Forth,* p. 113. Margaret Visser, in *Much Depends on Dinner* (Toronto: HarperCollins, 1992), p. 314, notes that a taste for architectural displays of food, especially moldable food such as ice cream, persisted in France for some time. Proust's Albertine teases her companion with her relish of such confections.

4.5. Carême's Grand Pavillon chinois. *(From Antonin Carême,* Le Pâtissier pittoresque *[1828].* Courtesy, the Lilly Library, Indiana University, Bloomington, Indiana.)*

sign indicates. The columns of the two pavilions ought to be executed in rose color; the capitals and the bases in yellow; the roofs of a pale green, the draperies white and their fringes rose. The Chinese characters on the draperies are painted in yellow.

The ornaments of the roofs, the bells, the trellises, and the gallery of the bridge ought to be yellow and pistachio green.[38]

The great displays such as Carême's are the works of master chefs, those whose job is also to please the tastes of their patrons with foods fit for fine dining. Extravagances such as these are relatively rare, but only because of their difficulty and the time, expense, and opportunity they require. While such lavish productions are possible only in the restricted context of wealth and leisure, a little reflection reveals that representation in food of a similar sort, if less elaborately crafted, is fairly common, though it is most dramatic when the meal involved is part of a ceremony. (The sugar skulls in the list above are a component of the celebration of the Day of the Dead in Mexico. Their design is contiguous with the practice of serving an entire ceremonial meal to the dead.) Ceremonies provide some of the most sustained and complex instances of symbolic function, and in spite of Carême's culinary innovations, his displays were continuous with older practices. In the European Middle Ages commemorative set pieces accompanied certain state or ecclesiastical banquets, at which the events or people being honored were represented in food sculptures displayed between courses: scenes from the Holy Land presented to knights returning from a crusade, or biblical tableaux and saints for archbishops. Often central components of such displays required that the skins of animals and birds be reassembled with their cooked contents, which presented chefs with the considerable challenge of resurrecting a peacock, deer, or swan and posing it in a convincingly lifelike posture. These creations perhaps skirt the borderland of "foods," for they were chiefly for display and parade and were not eaten, though the fact that their media were edible is part of their artistry. (Edible in theory, anyway. Revel reports that such presentations were often accompanied by an unappetizing stench from the decomposing skins into which the spiced and cooked meats were stuffed.) These creations raise the question of the boundaries of culinary art, and just where the experience of eating stops and starts. Shortly I shall address the ceremonial function of foods. At issue now, however, is the extent to which the sheer artistry of symbolic foods alone—the difficulty attendant on rendering them, the skill required, and the accomplishment of the finished product—qualifies these sorts of displays as art.

Obvious reference to objects and events make these foods representational, and to that degree the claim that foods cannot represent or refer to anything outside

---

[38] Carême, *Le Pâtissier Pittoresque* (Paris: Imprimerie de Firmin Didot, 1828), p. 29.

themselves is demonstrably false. The types of representation include denotation (reference to an existing individual or actual event) and representation-as (food that is shaped like something else but does not refer to any particular thing). The problem at this stage of analysis seems to be that such representations appear to have a frivolous, unnecessary quality that makes the food interesting and curious but not necessary profound or important. Admirable as feats such as Carême's may be, their intricacy seems important chiefly as a culinary stunt, the rendering in sugar and flour and fish paste of what is customarily done with mortar and bricks and lumber. Without detracting from the amusement and wit of such pieces, and indeed sometimes their genuine commemorative significance, we may say that the use of food for this kind of display seems at best derivative of the art forms it emulates—architecture, sculpture, and theater, as a rule. Shortly I shall supply a way to understand food that minimizes this suspicion, but even then stunt cuisine alone will not serve as a central or paradigm example of what is most important about eating. At best, it sustains the characterization of cooking as a decorative art, to use Douglas's classification. And indeed much food artistry is for decorative purposes, as traditions of techniques for carving and cutting demonstrate. For centuries before Carême noble kitchens employed carvers for the preparation of meats and fruits (Fig. 4.6), and a cookbook of the twentieth century continues this tradition with an appendix devoted to garnishes that announces that "garnishes are to foods what lace collars, belt buckles, and costume jewelry are to dresses."[39] The decorative capacities of food appear to be well established. So far, however, even the extravagant displays of Carême can do little to extend the artistic value of foods beyond decoration.

Moreover, we may also note an objection to decorative food that points to an adventitious element to the representational capacities of food: the examples of symbolic function in food discussed above are largely the result of *visual* manipulation.[40] An artist such as Carême is treating foodstuffs the same way a sculptor of more customary materials manipulates his bronze or marble. His *pièces montées* represent because they *look* like identifiable objects. Similarly, an Easter egg is a symbol of rebirth and renewal, partly because an egg literally houses new life but also partly because of its roundish shape—the endlessness of the edge of a sphere. The pretzel denotes a praying figure because of loops it makes that also could be made with a pencil. The churlish could complain that nothing especially "culinary" resides in these examples, and that their representational forms are simply derived from the repertoire of the objects of vision.

This objection indicates the need to extend recognition of the symbolic features of food yet further, to which task I shall turn momentarily. First, however, I acknowledge that much of the representational value of foods does indeed rely on in-

---

[39] *The Village Cookbook* (Scarsdale, N.Y., 1948), p. 325.
[40] Kevin Sweeney raised this point to me.

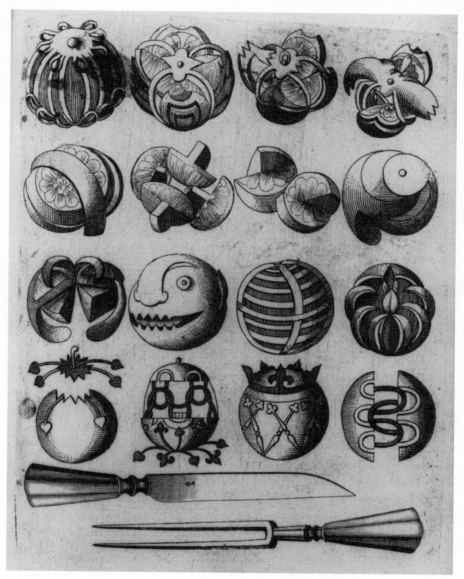

4.6. Decorative carved fruits. (From Jacques Vontet, L'Art de trancher la viande [c. 1647]. Courtesy, the Lilly Library, Indiana University, Bloomington, Indiana.)

formation provided by other senses, particularly vision. To me this is not an indication of a poverty of symbolic possibility for food but an illustration of the unremarkable fact that the experience of eating involves more than one sense. We have already invited smell into the company of taste, fully considered, and texture as well, which makes use of the sense of touch. The crunch and slurp of food involves hearing (there are Japanese dishes for which audible slurping is prescribed), and the preparation of a table is carefully attuned to visual pleasure.

But more can be said by way of response, both for the fact that sometimes what is seen is also eaten and for the symbolic function of the taste sensation itself. The fact that when a croissant was eaten the defeated Ottomans were metaphorically consumed involves the medium of food intimately. The croissant is still a symbol relying on visual representation, though its edibility enters dramatically into the enactment of its meaning. Nonetheless, representation (both denotation and representation-as) is but one mode of symbol that food achieves. It is when we examine Goodman's concept of exemplification that the pervasiveness of the symbolic function of food is most clearly demonstrated.

Exemplification

Exemplification, the symbolic relation in which an object both possesses a property and refers to it, is possibly the most common symbol type that food offers, for virtually any food exemplifies. That is, it refers and calls attention to some of the properties of what is eaten, presenting them for special notice and assessment or enjoyment through direct experience. In fact, the gourmet exercising a discriminating palate is attending to the properties exemplified in food and drink. These are not simply qualities that the food happens to possess. The gourmet does not direct attention to incidental properties that do not represent the aspects of food that demand appreciation. She does not care, for example, about the weight of the sow that discovered the truffles on the plate; she cares only about the taste properties of the truffles themselves. If she cares about when they were gathered and where they were found, it is insofar as such facts account for exemplified properties of taste. Note that when the claim is put this way, it does not fall prey to the complaint that taste directs attention only to the subjective state of one's own body. Attention to exemplified properties is attention directed to the object of perception via the taste sensations that it is capable of delivering. Goodman's catalog of symbolic relations neatly demonstrates the cognitive elements of tasting and eating—even of taste savoring, which is so frequently dismissed as purely self-attentive pleasure. Exemplification thus provides a handy classification of perceptual / cognitive experience that illuminates what was previously only vaguely seen to be wrong about this element of the sense hierarchy and the claim that the bodily senses are recalcitrantly subjective. The symbolic relation of exemplification refers to qualities possessed by the object of experience. True, they are experienced in the mouth. But this is simply a signal that we are in the domain of taste.

Chicken soup, for example, possesses a variety of properties, such as flavor, saltiness, and a somewhat oily texture. The ingredients are more or less present in the final product, and the sipper of soup may attend to them appreciatively (perhaps while at the same time assuaging hunger or dosing a cold). The property of (say) a subdued hint of parsnip well cloaked by onion and dill is exemplified in the soup in much the same way that being in a minor key may be exemplified in music or being blue exemplified by certain Picasso paintings.

These aesthetic characteristics are taste's version of aesthetic savoring and are familiar under other descriptions. They are also the most frequent sorts of evaluations and encomia one encounters in food writing. Exemplification enfolds the sensuous elements of taste experience—the quality of flavor, the blends or conflicts of sensations, as well as the pleasures. Thus this particular symbolic function, inseparable from the felt qualities of sensation, recasts in other vocabulary the most common defense of the aesthetic experience of food, but makes clear that the relish and enjoyment is more than subjective delectation, though it is that as well.

Because food exemplifies a multitude of complex sensory relationships of different tastes, smells, and textures, any meal (perhaps excepting K-rations, astronaut food, and the airline snack) also possesses what Goodman terms relative repleteness—that condition in which "comparatively many aspects of a symbol are significant." "Relative repleteness" is just a way of stating that a large range of the properties available to the sense are relevant to its appreciative assessment. Interestingly, this term of the aesthetic, "repleteness," like "taste" itself, is also part of the gastronomic vocabulary.

These types of exemplified properties, all of which refer to the taste qualities to which attention is drawn, are familiar in terms of the savoring and enjoyment of eating. Exemplification extends further than taste experience per se, however, and enters into the kinds of meanings that we absorb so deeply from our cultural practice that they are often lost to conscious awareness. The sorts of foods we eat at different times of the day vary, and in fact certain kinds of foods come to "mean" the meal that they provide. Oatmeal conveys the meaning of breakfast, for example, in those cultures where cereals constitute a typical first meal of the day. Examination of this sort of meaning gives us more senses in which foods may exemplify.

Possibly the nearest relative to a cognitivist account of food has been articulated by structuralist anthropologists. They assume that human behavior falls into patterns or structures that are similar no matter what the task at hand, and that activities such as cooking and eating, and indeed choosing what is considered edible, make most sense when compared with other aspects of a society's activities and belief systems. In Claude Lévi-Strauss's famous trope, for example, "raw" and "cooked" are oppositions that are isomorphic with other binaries (such as nature–culture and male–female), which taken together illuminate the myths and social practices of vastly divergent societies.[41] Mary Douglas considers food as a "system

---

[41] Claude Lévi-Strauss, *The Raw and the Cooked*, trans. John and Doreen Weightman (New York: Harper & Row, 1969). Lévi-Strauss is widely criticized among anthropologists—including those who share a structuralist approach, such as Mary Douglas—for imposing too rigid a structure of analysis on the phenomena under question.

of communication," and she speculates about how food might be understood as an art form.[42] "If food is to be considered as an art form it would be necessary first to choose questions which could be asked equally well of other art forms, and then to identify an area of problems which are specific to the food medium. Having first distinguished what kind of art form food is amongst the others in that culture, it would then be right to ask how does the local food art compare with other food arts in other cultures."[43]

Considering eating practices in her home country, England, Douglas observes that because food has a practical function, nourishment, it is appropriately grouped with the applied arts such as clothing, architecture, and utensils, rather than with the fine arts of music, sculpture, and painting. (When food is for display, as we have already noted, Douglas classifies it more specifically as an applied decorative art.) Hence the aesthetic elements in foods are those that are distinct from nutrition and are "subject to pattern-making rules" just like the fine arts. The sensory qualities of food are a big part of its aesthetic aspect. Food can have its own distinctive patterns of acceptable textures, smells, tastes, and colors; or sometimes (as with representational foods) it borrows from the registers of other art forms. Appropriate qualities for foods may transfer from standards of social behavior: for example, smooth, refined foods for formal occasions (structurally similar to silks and satins) and rough-textured foods for informal gatherings (where denim or tweed may be worn). Eating practices are also heavily patterned by social relations and class: what people eat and when, as well as with whom, varies according to their job and economic status. Generally speaking, "if food is treated as a code, the messages it encodes will be found in the pattern of social relations being expressed. The message is about different degrees of hierarchy, inclusion and exclusion, boundaries and transactions across the boundaries."[44]

Not only can eating be analyzed according to the social patterns it manifests, single meals have their own structure as well. Which combinations of foods count as meals depend on their sequence, their mixture of liquids and solids, of meats and vegetables and starches, the utensils required for their consumption, and the time of their service. Little of these patterns is supplied by the biological need for nutrition; they are the result of accumulated traditions and practices that culminate in the recognition of certain foods as edible, as constituting meals, as tasting good. All these recognitions, exercised so routinely that they are rarely even present to awareness, demand complex "cognitive energy."[45]

---

[42] Douglas, *In the Active Voice,* pp. 85–87. This "system" is closely connected to the social systems of rest, health and body care, clothing, and family. Ultimately, the patterns revealed in a study of such systems are heavily influenced by social power relations.

[43] Ibid., p. 106.

[44] Mary Douglas, "Deciphering a Meal," *Daedalus* (Winter 1972): 61; reprinted in Douglas, *Implicit Meanings* (London: Routledge & Kegan Paul, 1975).

[45] "Each meal carries something of the meaning of the other meals; each meal is a structured social event which structures others in its own image. The upper limit of its meaning is set by the range incorporated

Douglas's disclosure of the structures that order eating and the classification of foods is illuminating for several elements of the "meaning" of food. Particularly insightful are her discoveries about what is recognizable as edible and the isolation of "meals," as well as what we may call the social hierarchies present in eating habits: the kinds of foods eaten, who eats with whom, and so on. (One shares meals with friends and equals, for example.) The structures of eating reveal a good deal about large social patterns and are thus aptly descriptive of behavior. Often they are so inculcated in practice that they are not sufficiently obvious to consciousness to constitute an "experience" at all, but they may be brought into the focus of awareness with a little attention. Such implicit meanings may be understood as exemplified properties.

To wit: One wakes up in the morning and brews coffee. Toast, butter, and cereal complete this American-style breakfast. That the coffee is freshly ground and particularly savory, or that the toast is whole wheat rather than white this morning, may be the only exemplifications noticed by a sleepy eater. The other properties exemplified by this breakfast, however, are unnoticed only because they are habitual. Transport this person to Norway and serve him small silver fish and dark orange cheese redolent of goat, and he will surely take note of the fact that these foods do not "mean" breakfast to him. Not only are they not the types of foods he ordinarily encounters upon waking (a rather conservative time of ingestion) but they offer the kinds of tastes that seem more appropriate to lunchtime. Even more dramatic is the difference between cereal and the cooked rice dishes that he would be offered in China. Such national differences in what is eaten and when produce different exemplified properties, different "meanings" embodied in the foods. It is an obvious point, but the fact that tastes are always embedded in meanings is so often overlooked that the obvious is worth stating.

Expressive Foods

Exemplification has offered us two types of features of foods and their tastes: the particular properties that are savored and enjoyed in foods, which qualify conventionally as the aesthetic experience of taste according even to noncognitivist analyses; and the implicit properties that food acquires when it occupies a particular place

---

in the most important member of its series. The recognition which allows each member to be classed and graded with the others depends upon the structure common to them all. The cognitive energy which demands that a meal look like a meal and not like a drink is performing in the culinary medium the same exercise that it performs in language. First, it distinguishes order, bounds it, and separates it from disorder. Second, it uses economy in the means of expression by allowing only a limited number of structures. Third, it imposes a rank scale upon the repetition of structures. Fourth, the repeated formal analogies multiply the meanings that are carried down any one of them by the power of the most weighty." (Ibid., pp. 69–70.)

in the rhythm of nourishment that is represented by mealtimes. We have not yet explored to any extent what Goodman would term "metaphorical exemplification" in foods, that is, expressive properties.

In these instances, the property possessed and referred to by the food is one that applies metaphorically. The example given earlier was the property "sinister" applied to an apple. Obviously, this is not a property that usually applies to apples, metaphorically or literally; in the context of the story of Snow White, an apple is sinister because it is poisoned and because it was malevolently prepared to bring about the death of Snow White. There are numerous cases in which expressive properties attach to foods because of the particular context of a story, but there are also more ordinary cases in which foods come to express certain properties because of the traditional or routine circumstances of their preparation.

Chicken soup, again, is a home remedy of sorts in a number of cultures. There may be some medical reason for this custom; the healthful reintroduction of salt and liquid into a body that is dehydrated from fever has been suggested. Such palliative features are not likely to be a part of the experience of the soup, however; more relevant for the expressive properties such as "soothing" and "comforting" that are exemplified by chicken soup is the very fact that it *is* a home remedy and *means* that one is being taken care of. The expression of care that soup exemplifies is supported by the literal properties that soup also has: a rich but not taxing flavor, ingredients that are easy to swallow, and so on. The expression of this kind of property by foods may be culturally dispersed, localized in smaller groups such as families, or even perhaps a product of the habits of individuals.

Sometimes the expressive potential of foods exploits what seem to be the natural disposition of some flavors to be liked or disliked. Sweet, as we have seen, is one of the basic flavors that all people like, whatever their differences in securing particular sweet substances. It comes as no surprise, therefore, to find that sweet foods are used in ritual ceremonies to signal prosperity or luck. At the Jewish New Year, for example, bread is dipped in honey to signal a promise of hope and prosperity for the coming year. During ritual meals Hindus offer something sweet to eat in honor of the gods. Salt is needed for survival; it is also a universally sought-after taste in moderation, as physiological studies have demonstrated. Recognition of the significance of salt is formalized in the hospitality practices of several cultures. According to traditional code, one who breaks bread and shares salt with a Bedouin thereby achieves that person's protection, a custom that has also entered into literary tradition and into the expression "to share the salt with" or to "break bread with" in English. One word for hospitality in Russian means literally "bread-salt."[46] Conversely, the

[46] Leonard R. Kass discusses this and other aspects of hospitality in food practices in *The Hungry Soul* (New York: Free Press, 1994), pp. 111–27.

Weyewa of Indonesia may quietly rebuke one who violates the social code by offering him nuts of particular bitterness.[47] Such examples confirm a certain common expressive quality recognized in the basic tastes reviewed in the last chapter, which seem to lend themselves to being considered natural symbols when deliberately employed as flavors of food and drink.

The potential for even a simple, basic flavor to convey complex propositional understanding is illustrated at some length by an old English fairy tale, which shows us something of the direct, intimate force of understanding possible by means of the sense of taste. The title of the story is the nickname of its heroine, "Caporushes." It tells of a rich man who demanded professions of love from his three daughters. "I love you as I love my life" was the satisfactory answer of the first. "Better than all the world beside," said the second, and was also approved. The youngest (and of course the prettiest) daughter avoided clichés and described her love thoughtfully with a humble kitchen comparison: "I love you as fresh meat loves salt!" she said. Believing himself slighted, the father banished her from his household. The girl wandered until she came to a fen; then, fearing robbers, she wove herself a concealing cloak and hat of rushes to cover her rich dress and jeweled hair. So disguised, she took up an anonymous life as a scullery maid in the house of a neighboring noble. Some time later the son and heir of the manor fell in love with the beautiful scullery girl, and they became betrothed. Her father, grief-stricken and now blind, was invited to the wedding feast. Knowing he would be present, the bride ordered no salt to be used in preparation of the meal. As the story is told:

> Now when the company sate down to table their faces were full of smiles and content, for all the dishes looked so nice and tasty; but no sooner had the guests begun to eat than their faces fell; for nothing can be tasty without salt.
>
> Then Caporushes' blind father, whom his daughter had seated next to her, burst out crying.
>
> "What is the matter?" she asked.
>
> Then the old man sobbed, "I had a daughter whom I loved dearly, dearly. And I asked her how much she loved me, and she replied, 'As fresh meat loves salt.' And I was angry with her and turned her out of house and home, for I thought she didn't love me at all. But now I see she loved me best of all."

And then—for it is a fairy story—"as he said the words his eyes were opened, and there beside him was his daughter lovelier than ever."[48]

---

[47] Joel C. Kuipers, "Matters of Taste in Weyewa," in *The Varieties of Sensory Experience*, ed. David Howes (Toronto: University of Toronto Press, 1991), pp. 111–27.

[48] *English Fairy Tales*, retold by Flora Annie Steel (New York: Macmillan, 1918), p. 308.

This simple story illuminates several features of a discovery of a "truth" through immediate sense experience. Both literally and figuratively, the father is made to "see" his daughter's love through the taste of unseasoned meat. Moreover, what he comes to see or know through the exercise of the sense of taste is clearly an instance of propositional knowledge (that his daughter loved him and captured that love with reference to meat and salt). At the same time, what he discovers qualifies as a more or less commonplace truth, an obvious insight demanding little cogitation. The reader has had no difficulty from the start in recognizing the declaration of love in the words of the youngest daughter; the reader does not require the taste of the meat to know the meaning of her words. Everyone knows that food is more tasty with salt. What delivers the particular revelation to this sad father?

The circumstances of the wedding feast provide a context for his discovery. There is a wedding, an occasion for celebration; yet there is also grief and remorse over a lost, beloved child. We assume that the father has dwelt upon her words and his harsh response repeatedly. The sudden, unexpected, unmistakable *taste* of unseasoned meat brings home the pain of her rejected declaration of love. He *knows* viscerally, intimately, literally at a "gut level" that she loved him and that he cast her out unjustly. The sequence of events in the story and the particular position of the father focus the sense quality of saltless meat and its meaning in a discovery, an epiphany: *This* was her profession of love; *this* was my loss.

Philosophers have long struggled to reconcile two apparently opposing insights about aesthetic apprehension, especially when the object of attention is a work of art: On the one hand, art seems to afford unique, particular, and indispensable insights about life and experience. Yet on the other hand, when one is pressed to say just what a particular work of art "says," the reply is often something close to a truism. This tale helps us to see how both insights are reconcilable. It is significant that the father became blind after he banished his daughter, a signal of his stubborn refusal to recognize her love, even of his limited understanding of language, for he was expecting a more lofty statement and was not flexible enough to recognize the originality and force of her words. Through the revelation afforded him by taste, he gains wisdom, happiness, and vision both literal and figurative. He had not only to know her love "intellectually," as it were, but to *feel* the force of it. The power of the sensory experience of saltless meat can be delivered *only* through this "subjective" route: apprehending with one's whole being—mind and body—what before was recognized only intellectually. This is the force of "aesthetic" apprehension: that some truth or realization or discovery is delivered in a way that touches one intimately, that focuses and concentrates insight with the poignant immediacy of the blind father's taste of saltless meat. (So read, this little story confirms the reason taste was considered so suitable as a metaphor for aesthetic experience.)

Another story further demonstrates the complexities of meaning and the metaphorical exemplifications that taste experiences can achieve, in this instance on the basis of a very individual set of experiences and reflections. Though I devote my last chapter wholly to narratives in which eating is especially prominent, I invoke a section of a novel at this point to illustrate how an unexpected and profoundly moral metaphorical property can attach to taste. Charles Frazier's novel *Cold Mountain* is the double story of a man and two women scrabbling a difficult existence out of the Appalachian Mountains in the waning months of the Civil War. Facing starvation, they confront with necessity and regret the slaughter of animals they normally would not eat. They are appalled by the brutality of the behavior that their own bodies command in order to gain the sustenance needed to live, but at the same time their dismay is tempered by the recognition that their bodily need overtakes both manners and practices so deep that their violation approaches moral transgression.

Inman is a wounded Confederate soldier who has deserted from a military hospital. He is making his way home at great peril both from the approaching winter and from detachments of the Home Guard who are rounding up deserters. After the battle in which he was grievously wounded, he has dreamed repeatedly of his gradual transformation into a black bear who lives on grubs and honey in the mountains. His dreams, vivid and hallucinatory, induce in him a visceral sense of being one with bear, roaming the mountainside, feeling the lumbering strength of his limbs, the warm, loose shag of his fur. In his last dream, the bear he had become is killed and skinned by hunters. From these dreams Inman concludes that the bear "was an animal of particular import to him, one he might observe and learn from, and that it would be on the order of a sin for him to kill one no matter what the expense, for there was something in bear that spoke to him of hope."[49] But Inman cannot sustain his kinship with bear, for on his way home he is attacked by a mother bear in the dark hours of early dawn. Inman avoids death by stepping aside as the bear, confused by the murky light, rushes past him and blunders over a precipice, leaving behind a tiny cub clinging to a tree. The motherless cub will die, and in an act that may be mercy, for he does not have the resources to rescue and nurture the youngster, Inman kills it. And because he is starving and it would be a pity to waste the meat, he roasts and eats it.

> Inman sat and admired his country until the bear pieces were cooked, and then he dredged them in flour and fried them up in the last lard from the twisted paper the woman had given him days before. He ate sitting at the cliff top. He had not eaten bear of such youth before, and though the meat was less black and greasy than that of older bear, it still tasted nevertheless like sin. He

---

[49] Charles Frazier, *Cold Mountain* (New York: Atlantic Monthly Press, 1997), p. 279.

tried to name which of the deadly seven might apply, and when he failed he decided to append an eighth, regret.[50]

Even in his starved state Inman prepares this slaughter carefully. And in his sorrowful violation of his vow never to eat bear again in honor of his dream-discovered communion with this creature, he discovers meaning in the very taste of the meat, formerly so succulent on his tongue: regret.

Some might grumble at the degree to which a plot, a sequence of circumstances, and a moral sensibility must be employed to culminate in the ascription of metaphorical properties to the taste of young bear. This gripe points to an interesting difference between expression in foods and in art that I shall address in due course; for now it suffices to point out that no visual or auditory sensation alone delivers aesthetic complexity either. Independent of tradition and context, tastes are not by themselves the bearers of meaning any more than are the colors of paints straight out of the tube. But the meanings that tastes accrue are not arbitrary or capricious either. Meanings of many sorts become a part of eating experiences, sometimes emerging from the larger social context of eating, sometimes embedded in the very tastes of what we eat. Those meanings may admit readily shared discovery when the narrative contexts in which they emerge are common or public, or they may depend upon idiosyncratic and individual personal histories. Either way, taste is little different from other sense experience in its ability to possess meaning, to achieve cognitive significance.

In some form or other, virtually all eating participates in at least one of the symbolic systems disclosed by Goodman's analysis. Many of the cases I have invoked are instances of exemplification, which may occur as nothing more than attention to the flavor of one's dish. Though I have been stressing that even such commonplace taste experiences demonstrate the cognitive element in taste and in foods, pointing out that tasting itself requires recognition and a type of reference goes only a short distance toward showing how foods and artworks share essential features. The more profound uses of tastes and foods are in fact relatively infrequent, though no less important for that. The most significant instances of all of these symbolic types are to be found in ritual and in ceremonial meals.

Ceremonies and Rituals

The cognitive significance of food is an effect of reference, representation, expression, exemplification, and the social conditions of its preparation and serving. Not all eating has much significance, but any ceremonial meal possesses it in abundance.

---

[50] Ibid., p. 281.

Virtually all cultures and religions practice ceremonial eating, and so again a few examples must suffice to demonstrate the symbolic functioning of this kind of activity.

Festival meals can be analyzed by considering their individual components, their social context, and the fact of the meal as a whole. In the United States the fall holiday of Thanksgiving supposedly reenacts and thereby refers to the survival of an early European settlement through the harsh Massachusetts winter of 1621, during which time they would have starved without the good offices of the local Indians. This allusion to a happy relationship between peoples who were often at odds is vague and romantic, and the cynical might call this a case of fictional representation rather than denotation. Nonetheless, the reference to this historical event, whatever its actual character may have been, is important and makes the entire dinner itself representational. In keeping with the idea that the meal commemorates fellowship and community, it is ideally a large dinner among family and friends. There is a limited menu that recreates what is popularly believed to be the first Thanksgiving feast, including turkey and root vegetables. The food is hot, savory, and heavy—the kind of slowly digested sustenance that ushers in cold months. Literal exemplified properties such as warmth, flavor, texture, and weight contribute to the metaphoric exemplified properties of comfort, well-being, and plenty. In commoner parlance, the meal has a languid, comforting quality that is exaggerated by the habit of putting too much on the table and inducing torpor. The menu relies very much on tradition; innovation is frowned upon. There must be a turkey with stuffing and cranberry sauce, gravy, and several pies, including pumpkin or sweet potato, harvest vegetables not ordinarily associated with dessert at other times of the year. The choice of green vegetables, breads, and additional foods is optional, but without the core turkey the meal is unrecognizable as Thanksgiving. The selection of foods is so prescribed by tradition that many are prepared only at this time.

With the Thanksgiving meal, as with many ritual occasions, the conservative combination of foods indicates the degree to which it is the entire meal itself that acts as a symbol. The various dishes contribute to the expressive quality of the whole, and some of them also refer to events of the first Thanksgiving (the turkey to a bird native to the North American woods, the squash and other root vegetables to seasonal fare and approaching winter, cranberries to a food uniquely available to the region in colonial America). Their seasonal position is experienced as part of the experience of eating, which imparts awareness of a particular time of year. The fact that seasonal festivals are repeated is a critical part of the experience of eating. One is aware of oneself participating yet again in a cyclical celebration, one that is never quite the same as festivals of time past yet retains an enduring identity over time.[51]

---

[51] For observation on the nature of festivals and their continuity with art, see Hans-Georg Gadamer, *Truth and Method* (1960), trans. Joel Weinsheimer and Donald G. Marshall (New York: Continuum, 1994), pp. 122–23.

This is an indispensable element of all rituals, that they occur over and over, that the diner takes his or her place among others participating in similar rituals of dinner; that one time is ending and another beginning. Possibly one reason why sometimes foods taste good only during their relevant festivals is that their meaning is so restricted to that time.

Another festival meal illustrates even more legislated symbolic functions for foods. The Jewish Passover seder commemorates the exodus of the Jews from captivity in Egypt, and by extension the freedom of all peoples from slavery. A religious ritual meal such as this is rich with symbolic relations manifest not only in the visual presentation of foods but also in their very tastes. In the center of the table is the seder plate, and on it are placed six foods that are part of the ceremony that opens and closes the meal: the roasted shank bone of a lamb, a roasted egg, bitter herbs, *charoses* (a mixture of ground nuts, honey, and apples), parsley or chervil, and a dish of salt water. The bitter herbs signify bondage and sorrow in Egypt. This symbolic value does not depend on visual properties; the herbs metaphorically exemplify sorrow by means of their sharp taste. The small bowl of salt water denotes (and indeed chemically replicates) the tears shed in captivity, and the parsley, indicating the renewal of spring, is dipped in the salt water and eaten. The *charoses* symbolizes with its texture the mortar the Jews used in building temples for the Egyptians, and it is eaten in combination with the bitter herbs (which may be horseradish or a sharp-tasting green herb). The egg stands for renewal of life, and the shank bone for the Paschal lamb eaten in commemoration of the passover itself, the fact that God passed over the houses of the Jews and slew the firstborn of the Egyptian captors.

No risen bread is eaten during the ten days of Passover observance, in commemoration for the flight from Egypt, which necessitated taking bread from ovens before it had time to rise. The matzoh that signifies this aspect of the exodus exemplifies the properties of unleavened bread, as opposed to merely possessing the properties, as any cracker may do. It also metaphorically exemplifies or expresses haste and urgency, and by all these means it commemorates the biblical event and its continued significance.

Some ritual foods of the seder plate are present and tasted but not actually consumed. The lamb shank bone simply sits on the plate and is raised and replaced during the ceremony. Salt water has emetic properties and cannot be more than tasted. Thus many foods with important symbolic functions are not actually to be eaten, in the sense that their role is not one of nourishment or of sensory enjoyment and delectation. Nevertheless they not only are part of the meal, they also have a significance that is manifest in the act of tasting. Passover also has standard foods that are eaten chiefly at that time, as does Thanksgiving. (Because it is a much older and more dispersed festival—many centuries old and celebrated all over the world—local customs for choice of those foods vary.) And as with many religious practices, there are also prescribed means of preparing foods, some of which alter their taste from the way they would be experienced at other seasons. (Matzoh flour, for example, must be substituted in any recipe that otherwise would call for wheat flour.) The regional differences in the enactment of the Passover seder, including the different foods considered traditional, do not disturb the identity of the ceremony.

The profound importance of foods that are not actually to be eaten as part of a meal is also illustrated by the Christian sacrament of the Eucharist.[52] This is the liturgical rendering of the Passover seder Christ held with his disciples, though the meaning of the substances and what is considered "tasting" and "eating" have altered with the change of religious belief and the circumstances in which the foods are encountered. The wafer and wine of Communion denote the body and blood of Christ. If one subscribes to the doctrine of transubstantiation, they actually become those substances, in which case the body and blood are literally re-presented: present again to the congregation. The Communion bread and wine metaphorically exemplify or express the events foreshadowed by the Last Supper—the agony in the garden of Gethsemene, the crucifixion, and the resurrection. These instances of bread and wine are both food and not food. They are tasted and swallowed, but not for nourishment. The tastes of the bread and when permitted of the wine—for not all churches allow the laity to drink of the blood of Christ—occasion reflection of the profoundest sort. The fact that the sacrament is actually taken into the body indicates the most direct participation in the mystical reenactment of God's sacrifice, one that the exercise of any sense other than taste might not render so intimate.

Not only eating but also its opposite should be considered as part of the ritual meanings of foods, for fasts as well as feasts are observances of many religions, such as Lent, Ramadan, Yom Kippur. When expedient, fasting may be incorporated into the religious practices of daily life, as with the Ethiopian church that demands one fast day a week—not only penance and self-discipline, perhaps, but prudent rationing of food resources in a country where food distribution is difficult.[53] Periods when one should neither exercise the sense of taste nor nourish the body are significant; they nourish the soul, for the assumption is that the body's comfort is a hindrance to probing reflections of the spirit. In this way the very hierarchy of the senses is incorporated into the rhythms and meanings of eating practices.

These examples indicate that the customs and beliefs of the ambient culture contribute to the meanings of foods, and reciprocally foods themselves contribute to the defining characteristics of a culture. The tea ceremony of Japan is a practice of Zen Buddhism and manifests (exemplifies) the values of that philosophy. It involves far

---

[52] On the Eucharist, see Louis Marin, *Food for Thought,* trans. Mette Hjort (Baltimore: Johns Hopkins University Press, 1989), pp. 120–24.
[53] This observation was suggested to me by Tereffe Asrat.

more than just drinking tea, for the ceremony is a staged event that prescribes ideal qualities for the physical surroundings and for the utensils to be used. It invites engagement with all the senses and fosters meditation on the meaning of the experience. D. T. Suzuki describes the art of tea drinking in terms of the Zen value of simplicity. The hut for the ceremony is spare, nestled in a spot chosen for vegetation, view, water, wind. The preparation of the tea is unhurried; the tastes are delicate, indeed all the sensations surrounding the event are soft and harmonious. Here is Zen Master Takuan's description of a tea ceremony:

> Let us then construct a small room in a bamboo grove or under trees, arrange streams and rocks and plant trees and bushes, while [inside the room] let us pile up charcoal, set a kettle, arrange flowers, and arrange in order the necessary tea utensils. And let all this be carried out in accordance with the idea that in this room we can enjoy the streams and rocks as we do the rivers and mountains in Nature, and appreciate the various moods and sentiments suggested by the snow, the moon, and the trees and flowers, as they go through the transformation of seasons, appearing and disappearing, blooming and withering. As visitors are greeted here with due reverence, we listen quietly to the boiling water in the kettle, which sounds like a breeze passing through the pine needles, and become oblivious of all worldly woes and worries.[54]

The meaning of tea in this setting—its simplicity, its harmony, its conduciveness to mental clarity and awareness of the flow of life—indicates that the taste and other experiences afforded through this ceremony should be inflected and guided by a suitable and informed philosophic attitude. Indeed, simply tasting the tea alone would be an impoverished experience. It would lack the meaning, the significance, of tea. The tea itself may be said to exemplify some of these properties, for the quality of the liquid and of its service draw attention to the delicacy and subtlety of its flavor. Like any of the single dishes served at the festival meals mentioned above, however, it is a part of a complex whole and its meaning emerges from the entire event and the philosophical tradition it embodies and perpetuates.

Food and Art Compared

I have been presenting the case for the similarity of foods with works of art by demonstrating how the requirements of Goodman's symbol types are fulfilled by

---

[54] Takuan (1573–1645) quoted in D. T. Suzuki, *Zen and Japanese Culture* (Princeton: Princeton University Press, 1970), pp. 275–76.

food and drink and the taste experiences of eating and drinking. These symbolic functions seem to be enacted by foods in much the same way that they are by works of art. As we have noted, Goodman refers to "symptoms of the aesthetic" without defining that contested concept. Symptoms of the aesthetic include exemplification and relative repleteness, requirements satisfied by the tasting and eating of foods. At this point it seems clear that his approach affords us grounds to assert that eating and tasting are activities with a sound claim to aesthetic attention, one that may be considered consistent with and supplementary to the defense of the aesthetic perception of foods advanced by Prall and Telfer. Ought we now to take the next step and conclude that foods also qualify as works of art in the full sense of the term? That they represent in their own medium the same sorts of objects as paintings, sculptures, poems, and symphonies? I do not believe we should. For one thing, the concept of art, dominated as it is today by the idea of *fine* art, is a poor category to capture the nature of foods and their consumption. While one earns a bit of stature for food by advancing it as an art form, the endeavor is apt to divert attention from the interesting ways in which the aesthetic importance of foods diverges from parallel values in art. Much of my argument has been devoted to correcting misunderstandings about the sense of taste and to defending the theoretical significance of food, but the discontinuities between meals and art should not be gainsaid. How ought we to characterize these dissimilarities without at the same time losing sight of the important similarities between foods and arts?

We may begin by considering again a possible objection to aesthetic meanings for foods that I have flagged from time to time: foods seem to be heavily dependent on either ceremonial context or personal or cultural narrative to attain their cognitive and aesthetic significance. The symbolic functions of food of the wider variety— those that involve expression and denotation in particular—seem to require a place in some cultural practice in order to come into being. Consequently, one may suspect that it is not the food itself that has meaning. Without its placement on the appropriate Thursday in November, for instance, Thanksgiving is just another heavy meal; the food alone does not express the festival.[55] Without the surrounding story and the history of ritual, the individual items on the Passover table are just things to eat; without the tradition of Zen philosophy, displayed equally in the setting, the utensils, and the surroundings of the ceremony, the cup of tea is only a cup of tea. In short, foods and their tastes appear to depend inordinately on defining context if they are to achieve the cognitive significance that I am claiming underwrites their aesthetic standing.

---

[55] As Barbara Salazar pointed out to me, festival timing is not open to arbitrary manipulation. During World War II President Roosevelt moved Thanksgiving up a week or two, to nationwide outrage. It was moved back as soon as the war was over.

Of course, one could grant this point and retreat to just one symbolic function, exemplification, as the basis for the aesthetic import of foods. Foods that are presented for the delight of the palate can be understood to exemplify their tastes. Yet it would be a sacrifice of richness and breadth for the significance of foods if this were the only grounds on which it could be aesthetically justified. It would be another way of claiming that well-prepared food tastes really good—and we knew that already. Therefore this suspicion regarding context dependence is to be taken seriously. Rather than constituting a brief against the cognitive and aesthetic dimensions of tastes and foods, however, these considerations illuminate two important discontinuities between foods and fine arts: the aesthetic functions of food exceed the qualities of the food itself, and food and art do not have parallel histories and traditions.

Consider the disparaging contrast one artist was moved to make between food and art. The composer Hector Berlioz was an acerbic critic of the music of his day, and on his travels in Italy he complained that the audiences of Milan were so boisterous and inattentive to the operas performed that one could hardly hear the music. In his *Memoirs* of 1832 he recorded this gripe: "To the Italians music is a sensual pleasure, and nothing more. For this most beautiful form of expression they have scarcely more respect than for the culinary art. They like music which they can assimilate at a first hearing, without reflection or attention, just as they would do with a plate of macaroni."[56]

One may have a higher opinion of both Italian opera and pasta and still acknowledge that Berlioz's complaint expresses an insight about the difference between eating and encountering art. It is not, however, that eating never provokes "reflection and attention," as he surmises. I hope that the examples of ritual and ceremonial eating and the complex situations in which foods and tastes exemplify metaphorical properties lay to rest the idea that tasting and eating are to be appreciated only for sensuous enjoyment. The uses of foods and drink for religious and commemorative purposes clearly foster, even force, reflection on the meaning of the event taking place, its location in culture and history, and its personal emotional import. Unlike music or other fine art, however, this sort of reflection—important as it is—is not a mark of greatness for food *as food*. Berlioz might complain about the quality of Italian comic opera, and his objection to the shallow fare served up by the composers of that genre—the fact that they appeal to the ear more than to the heart or mind—would be at the same time a complaint about the quality of the music, about whether it merits being considered "great art." By contrast, many of the symbolic features of food may be fully present in food that is not particularly tasty but still serves the significant function of being part of a ceremonial event. To be sure, this is not the case for all aspects of taste and of food. For food to be "great" *as food*,

---

[56] Hector Berlioz, *Memoirs of Hector Berlioz from 1803 to 1865*, trans. Rachel Holmes and Eleanor Holmes, rev. Ernest Newman (New York: Tudor, 1935), p. 183.

its sensuous exemplified properties—those delivered for particular attention to the thoughtful diner—need to be especially fine. But it may represent, express, and otherwise signify without being haute cuisine; without, in other words, being particularly fine insofar as the "culinary art" is considered.

This feature of food is connected to the observation that foods require extended context to achieve their denotative and expressive meanings, that the items to eat *by themselves* do not always manage to carry their ritual or traditional or cultural significance. In certain cases meaning may become so attached to particular items that they indeed do stand alone by virtue of unique association. But in most instances fuller context is required for the foods to possess their symbolic functions. The reason is both very complex and rather obvious, though it tends to be obscured by the tendency to compare works of art to items of food on a case-by-case basis: the history of art and the history of food are not parallel. Thus what art has come to be and what food has come to be in our contemporary culture are not the same. This observation could lead to some intricate historical investigation, but I shall invoke only one fairly evident distinction: In the Western tradition there has developed a concept of *fine* art that is held to contrast to craft or to applied or decorative arts. Moreover, within the tradition of fine art, we also have the recent and still powerful legacy of the idea that aesthetic value is autonomous and intrinsic, that art is valuable for its own sake alone. The influence of this historical shift on the concept of art and on aesthetics has led us to consider the various cognitive and aesthetic qualities of works of art to inhere in the works themselves, free of surrounding context. Foods have no such history. Their aesthetic qualities emerge from practice and are embedded in the festivals and ceremonies and occasions in which they take on their fullest meanings. To try to compare a single meal or individual food with any given work of art is to yank that item from its context and impoverish its aesthetic import. It directs attention only to its exemplified qualities, and not even to all of those: the ones that remain to be relished free from ceremonial practices are just those *sensuous* exemplified qualities—the savor of the tastes themselves—that for all their undeniable pleasures do not fill the terrain of deeper aesthetic significance that foods display in their practical contexts, including ritual, ceremony, and commemoration. On its own food is assessed only for a relatively narrow band of exemplified properties; art is assessed for all symbolic functions.

Thus despite the similarities between food, drink, and artworks in terms of their cognitive significance and related aesthetic dimensions, there is a lack of symmetry between the features of foods that are comparable to central aesthetic features of art and the measure of the quality of the individual objects under assessment. This is probably why those who have advanced briefs on behalf of both the aesthetic and the artistic significance of foods have fallen short of being able to assert their full status as works of art. Either food is denied the status altogether while being granted aesthetic value, as Prall argues, or foods are recognized as permitting a certain degree of artistic achievement but are relegated to a minor art form, as Telfer, Douglas, and perhaps even Revel maintain. I believe that insofar as they carry the same sort of aesthetic significance, understood as constituting a cognitive dimension in the sort of way that Goodman accommodates, food and drink merit aesthetic standing, and at the same time serve many of the same symbolic functions as do works of fine art. However, the latter role, which I believe makes foods deeply important and not just sensuously delightful, is not always paramount when the quality of cuisine is being evaluated. In this instance, the sensuous enjoyment of eating and drinking often legitimately takes the foreground, and the other symbolic functions of foods (expressive, representational, and so on) recede—unless, of course, fine cuisine is also a part of a ceremony, ritual, or commemoration. Even when the fare is scanty or poor and the sensuous enjoyment thereby lessened, however, the other symbolic functions of foods may still be of such importance that the festival, practice, or ritual of which eating is a component is in no way diminished.

So is food an art form? This does not seem to me to be the crucial question, though the commonalities between food and art are centrally significant for understanding what food is in its own right. Certainly food does not qualify as a fine art; it does not have the right history, to make a complex point in shorthand. Culinary art can still be considered a minor or a decorative art, or perhaps a functional or applied art (for we should not minimize the fact that eating is a daily aspect of living in the most literal sense of that term). The reasons advanced by Telfer, Revel, and Douglas are sufficient to support in this sense the artistic achievement of fine cooking, distilling, and winemaking. However, this warrant for the label "art" is not the most important link between food and art. It is much more significant that both form symbolic systems with similar components, though those components are not symmetrically related to the merits of the created products. The fine achievements of the cook, the winemaker, and others who prepare what we ingest are sometimes but not invariably a part of the most important aesthetic experiences of eating and drinking. These achievements need to be understood in related and overlapping ways, but ways that also acknowledge and preserve the distinctive roles that foods, tastes, and eating may assume.

Moreover, though I have disputed the dismissal of taste as a low, bodily sense from the beginning, my purpose has been not to elevate taste to the status of the distal senses but rather to point out the ways in which taste invites philosophical interest. Some portion of that interest is in the ranking of the senses itself, for the bodily element of the experience of eating has its own significance that contributes to the asymmetry between foods and fine art forms. It is not only that so many of the exemplified properties savored in food are sensuous (which is to say it tastes good). An important part of eating, drinking, and tasting is precisely that they signify the bodily, the mortal part of existence. There is only a superficial irony in this claim: part of the importance of food, eating, and awareness of tasting, swallowing, digesting is that they do direct attention to the supposedly "lower" aspect of being human—the fact that we are animal and mortal. Eating is and must be rooted in a relentless routine of hunger, swallowing, satiety, and hunger again. No wonder sometimes we do not have the time for aesthetic attention to this demand. The significance of eating is ineluctably bodily, and the constancy of the rhythms of eating remind us of the transience of the activity. (In Hegel's words, "we can smell only what is in the process of wasting away, and we can taste only by destroying.")[57] Despite the fact that tasting and eating provide fully aesthetic cognition, I do not want to try to level the senses or their objects in such a way that the traditions that rank the senses disappear altogether. It will be more illuminating to probe the meanings assigned to foods and to eating, including aspects of what may appear at first to be their negative valence. This needs to be acknowledged so that the different reflections prompted by food and by tasting and eating may be rightly understood. The inescapable cycle of hunger and eating is in a sense commemorated by the fragility of food itself, which melts, collapses, is eaten and digested, rots, molds, and decays. Because eating is a repetitive and transient experience, because food does not last but spoils, because it not only nourishes but poisons, eating is a small exercise in mortality. Rather than transcend time, as romantic ideas of art suggest is the goal of masterworks, food succumbs to time—as do we ourselves. This perhaps is the final reflection that tasting prompts: not just that it is pleasurable but that it fades so quickly.

---

[57] G. W. F. Hegel, *Aesthetics: Lectures on Fine Art,* trans. T. M. Knox, 2 vols. (Oxford: Clarendon, 1975), 1:138.

CHAPTER 5

The Visual Appetite: Representing Taste and Food

As we have seen, reflection on eating, and especially on certain special or ceremonial meals, affords considerable food for thought as well as for the body, and
the meaning of taste may be apparent in the taste of meaning in the very act of eating. Investigation of actual eating, however, is not the only way to reveal what
taste and foods can mean, and indeed in spite of its directness, it is often not the
most illuminating way, either. For most people, eating is part of life's daily routine.
Extremes of deprivation interrupt the rhythms of ingestion, but unless one is af-
flicted by famine or acute poverty or has elected to fast, the business of fueling the
organism is apt to take on the aura of the ordinary and to be regarded in the same
unreflective way that any routinized activity is. Indeed, hunger may distract one
from other callings and thereby assume the appearance of an intruder who must
be appeased as expeditiously as possible. This train of thought is but one step
away from thinking of appetite, eating, and their associated sensory apparatus as
unworthy of much consideration beyond making that appeasement as efficient
and pleasant as possible.

Therefore let us consider how foods and taste appear in cultural products that
lack the nutritional necessities of eating and that invite—indeed demand—thoughtful reflection: the representation of tasting and eating in visual art and in narrative.
This vantage removes us from the routines of actual eating and affords some distance
from which to assess the meanings of an experience that engages the body so intensely and so frequently. We shall find some overlap between the meanings food attains in art and its meanings in use, but while continuity is to be expected, we shall
also find artistic exaggeration, selection, and invention. More than an illustration of
meaning in food, art provides a perspective on the broad historical context in which
the meanings of tastes, foods, and eating emerge.

It should come as no surprise to discover the familiar sense hierarchy at work in
artistic representations, and their iconography augments our understanding of the
ranking of the senses. The very features that have seemed to disqualify taste as an
object of extended philosophical interest are complexly portrayed in art. The presumption that taste and smell are closer to nature than other senses, for example, is
both presented in art and challenged in the very act of its presentation. The render-

ing of sense experience in visual arts reveals the degree to which all the senses are already (or always already) the subject of interpretation, never functioning as simply the natural, animal elements of complex human activity. This general observation may come as no surprise, either. When we discover the range of interpretations attached to the sense of taste and its objects in visual depictions of them, however, we have to wonder how eating could ever be considered a purely natural act, especially one that merely reflects the fact that bodies require nourishment.

There is an entire genre of painting devoted to the depiction of items of the table. So-called still life painting does not traditionally occupy a place of high esteem in art theory, and in the standard belittling assessment of this genre we may see an echo— or perhaps a version—of the philosophical hierarchy of the senses. I have argued that there is a gender dimension to that ranking, and in the zone of art history we discover similar factors that contribute to the second-place standing of still life. Thus consideration of this genre not only reminds us of the meanings that food attains but also deepens our exploration of certain gendered aspects of the intellectual tradition under study. A perennial moral dimension of the sense hierarchy concerns the worry that appetite is prone to be overindulged. As a subject of depiction in visual art, appetite brings to awareness the erotic connections of food with sex and the potentially unruly power of both.

The very shapes and colors of foods have provided decorative motifs in architecture and crafts; both sensuous properties and traditional meanings of foods furnish subject and form in the still life compositions of modern painting. Many of these paintings perpetuate the role of food depictions as decorative, pleasant, and enticing; but we shall find as well that food is a powerful vehicle for the expression of that which is dangerous, terrible, and abhorrent. This latter role for food is an additional reason why we now turn to the representation of matters of taste, eating, and appetite, rather than actual acts of eating, where health, nutrition, and toxicity limit the very idea of the edible. While sometimes the artistic rendering of foods seems virtually to mirror daily life and real patterns of eating, at other times art moves into worlds where foods are palatable only as representations, for art reaches toward limits of tolerability that practice cannot approach.

Representing Taste: The Sense Hierarchy in Art

At the Cluny Museum in Paris hang a series of six Gothic tapestries that together bear the name *La Dame à la licorne*, or *The Lady with the Unicorn*. Each tapestry depicts a noble lady, sometimes accompanied by an attendant, a lion, and a unicorn; sundry animals are scattered amidst the surrounding millefleurs that fill a red-rose ground. The human figures, the lion and the unicorn, and some of the small animals are placed upon an oval of dark blue, an island of sorts on which their arrangement

5.1. The tapestry panel depicting taste in the series The Lady with the Unicorn. *(Musée du Moyen Age [Cluny], Paris. Giraudon / Art Resource, New York.)*

lends a degree of visual depth to the composition.[1] Five of the tapestries portray the five senses; the enigmatic sixth hanging appears to comment on them all.[2]

    The tapestry identified as depicting sight features the lady sitting alone. She holds a mirror, and the unicorn, its forelegs resting on her lap, observes its own image. Hearing is represented by the device of music, as the lady plays on a small organ while her attendant works the bellows. In the panel depicting taste the lady stands with her hand poised over a comfit dish filled with sweets that look like berries or small candied fruits (Figure 5.1). Her right hand pauses over the dish, fingers toy-

---

[1] The manifold details of this series have invited speculation and interpretation ever since the hangings were brought to public attention in 1844. George Sand discovered the hangings at the Château de Boussac sometime in the 1830s and mentioned them in her novel *Jeanne* (1844), as well as in three later publications.

[2] The proper order of the tapestries has been a matter of debate. It was formerly thought to proceed as: touch, odor, taste, "A mon seul désir," hearing, sight (Pierre Verlet, *Le Musée de Cluny* [Paris: Musées Nationaux, 1966], p. 83). My discussion follows Alain Erlande-Brandenburg's more recently established order, which places "A mon seul désir" last to stand as a comment on the subjects of the first five hangings (*Musée de Cluny: Guide* [Paris: Musées Nationaux, 1986], pp. 66–67).

ing with a berry, though her attention is directed to a bird that has lit on the fingers of her left hand and is nibbling at a berry it clasps in its claw. The lady herself neither eats nor tastes, but a small monkey at her feet is more enthusiastically engaged: it gobbles up one of the sweets. Similarly, in the panel depicting smell, the lady gazes at a flower she holds, one she has just taken from a basket held by her attendant; the monkey behind her has rummaged through a basket of flowers and has buried its nose in a large blossom. In the panel depicting touch the lady, turned slightly away from the unicorn, grasps its horn with one hand and holds a standard bearing an armorial banner with the other.[3] In the sixth tapestry the lady and her attendant stand under a tent flanked by the lion and the unicorn. The attendant holds a small open casket, and the lady's hands are either withdrawing or replacing a long jeweled necklace. The border at the top of the tent contains the series' only inscription: "A mon seul désir." The import of this simple phrase is ambiguous, as its several possible English translations indicate: "For my only desire," "To my one desire," "At my sole behest." Just what it signifies has been the subject of particularly intense scrutiny.

At first it seems that the lady is taking jewels from the casket, but the soundest interpretation reverses this reading: the lady is placing the jewels into the casket, not taking them out. The necklace in her hands is one of the elaborate collars she has worn in the other panels. Her action signals that she is renouncing the domination of the passions that result when the senses are indulged; she indicates her acknowledgment of the superiority of the intellect over the bodily senses. By this reading, this cycle of tapestries does not at all celebrate the senses, despite the first impression received from the detail and care devoted to each; rather, the whole confirms the fallibility of the world of sense and an acceptance of a Platonic understanding of the nature of reality. The enigmatic words decorating the tent indicate not "For my one desire" but "According to my only wish": the lady voluntarily renounces the authority of the senses.[4]

Scrutiny not only of this individual tapestry but also of the rendering of the senses in the five other panels confirms this reading, for the human agents are notably little involved in the exercise of the senses. Only in *Hearing* is the lady really actively engaged, and in the production of music, arguably the most mathematical and abstract of the arts. It is the unicorn that exercises sight and the monkey—not one of God's exalted creations, according to European iconography—that ardently indulges in the lower senses of taste and smell. Touch is perhaps treated the most

---

[3] The arms represented by the banners that appear in every panel are those of the Le Viste family. Erlande-Brandenburg believes that the tapestries were woven to commemorate the appointment of Jean Le Viste (d. 1500) to royal office in 1489 (Alain Erlande-Brandenburg, *La Dame à la licorne* [Paris: Musées Nationaux, 1978]).

[4] Erlande-Brandenburg makes the case for this interpretation. "'A mon seul désir', c'est à dire 'selon ma seule volonté'. Le collier déposé est symbole de renoncement aux passions que déchaînent en nous les sens mal contrôlés" ("Etude," ibid., n.p.).

ambiguously: the lady touches an animal of great spiritual meaning and purity, yet she turns away. (It is tempting to read her grasp of the unicorn's horn as a vaguely phallic gesture.) Touch is often considered the sense most related to sexual passion, and notably, the monkeys in this hanging are manacled, one of them to a roller-shaped weight rather like a ball and chain.[5]

Michel Serres interprets the tapestries not only as a statement about the realm of the senses but also as a portrayal of the most primitive construction of the human self.[6] Serres stresses the fact that only the sixth tapestry contains language, and language constructs the human world. By themselves the external senses remain mute, inchoate, impossible to bring to reflective consciousness, a process that requires language. Of course, the idea that the senses *tout court* are "animal" is an interpretation founded upon familiar philosophical assumptions, not a discovery in nature. One can make claims about some nonhuman, animal world of the senses only by means of human reflection within a choice of systems of representation. As Serres puts it, we cannot leave the tabernacle of language; there is no way to describe the senses from outside the tent of words.[7] Therefore that "natural" sense, taste, is already interpreted *as* natural: the lady hesitates over the bowl of sweetmeats; the monkey, succumbing to its animal appetite, greedily pops one into its mouth. This rendering of the simultaneous bodily need to eat and the intellectual and spiritual need to recognize the fallibility of sense experience casts the notion of the human self in a network of ideas that includes the superiority of intellect over body. The senses, though components of human biology (and in that sense part of "nature"), when considered reflectively as they must be in theoretical analyses and artistic portrayals, are given meaning on a foundation of presumptions about order and significance. And this order enters our own experience; arguably we employ an interpreted understanding of our senses even as we use them in our excursions through the world.

La Dame à la licorne is an early prototype of artistically rendered allegories of the senses, a genre that peaked in popularity in the seventeenth century, especially in

---

[5] While other interpreters have not looked for indications of the sense hierarchy in these panels (indeed, the last panel suggests the unimportance of all sense experience), suggestions of the familiar sense hierarchy can be found in their iconography. Not only do we find the kinds of depictive details mentioned above, but the clothing of the lady suggests symbolic function. In the panel illustrating touch, her necklace eschews the flower motif of the others in favor of round metal links rather like fetters, and from her belt hangs a linked chain suggestive of the monkey's leash. The superiority of sight and hearing over the other senses may be indicated by the lady's headdress: in the panels illustrating these two senses she wears a wrapped veil peaked by an aigrette—a crest or tuft over the brow. Only in the last panel, "A mon seul désir," does this motif appear again; perhaps it signals the greater intellectual affinity of sight and hearing, despite their fallibility as senses.

[6] Michel Serres, *Les Cinq Sens* (Paris: Bernard Grasset, 1985), pp. 52–63.

[7] "Je ne peux écrire ni dire les cinq tapisseries, car si je dis ou écris, je ne parle que de la sixième": ibid., p. 58.

Northern Europe and in France.[8] Many of these paintings follow a loosely Platonic line of thought that considers the world of the senses to be a pale echo of the world of the spirit or the intellect (for Christianity adapted Platonic universals to its own spiritual ends). But the philosophy befitting these allegories need not be one that always distrusts the senses altogether. Nature is God's handiwork, and as such it possess divine meaning, albeit hidden. In this case, the five senses are interpreted as means to apprehend this natural dimension of divine creation. Judicious and temperate exercise of the senses could reveal the hidden meanings of nature, though of course their pleasurable indulgence would be a misuse of the sensuous mode of apprehension.[9] Related philosophical interests concentrate on the distinction between appearance and reality by pondering sense experience, the common illusions of which provide standard examples of how one may be misled about the true nature of the world. This too can be the import of a sense allegory.[10] Extended argumentation on such subjects must remain the province of discursive philosophy, but for balance of interest across the senses, artistic treatments have a certain advantage in comparison with their philosophical counterparts. Many philosophers simply dismiss the lower senses after cursory thought or neglect them altogether. Representational allegorical treatments, while they may assert the same judgments of value about the senses both individually and as a group, treat the senses equally as far as artistic attention goes. The indulgence of appetite and of the sense of taste is rendered with as much detail and care as the spiritual benefits of music.

Taste, as befits its reputation, is often represented as particularly vulnerable to abuse. An illustrative case is provided by the *Allegory of the Five Senses* (1618) of Jan Brueghel the Elder, now in the Museo del Prado in Madrid. The heavily detailed paintings that make up this series are full of tokens of each sense, many with meanings that time has obscured, though one can recognize some standard signs for each sense even without an iconographic guide: a woman gazes at a painting in the allegory of sight; she is surrounded with optical devices such as a telescope. Musical instruments signal hearing; flowers, smell. *Touch* is filled with tactile trappings, chiefly armor and weapons, though featured in the foreground is a fond (and slightly erotic) embrace between Venus and Cupid. *Taste* displays a foreground littered with eatables and dead game; a woman sits at a long, laden table eating greedily (Figure 5.2).

In each of the paintings except *Smell*, which is set outside in a garden, the walls of the depicted rooms are filled with paintings of both antique and biblical scenes relating to the exercise of the relevant sense. Each painting features a naked or loosely

[8] Michel Faré, *La Nature morte en France: Son Histoire et son évolution du XVIIe au XXe siècle* (Geneva: Pierre Cailler, 1962), pp. 105–7.
[9] Ildiko Ember, *Delights for the Senses: Dutch and Flemish Still Life Paintings in Budapest* (Wausau, Wis.: Leigh Yawkey Woodson Art Museum, 1989), p. 32.
[10] Faré, *La Nature morte en France*, p. 10.

5.2. Jan Brueghel the Elder, Allegory of Taste. *(Museo del Prado, Madrid. Alinari / Art Resource, New York.)*

clad woman exercising the sense and a cherub participating with her—with the striking exception of *Taste*. The antique figure attending this sense is no innocent rosy baby but a wicked-looking satyr or faun, who pours wine for the gluttonous woman and gazes lustfully at her display of appetite.

The satyr is a riveting anomaly in this series of pictures. His presence singles out indulgence in taste as the especially risky venture among the senses, for the gobbling woman is wholly occupied with her gustatory pleasure, and lust awaits the satiation of one appetite so that it may be supplanted by another.[11] Nor is this an idiosyncrasy of this set of pictures, for as we shall see, the appetite for foods and the savoring of the sensations afforded by taste are prevalently associated with an appetite for sex and the lusty pursuit of objects of that desire. This is not to say that taste is the preeminent sense that stimulates sexual desire, for such is clearly not the case. All five senses provide their routes to arousal, and in much visual art it is the eye itself that is most often appealed to when what is depicted also stimulates desire. Nonetheless, when it is the senses themselves that are the subject for art, we do find the appetite for food and for the relish of its taste linked to an appetite for sex. It is as though this sense provided the most direct conduit that joins the two desires, or as if appetite were one phenomenon with two routes to satisfaction.

---

[11] Fabrizio Clerici, in *Allegorie dei sensi di Jean Bruegel* (Florence, 1946), pp. 23–24, interprets the satyr as urging the woman to overcome her hesitation or reluctance to indulge in appetite. Whether the woman is hesitantly or enthusiastically devouring her food is difficult to say definitively. Whichever, the satyr is clearly an image of somewhat menacing enticement.

5.3. *Lubin Baugin,* Still Life. *(Musée du Louvre, Paris. Giraudon / Art Resource, New York.)*

While Brueghel's series of paintings illustrate the senses in action, another type of allegorical painting represents the senses by means of their objects and constitutes a genre of still life painting. Lubin Baugin's *Still Life* (Figure 5.3), for example, shows a portion of a table covered with objects, each of which represents one of the senses: a mirror for sight, a lute or mandolin for hearing, a vase of flowers for smell, a deck of cards and a chess set for touch, and a goblet of wine and loaf of bread for taste. At first glance we are looking at a realistic representation of a rather crowded table in a home, casually set for a snack and some entertainment. Reflection and familiarity with the genre aid our understanding of the artifice of the composition and our realization that the five senses are the subject of depiction.

Still life renderings of the senses are metonymic in that the sense is signaled by one of its objects. The iconography deployed in this type of depiction frequently features mirrors as symbols of vision; they are visual objects par excellence, mimetic devices that give the world back as seen, albeit reversed. In a sense any paintable object could stand for sight, since by the very fact that it can be visually depicted it necessarily is an object of vision. But such wide choices for iconography would obscure the reference to vision altogether. A mirror not only is visible, it is a manufactured object with a purpose: to be used to *see* things by way of reflection. Thereby mirrors call attention to vision itself: "reflecting media, mirrors, water surfaces, metals, and other eyes are necessary, through which the seeing of seeing becomes visible."[12] Certain moral meanings attached to the senses may be aptly conveyed by means of their tokens. Because mirrors are frequently employed to check one's own appearance, this object also suggests human vanity and unwise preoccupation with matters of adornment. When the allegory depicts human figures as well as objects, the gazer in the mirror is almost always female.

Musical instruments frequently represent hearing, for again their chief purpose is to make a sound that catches the attention of the hearing sense. Moreover, musical instruments also signal a civilized, artful use of this sense, one that is refined and developed and by no means "natural." Both musical and scientific instruments figure, however, in *vanitas* motifs as symbols of the futility of human endeavor, the ultimate waste of effort that human achievements amount to in the grand course of time. Similarly, vision may be depicted by means of optical instruments such as telescopes or lenses; these objects also convey a double message, signifying both a sense and the vanity of the human development of its exercise, even when that has produced considerable scientific expertise and knowledge.

Smell, by contrast, is most frequently denoted by a flower—an object plucked from a field or garden. The scent of a blossom is a gratuity of nature and requires no human invention. If the petals of the flower are beginning to wither and drop, then the flower serves also as a memento mori ("remember that you must die") to remind the viewer that time is fleeting and the pleasures of perfumes short-lived. (Occasionally smell is depicted by means of a manufactured scent, such as perfume or pipe tobacco.)

The symbols of touch have more variation, but this sense is typically represented by something held in the hands and explored with the fingers, such as a gamepiece or playing cards. These objects are kin to musical and scientific instruments in that they are fully human achievements but do not endure in the long run. The frivolity of games makes chess boards and playing cards indicative not only of touch but also of *vanitas*.

Taste, like smell, may be denoted by a natural object such as a piece of fruit or it may be signaled by a prepared food. Opulent foodstuffs indicate luxury, and in early progenitors of still life paintings the foregrounds often feature excessive piles of food that frame a distant biblical scene, as in Pieter Aertsen's painting of heavily laden tables behind which Jesus speaks with Mary Magdalen and Martha (Figure 5.4).[13] However, still life allegories such as Baugin's depict taste with a humble loaf of bread

---

[12] Peter Sloterdijk, *Critique of Cynical Reason*, trans. Michael Eldred (Minneapolis: University of Minnesota Press, 1987), p. 145.

[13] A domestic scene of Christ in the house of Mary and Martha is a frequent setting for foregrounds of piled foods. See Ingvar Bergström, *Dutch Still-Life Painting in the Seventeenth Century*, trans. Christina Hedström and Gerald Taylor [1947] (New York: Hacker Art Books, 1983), pp. 16–24.

5.4. Pieter Aertsen, Vanitas. *Still life, 1552. In the background Jesus with Saint Mary Magdalen and Saint Martha, sisters of Lazarus. (Kunsthistorisches Museum, Vienna. Erich Lessing / Art Resource, New York.)*

and a cup of wine. An edible object such as bread actually could serve as a symbol of all five senses, for bread is seen, smelled, tasted, and (when crunched) heard; and of course it is touched, not only by the hands but also by the lips, tongue, and throat. But Baugin's painting demonstrates something even more important: the potential of the icons of taste to carry spiritual meaning. For here the usual lowly role of this bodily sense is dramatically reversed. The bread and the wine, singly or together, suggest neither the vanity of human endeavor nor concupiscence but the spiritual encounter offered by the Christian Eucharist.[14] While the tokens of the other senses suggest preoccupation with the transient activities of this world, taste engages with the transcendent world of the divine. In a painting such as Baugin's taste assumes a less bodily role than the sense hierarchy ordinarily allows, alluding to a spiritual dimension to tasting and the reflective understanding sometimes possible in ritual eating. It is not that the bodily sense is transcended or denied, as in *The Lady with the Unicorn,* but in fact the reverse: the intimacy of tasting unites the communicant with God. The wine—the blood of Christ—stings the tongue, slides down the throat, enters the body, infuses the soul.

The fact that taste can signal communion with the divine as well as gluttony and self-indulgence, that it can be the sense of transcendent experience as well as the one locked in carnal appetite, indicates that the analysis represented by the sense hierarchy is by no means exhaustive. Even when the purpose of a painting is to warn of the

---

[14] Faré, *La Nature morte en France,* p. 106.

dangers of the bodily senses and their overindulgence, the meanings that taste, foods, and appetites can convey vary hugely. This complexity of meaning is frequently overlooked, even by theorists and commentators who have directed their attention to visual representations of food, for paintings wholly devoted to the depiction of items of the kitchen or the dining room have come in for their share of derogatory analysis. In fact, commentary about still life depictions is as revealing as the depictions themselves on the subject of the senses, their objects, and their exercise.

Still Life Painting and the Depiction of Food

Art history and criticism provide a counterpoint to philosophical treatments of the sense hierarchy. Since classical antiquity, the rendering of food and other domestic, quotidian objects for their own sake alone has prompted condescension among theorists of art, sometimes even amounting to scorn.[15] When foods form a part of a grander painting that tells a story from the Bible, legend, or history, they can play an important narrative role. Indeed, the symbolic valence of certain foods often enhances the depth of meaning of accompanying images. In such contexts foods and other humble objects do not draw attention to themselves as such, but lend their meanings to a more important story that inspires the mind and the moral understanding of the viewer. If a painting depicts foods as the central subject of representation, however, it has been standardly considered a lowly example of the pictorial arts. Criticisms of food and other mundane objects as unworthy subjects for the painter's art pertain chiefly to the choice of these items as the sole subject of art.[16]

This is a recurring theme of art treatises of the early modern period. Seventeenth- and eighteenth-century European art theory is particularly articulate in its denigration of such depictions, which come to be known by the general label of "still life"— the painting of objects that do not move. The very terms for this genre reveal its low estate: the origin of the English term "still life" is the Dutch *still-leven,* a term coined to refer to paintings of things incapable of movement. This expression, with its connotations of still and tranquil life, entered languages with German roots. In French in the seventeenth and eighteenth centuries, the common term was *nature reposée,* or things at rest. The French term now used, *nature morte,* came into use in the mid–eighteenth century, probably under the influence of academicians who expressed their contempt for the genre with the notion of "dead nature."[17] There are at

---

[15] Summaries of the low estate of this genre may be found in Charles Sterling, *Still Life Painting from Antiquity to the Present Time,* trans. James Emmons (New York: Universe Books, 1959), p. 11; and Norman Bryson, *Looking at the Overlooked: Four Essays on Still Life Painting* (Cambridge: Harvard University Press, 1990), Foreword, pp. 136–37, and passim.

[16] Depicted objects in still life painting range from flowers to machinery. My discussion focuses on kitchen objects, chiefly foods.

[17] Sterling, *Still Life Painting,* pp. 43–44. See also Bergström, *Dutch Still-Life Painting,* pp. 3–4.

least four elements to the traditional objections to still life painting, all of which bear interestingly if indirectly on an understanding of taste and food: the supposed triviality of the subject matter; the illusions presented by trompe l'oeil techniques, with which still life is often rendered; the appeal of depicted foodstuffs to appetite; and the complicated "feminine" qualities of edible subjects in domestic settings.

In the seventeenth century André Félibien ranked the themes of painting in lectures delivered to the French Royal Academy, beginning with the lowest: the painting of fruits, flowers, shells, and dead animals.[18] As theories of the grand style of painting further develop, this ranking continues: paintings of foods and of household objects are inferior to paintings with narrative content that take their themes from the Bible, classical mythology, or the great events of history. While the skill of the Dutch masters of still life is acknowledged, their accomplishments are not credited with merit of the highest sort.[19] In his lectures to the Royal Academy in England, Sir Joshua Reynolds similarly damns the still life painter with faint praise: "Even the painter of still life, whose highest ambition is to give a minute representation of every part of those low objects which he sets before him, deserves praise in proportion to his attainment; because no part of this excellent art, so much the ornament of polished life, is destitute of value and use. These, however, are by no means the views to which the mind of the student ought to be *primarily* directed."[20]

Metaphysical considerations enter into these reservations about still life painting in neoclassical and early modern theory. The goal of the art of the brush was long held to be the portrayal of truth, conceived in a Platonic way as an image that leads the mind to a concept of the form of the object portrayed.[21] This is also the nub of argument between the so-called classicists and modernists. Those who held that the principles of art manifested in the art of classical antiquity should remain the models for painters did so on the grounds that just those forms best represent the ideal proportions of their subjects, for example, the human body. Depicting grand and mythic subjects was considered the best way to lead the mind to general truths and to knowledge. Given these standards, foodstuffs appear simply trivial. While an apple in a bowl before the Virgin Mary is imbued with moral and spiritual meaning that leads the mind to contemplate important truths about original sin and redemption, an apple browning on a sideboard simply duplicates the daily round of body

[18] André Félibien, *Conférences de l'Académie royale de peinture et de sculpture* (Paris, 1669).

[19] Jonathan Richardson, for example, noted the degree of merit to be acknowledged in the exact copies of low subjects in which Dutch and Flemish masters excel: *An Essay on the Theory of Painting* (1725), facs. ed.(Menston, Eng.: Scolar Press, 1971), p. 171.

[20] Sir Joshua Reynolds, *Discourses* [1797] (New York: Penguin, 1992), p. 114.

[21] See my "The Eclipse of Truth in the Rise of Aesthetics," *British Journal of Aesthetics* 29.4 (Autumn 1989). Both Richardson and Reynolds were empiricist in their philosophical leanings but classicist in their taste for art. See Richard Woodfield's categorizations of art theory of the eighteenth century in his introduction to Reynolds, *Seven Discourses* [1778], facs. ed. (Menston, Eng.: Scholar Press, 1971).

maintenance and occupies the mind with small and distracting details. So goes the first academic objection to still life: its mundane subject matter is unworthy of serious attention.

Ironically, the ability of many painters to depict the details of the objects of daily life with stunning skill leads to another frequent criticism of this genre: that it often achieves a high degree of visual illusion. The methods by which still life is often painted render these humble scenes startlingly "realistic." Light refracting through glass, peaches dripping juice, dew still clinging to freshly picked leaves, flies and beetles investigating the remains of a meal—such details created with a brush fine enough to erase its own strokes accomplish a high degree of illusion. Because of the modest dimensions of actual foodstuffs, still life paintings are also frequently more or less life-size, adding to their illusionary effects.

Art theory has often betrayed ambivalence with respect to trompe l'oeil techniques. On the one hand, the skill required to fool the eye to this degree is undeniable; combined with the sophisticated use of linear perspective, it signals a particular mastery of drawing technique as well as an understanding of optics.[22] On the other hand, such illusion is all too easily turned to trickery. Merely fooling the eye, more easily done when the painted object is depicted as its actual size, may give temporary delight. But it is ultimately an empty triumph because it teases the eye without informing the mind. Jonathan Richardson criticizes the poor judge of art who believes a picture good "because a Piece of Lace, or Brocade, a Fly, a Flower, a Wrinkle, a Wart, is highly finish'd, and (if you please) Natural."[23] All the incidental items Richardson singles out might be made into details of an important story, but by themselves they do not raise painting to its fullest potential as an important art. As Reynolds puts it, "If deceiving the eye were the only business of the art, there is no doubt . . . but the minute painter would be more apt to succeed; but it is not the eye, it is the mind which the painter of genius desires to address; nor will he waste a moment upon those smaller objects which only serve to catch the sense, to divide the attention, and to counteract his great design of speaking to the heart."[24]

Allegiance to history painting in the grand style leads theorists such as Reynolds and Richardson to regard Italian schools of painting as superior to those of Northern Europe, which perfected domestic, village, or intimate settings. Relatedly, Reynolds's directive to paint "general nature" rather than to focus on the details of

---

[22] Conventionalists such as Goodman would doubt the grounds on which such illusion was considered to rest: the duplication of the operation of eye and light on the part of the skilled painter such that from a given perspective the look of a painting imitates the look of a real thing. The classic discussion of illusory representation is E. H. Gombrich, *Art and Illusion* (Princeton: Princeton University Press, 1960).
[23] Richardson, *Essay on the Theory of Painting*, p. vi.
[24] Reynolds, *Discourses*, p. 112. Bryson, *Looking at the Overlooked*, analyzes what he sees as sinister and unsettling effects of trompe l'oeil on pp. 140–44.

particular objects feeds the preference for Italian-style history painting.[25] Encouragements to develop similar tastes can be found in the popular drawing instruction manuals of nineteenth-century America, which disseminated ideas originating in European theory.[26]

Trompe l'oeil appeals to the eye, and some critics worry that such pictures may appeal also to the sense of taste and gustatory appetite. Indeed, the more illusionistic the still life, the more direct the stimulation of gastronomic juices. Some still life pictures depict delectable edibles—fresh fish, gleaming fruit, ripe figs bursting with juice, steaming bread fresh from the oven. Long ago Philostratus caught the delicious continuity between the real and the represented in this ancient description of a painting of foods:

> It is a good thing to gather figs and also not to pass over in silence the figs in this picture. Purple figs dripping with juice are heaped on vine-leaves; and they are depicted with breaks in the skin, some just cracking open to disgorge their honey, some split apart, they are so ripe. . . . You would say that even the grapes in the painting are good to eat and full of winey juice. And the most charming point of all this is: on a leafy branch is yellow honey already within the comb and ripe to stream forth if the comb is pressed; and on another leaf is cheese new curdled and quivering; and there are bowls of milk not merely white but gleaming, for the cream floating upon it makes it seem to gleam.[27]

The Dutch still lifes of "abundance" popular in the seventeenth century lavishly present a world replete with eating pleasures. The fact that such paintings frequently carried a *vanitas* message or another moral caution carries little weight with their detractors, who imply that the stimulated appetite overpowers the intellectual lesson. Perhaps these pictures risk bypassing the appropriate sense of the painter's art altogether and arouse the appetite to eat. Inasmuch as they may do so, this is another feature of the representation of food that disqualifies it from the higher ranks of art, for it sacrifices the appeal to the intellect and the ennobling of the spirit. (Once again, the presumption is that the lower senses stimulate appetite and not cogitation.) It would not therefore offer what is best about the art of painting by (as Reynolds put it) "disentangling the mind from appetite, and conducting the

[25] See Reynolds, *Discourses,* Discourse IV. Svetlana Alpers argues that this preference for Italian style cast a long shadow over the achievements of northern painters: *The Art of Describing: Dutch Art in the Seventeenth Century* (Chicago: University of Chicago Press, 1983).

[26] Opinion against still life prevailed in eighteenth- and nineteenth-century art circles in the United States. See William Gerdst, *Painters of the Humble Truth* (Columbia: University of Missouri Press, 1981), chap. 1; Carolyn Korsmeyer, "'The Compass in the Eye,'" *Monist* 76.4 (October 1993).

[27] Philostratus the Athenian, *Imagines,* trans. Arthur Fairbanks (New York: Putnam, 1931), bk. 1, p. 31, quoted in Bryson, *Looking at the Overlooked,* pp. 18–19.

thoughts through successive stages of excellence, till that contemplation of universal rectitude and harmony which began by Taste, may, as it is exalted and refined, conclude in Virtue."[28]

Such a worry was expressed by Arthur Schopenhauer, a philosopher who incorporated commentary about art in his metaphysical writings. Schopenhauer appreciated certain types of still life painting for the tranquillity with which they rendered arrangements of mundane, insignificant things. When tasty-looking foods are numbered among those things, however, that tranquillity is liable to be disturbed by the arousal of appetite. Schopenhauer classed still life painting as a species of the "charming," conceived as the opposite of the sublime and the beautiful in painting. The involvement of charm in the suggestion of satisfied appetite is at stake, for "the charming or attractive draws the beholder down from pure contemplation, demanded by every apprehension of the beautiful, since it necessarily stirs his will by objects that directly appeal to it."[29] Two examples of the category of low, "charming" art are relevant to this discussion. One is still life painting of foods, and the other is a rendering of the nude body in a way calculated to titillate sexual desire. First, still life:

> The one species, a very low one, is found in the still life painting of the Dutch, when they err by depicting edible objects. By their deceptive appearance these necessarily excite the appetite, and this is just a stimulation of the will which puts an end to any aesthetic contemplation of the object. Painted fruit, however, is admissible, for it exhibits itself as a further development of the flower, and as a beautiful product of nature through form and colour, without our being positively forced to think of its edibility. But unfortunately we often find, depicted with deceptive naturalness, prepared and served-up dishes, oysters, herrings, crabs, bread and butter, beer, wine, and so on, all of which is wholly objectionable.[30]

Many of the items to which Schopenhauer objects possess (or once possessed) symbolic meanings that he overlooks. Oysters indicate luxury and sexual indulgence, and crabs and lobsters, because of their propensity to scrabble sideways and backward, are employed to indicate inconstancy. To the observer attuned to these meanings, such pictures should inspire thoughts about moral lapses, not just tasty eating. However, it is the whetted appetite of the viewer that lessens the value of a painting, and that appetite is whetted by succulent-looking dishes depicted with a

[28] Reynolds, *Discourses,* Discourse IX, p. 171.
[29] Arthur Schopenhauer, *The World as Will and Representation*, vol. 1, sec. 40 (1819), trans. E. F. J. Payne (New York: Dover, 1969), p. 207. Schopenhauer analyzes aesthetic experience as the contemplative calm possible when the will is subdued; appetite stirs the will and is always at odds with aesthetic attention.
[30] Ibid., pp. 207–8.

high degree of realism. Admiring a trompe l'oeil of a finely laid table, according to this line of thought, would be but one step removed from sitting down to a meal. One suspects that even were Schopenhauer reminded of the moral significance of the still life, he would object to the powerful stimulation of the appetite by the luscious representations of foods, arguing that the will to eat overwhelms the opportunity for contemplation.

In sum, still life depictions are inferior to paintings of important events or stories—so-called history paintings—on the grounds of the inferiority of their subject matter; the clever but tricky skill that is the chief accomplishment of their rendering; and their appeal to an inferior faculty, appetite, over intellect. Here we have in the language of art criticism the very worries that philosophers raise about the senses: anxiety about appetite and indulgence, and skepticism about the reliability of sense perception when illusion is an ever-present possibility. It should be no surprise to see these concerns come together with the visual representation of foods.

In Praise of Still Life

In spite of this history of low critical esteem, still life painting has always been immensely popular, as its commercial success attests.[31] Moreover, there are also artists and art historians who defend still life in response to the charges that have been brought against it. Interestingly, however, these defenses do not attempt to vindicate artistic interest in the taste experiences that would be available from depicted foods were they real and not paint; nor do they embrace the bodily experience of whetted and satisfied appetite. Rather, defenders of still life implicitly accept the values according to which this art is denigrated but argue that the condemnation is mistaken. The reason most often invoked is that artists imbue their compositions with moral messages that serve to detach the viewer from thoughts of the taste pleasures that may be aroused by the depiction of foods. Many of the fans of still life among art historians defend the genre by stressing both the moral depth of such paintings and their formal properties, vindicating the paintings by appeal to both their intellectual and visual allure.

That still life is often a venue for moralizing is indisputable. Schopenhauer's concerns about the stimulation of appetite that still life might prompt was at one time matched within the ranks of still life artists themselves, who in many varieties of the genre incorporated moral reminders in their paintings. In early modern Europe still life grew out of religious painting and book illumination, and what now seem inci-

---

[31] Paintings were purchased by the Dutch peasantry as well as the middle and upper classes (Bergström, *Dutch Still-Life Painting*, pp. 2–3). Gerdst, *Painters of the Humble Truth*, chronicles the popularity of still life in America (pp. 20–21 and passim).

dental details at the time were freighted with symbolic meaning. A butterfly hovering over a blossom, for example, appears to a secular viewer as a nice natural touch—an insect enjoying the same bouquet as its arranger. But butterflies are also symbols of the human soul, so the hovering insect signals the transience of life, for as fruit rots and flowers fade, so the soul inhabits its body briefly.

The most extreme form of moral message delivered by still life is to be found in the *vanitas* picture, named after the opening lines of *Ecclesiastes: Vanitas vanitatis, et omnia vanitas*, "Vanity of vanities, all is vanity." The typical giveaway detail of a *vanitas* arrangement is a human skull, though other symbols of the transience of life and the insignificance of human endeavor abound: guttering candles, wilted flowers, spoiled fruits and stale breads, hourglasses, soap bubbles, oil lamps, coins, and globes terrestrial and celestial. Many *vanitas* pictures do not feature food at all. They group together symbols of human effort—books, scientific instruments—and human pleasures—pipes, playing cards, musical instruments.[32] These objects in combination with signs of mortality put the viewer in mind of the futility of human endeavor in the sweep of time. Sometimes foodstuffs are present in the group as well, perhaps a spilled glass of wine or a split fig next to a dusty skull. The result is unmistakably didactic and not terribly appetizing. As Charles Sterling puts it, "If the banquet picture, thanks to its composition and the presence of a few symbolic objects, offered matter for reflection in addition to the pleasure it gave the eye, the *Vanitas* picture was wholly intellectual in conception."[33] Less obtrusive memento mori symbols can be found in still life paintings of foods, where their effect is to caution against indulgence in the appetites. Ingvar Bergström points out that pocket watches occasionally appear on the table of breakfast pieces or fruit pieces, and that the watch symbolizes temperance or moderation, suggesting a measured amount of food. Bergström remarks: "The watch became a slightly moralizing ingredient in still life art, which by its presence could protect the painters against the accusation that their paintings tempted people to gluttony and an extravagant life."[34]

Given the effort that artists made to impart a moral message in their paintings, it is perplexing that so many commentators worried about the senses and the gustatory appetite to which still life supposedly appeals. Some of the later ones may have been sufficiently unfamiliar with the iconography of the genre that these messages were muted. But it may also be that the preference for history painting in the grand manner was the chief driving force behind the denigration of still life. Certainly con-

---

[32] Bergström, *Dutch Still-Life Painting,* puts the items of the most fully developed *vanitas* motifs into three groups: (1) books, scientific instruments, symbols of the arts; (2) purses, deeds, precious items, weapons; (3) symbols of tastes and pleasures: goblets, pipes, musical instruments, playing cards, and dice. They represent respectively the contemplative life, the practical life, and the sensual life (pp. 154, 307n2).

[33] Sterling, *Still Life Painting,* p. 52.

[34] Bergström, *Dutch Still-Life Painting,* p. 190.

temporary viewers are unlikely to notice moralizing motifs immediately and are more apt to be entranced by the illustrative detail of a mouse scavenging crumbs at the edge of an uncleared table than set back by the memento mori message of such a creature rummaging in the remains of dinner.

An intriguing defense of still life that inverts the values traditionally invoked against it has been advanced by the art historian Norman Bryson, who adapts two Greek terms to summarize contrasting categories of painting: "rhopography," or the depiction of trivial, mundane objects, and "megalography "(or history painting), the depiction of mythic or historical events of unusual significance.[35] Still life, he argues, insists on attention to rhopographic details as an antidote to human pride and ambition. That is to say, some of these paintings present rhopographic images in implicit refusal of the importance of megalography altogether. Others may be understood as having the converse effect: the modes of rendering fruits, flowers, meals, wastes from the table often have a moral and intellectual message that can raise the significance of rhopography to a weight equal to that of megalographic history painting.

Part of the fascination of rhopography, on Bryson's view, is not that it is devoid of the values that give megalography its significance but that it reverses them. Without a narrative of human actions, the still life represents what is left when human beings exit the scene: things. It is in the nature of rhopography to challenge measures of human importance. Things persist with their own slow rhythm and covertly subvert the achievements of the humans who live among them. "Opposing the anthropocentrism of the 'higher' genres, it assaults the centrality, value and prestige of the human subject. . . . Human presence is not only expelled physically: still life also expels the values which human presence imposes on the world." Bryson observes that still life is potentially humbling to the viewer. "All men must eat, even the great; there is a leveling of humanity, a humbling of aspiration before an irreducible fact of life, hunger."[36] This defense of rhopography is tied to an additional reason for the low estate of the genre that Bryson reveals: the fact that rhopography depicts what may be termed a "feminine" space.

As ever, the notion of femininity relevant here is complex and opaque. In the most obvious sense, the space depicted by rhopography is feminine because it is largely domestic, and women are classed by ideology and history as keepers of the

[35] These terms were introduced by Charles Sterling in *Still Life Painting*, p. 11. Sterling argues that European still life has its origin in Renaissance imitation of the surviving wall paintings of Pompeii and Herculaneum, and he turns to the Greek to form the terms "rhopography" and "megalography" to describe the ranking of the two subjects. Bryson also adopts the terminology but argues that properly speaking the distinction one finds in the post-Renaissance European discourses about painting is modern and does not echo the classical debate. See *Looking at the Overlooked*, chaps. 1 and 2.
[36] Bryson, *Looking at the Overlooked*, pp. 60, 61.

hearth. The genre is also feminine in the sense that even in times when women's activities have been particularly restricted, painting fruits and flowers has been seen as appropriate exercise of their creative talents. Women may be assumed to be acquainted with the subjects for still life painting because of their domestic duties; moreover, they might learn the particulars of these subjects without needing access to teaching studios, the mathematics of perspective, or studies of anatomy that would expose them to nude models. Of course, at the time when women were granted the opportunities to excel at this type of painting, it was slipping in esteem and headed for its nadir of reputation as a "minor" branch of painting.[37]

More subtly, Bryson argues, rhopography is feminine in the sense that it subverts the claims of masculine heroism to break free from routine and the daily grind in order to achieve something of lasting importance: "The opposition between megalography and still life, between the values of greatness, heroism, achievement, and the values which rhopography pits against them, certainly operates. Yet the opposition does not exist in a vacuum: *it is overdetermined by another polarity, that of gender.*"[38] To eat, to wash, to sleep are requirements of all of us, whether heroes or serving maids. The world of meals and of kitchen detritus so often featured in still life paintings is a subtle but uncomfortable leveler: the achievements of individual efforts are ignored; the unchanging daily life holds sway. Thus rhopography is a "feminine" genre in the sense that the polarity between masculine and feminine describes the polarity between individual heroic achievement and the general routine of creaturely maintenance.[39]

Bryson's analysis of the feminine space of still life suggests some of the subtler politics of the evaluation of genres of painting. He focuses on the more abstract elements of gender and interprets still life as a gentle reminder of ultimate destiny, the whole genre defended as a general *vanitas* lesson, in effect. Indeed, his defense of the still life painters who embrace the humble domain of rhopography refers not to the appetite of hunger at all but to its transcendence.

One of the first artists to exploit the moral dimension made possible by pictures that shun the heroic was the Spanish monk Juan Sánchez y Cotán (1561–1627). Far

---

[37] Rozsika Parker and Griselda Pollock, *Old Mistresses: Women, Art, and Ideology* (New York: Pantheon, 1981), esp. chap. 2.

[38] Bryson, *Looking at the Overlooked*, p. 157.

[39] Bryson places the feminine space of still life in a psychoanalytic context: the enclosed, domestic interiors represent both the confinement and entrapment and the warmth and familiarity of the mother's body. "Still life bears all the marks of this double-edged exclusion and nostalgia, this irresolvable ambivalence which gives to feminine space a power of attraction intense enough to motor the entire development of still life as a genre, yet at the same time apprehends feminine space as alien, as a space which also menaces the masculine subject to the core of his identity as a male" (ibid., pp. 172–73).

5.5. *Juan Sánchez y Cotán,* Still Life with Cardoon. *(Museo de Bellas Artes, Granada. Giraudon / Art Resource, New York.)*

from a base appeal to appetite, Sánchez y Cotán's *bodegones*, kitchen pictures of open larders, appeal to vision and to the intellect (Figure 5.5). According to Bryson, they

> are conceived from the beginning as exercises in the renunciation of normal human priorities. . . . [Sánchez] makes it the mission of his paintings to reverse this worldly mode of seeing by taking what is of least importance in the world—the disregarded contents of a larder—and by lavishing there the kind of attention normally reserved for what is of supreme value. The process can be followed in either a 'descending' or an 'ascending' scale. From one point of view, the worldly scale of importance is deliberately assaulted by plunging attention downwards, forcing the eye to discover in the trivial base of life intensities and subtleties which are normally ascribed to things of great worth; this is the descending movement, involving a humiliation of attention and of the self. From another point of view, the result is that what is valueless becomes priceless: by detaining attention in this humble milieu, by imprisoning the eye in this dungeon-like space, attention itself gains the power to transfigure the

commonplace, and it is rewarded by being given objects in which it may find a fascination commensurate with its own discovered strengths.[40]

Religious painters such as Sánchez manage to endow rhopography with the same spiritual seriousness as biblical scenes.

To vindicate still life by this line of thought requires that the pictured vegetables and fruits be considered objects of vision and of contemplation only, not objects of the sense of taste. Bryson contends that Sánchez's *bodegones* "remove the interference of worldly attraction and . . . awaken vision to a sense of its own powers." In so doing, they free the visual sense from its habitual thrall to the desires and ambition of a human subject caught up in the schemes of importance, of achievement, fame, wealth. Sight is freed from passion and from worldly desire. This process of transcendence as described wholly conforms to the value scheme of the traditional sense hierarchy, for the defense of Sánchez is on grounds that are solely visual and intellectual; by implication Bryson accepts the indictment that Schopenhauer levels against paintings that stimulate appetite by portraying foods as delectable. In fact, Bryson describes the effect of Sánchez's pictures as almost anorexic ("food enters the eye, but must not pass through touch or taste") and argues that a component of their intellectual appeal is the mathematical combinations of the forms depicted, which the eye can trace and the mind analyze.[41]

Sánchez's pictures represent one type of rhopography that insists on the humility of its subject matter and forces a moral awakening through that humility, through refusal to become anything approaching the importance of megalography. This is by no means the only type of still life or the only defense of the importance of the genre as something more than a decorative art. Caravaggio, Bryson argues, achieves the converse effect, raising the objects depicted in his *Basket of Fruit* to the same level of importance as megalography. Modernist paintings, among which still life groups figure prominently, similarly insist on an equivalence of importance between rhopographic and megalographic subjects. Cézanne, for example, removes food from its function in his arrangements of fruits and tablewares, employing these quotidian objects in arrangements that call attention to the act of painting itself—that is, to his *art*. "The *Still Life with Apples* by Cézanne (1839–1906), for example, makes no attempt to refer its arrangement of fruit, bowl and table to any aspect of a recognisable meal, or scene within a house. On the contrary, it aims to remove itself from func-

[40] Ibid., pp. 63–64.
[41] Ibid., pp. 64, 66, 88. Bryson says of Figure 5.5: "The vegetable stalks are analysed as a collection of extraordinarily complex curves riding from staggered bases and tending towards separate asymptotes, within a general hyperbola falling from right to left" (p. 69).

tion altogether: the fruit are disposed with no rationale except that of forming a compositional armature for the painting."[42]

Bryson's defense of certain types of still life relies on showing how these artists manage to remove foods from the functions they ordinarily serve—that is, nourishment and the satisfaction of hunger or appetite—and transform the theme into something larger than its life. Caravaggio makes a basket of fruit heroic; Sánchez appeals to the intellect with a spiritual lesson; Cézanne exploits the formal possibilities of still life arrangement and denies the nutritional function of food altogether. This appreciation of still life notes the potential evocation of appetite by the genre, yet the actual importance of still life pictures requires denial of appetite and appeals only to a visually inspired intellectual message. By implication, the sense of taste is too attached to bodily appetite to be the sensory basis for the kind of intellectual appreciation that vindicates this genre. We have seen that this perspective on taste is not a necessary one, that foods may be the source of reflective insight both in their real places on the table and in paintings. This is not the majority view, however, and even Bryson's articulate defense of still life bases its claims on views that not only incorporate the sense hierarchy but repeat its standard derogation of bodily sense.

That the moral, spiritual, and intellectual values discovered in paintings should be rooted in visual experience is, on reflection, not very surprising. It is in fact thoroughly overdetermined, not least because painting is a visual art form. More deeply, however, this phenomenon indicates yet more about the sense hierarchy and about the difficulty of speaking about the experience and insight provided by the "lower" senses with their unruly appetites. Appetite, indulged and satisfied, represents an engagement with sensation and an embrace of the fleeting pleasures that the body offers. So represented, it may be lusty, poignant, inviting, and comic. It also may be distracting, misleading, and gross. Like its objects, gustatory appetite is represented in manifold ways that reveal its complexity and an endemic ambivalence concerning its power.

Representing Appetite

According to historical gossip, when in Venice Lord Byron liked to drift in a gondola on an evening ride, nibbling from a ball of polenta that his mistress kept warm between her breasts. History is silent about the details of this practice; possibly the feat was accomplished with the aid of Romantic corsetry. But "Byron's mistress skewered a ball of polenta on her stays" lacks the voluptuous relish of "warmed it between her breasts." The link between women's bodies and nourishment is perhaps too automatic to have occasioned many queries about how she kept the polenta from sliding

---

[42] Ibid., p. 81.

into her lap or tumbling into the canal, or how she avoided smearing grits on her dress. It seems unquestionably "natural" that the polenta—nourishing, bland, infantile—would ride comfortably in the cradle of her bosom, available for pecks and nibbles when the great poet wanted a snack.

The associations between a female body and food have an obvious genesis in something actual and indeed natural—a mother suckling an infant. But they continue in discourse about, depictions of, and behavior toward bodies in ways that expand well beyond the nourishment of the young, entering not only into the ontology of sexual difference that we saw in the first chapter and characterizations of the aesthetic that we saw in the second, but into discussions of literal taste and eating as well. A common denominator in all the associations of female bodies and edibles is the ambiguous meaning of "appetite," which connotes both sexual and gustatory craving for satisfaction, an association that appears to be more or less universal across dramatically different societies; indeed, the ambiguity of words referring to gustatory and sexual appetites is found in vastly different languages.[43]

With fair frequency, the two appetites are shown in mutually implicative combination. But as with the sexual appetites, the subject positions from which gustatory appetite is articulated are chiefly masculine, at least in the Euro-American tradition. When we inquire about the portrayal of appetite in visual representations of women's bodies and foods, we enter into the same world of ambiguities and contradictions as with the question, Who is looking? Art-historical discourse is by now quite used to the latter question and to the notion of the presumed maleness of the ideal viewer as constructed by the codes of visual art. Something comparable is to be found with the appeal to appetite and the related bodily senses when food is presented alongside female bodies. Not only is the female figure in these pictures posed as delectable visually, but she is also devourable, consumable. Not as a rule literally, although perhaps the upshot is a sort of metaphoric cannibalism: the ultimate subsumption of a feminine object to a masculine appetite. M. F. K. Fisher reports that the Greeks and Romans considered that women should be "served with the final wines and music"; those Greeks also ate cheesecake baked in the shape of a woman's breast.[44]

---

[43] Anthropological studies detailing the prevalence of the links between appetites for sex and for food include Claude Lévi-Strauss, *The Raw and the Cooked,* trans. John and Doreen Weightman (New York: Harper & Row, 1969); Jack Goody, *Cooking, Cuisine and Class* (Cambridge: Cambridge University Press, 1982); Peter Farb and George Armelagos, *Consuming Passions: The Anthropology of Eating* (Boston: Houghton Mifflin, 1980). The anthropologist Joel C. Kuipers reports that among the Weyewa of Indonesia, marriage is likened to eating and women not available for marriage are called "bitter" ("Matters of Taste in Weyewa," in *The Varieties of Sensory Experience*, ed. David Howes (Toronto: University of Toronto Press, 1991), pp. 122–23).

[44] M. F. K. Fisher, *Serve It Forth* (1937) (San Francisco: North Point Press, 1989), pp. 51–52; Martin Elkort, *The Secret Life of Food* (Los Angeles: Jeremy P. Tarcher, 1991), p. 76. When the subject position appealed to is masculine, the emotive and erotic tone of such depictions is often appealing and playful.

With regard to the visual representation of appetite, the worry about stimulation of actual hunger that we see in certain opinions about the depiction of food is echoed in views about the depiction of nude female bodies. Schopenhauer's objection to the "charming" in painting is not only directed to still life. The other type of painting he finds charming and antithetical to aesthetic contemplation concerns appetite of another sort. His comment about still life continues:

> In historical painting and in sculpture the charming consists in nude figures, the position, semi-drapery, and whole treatment of which are calculated to excite lustful feeling in the beholder. Purely aesthetic contemplation is at once abolished, and the purpose of art thus defeated. This mistake is wholly in keeping with what was just censured when speaking of the Dutch. In the case of all beauty and complete nakedness of form, the ancients are almost always free from this fault, since the artist himself created them with a purely objective spirit filled with ideal beauty, not in the spirit of subjective, base sensuality.[45]

The history of painting abounds with the association of women and food. As depicted subjects of painting, foods are frequently linked with the bodies of the women who simultaneously serve the dishes and offer up themselves. To be sure, such pictures are not always lustful. The same spirituality sometimes conveyed in pictures of foods can be found in this linkage. Pictures employing Christian iconography may position the breast of the nursing Madonna in proximity to fruits that are presented as another nourishment replete with religious significance.[46] Even in less reverent contexts, the artistic depiction of appetite is often playful or witty, and indeed it is not always overtly paired with women's bodies and the representation of

---

When the subject position appealed to is feminine and female appetite is in question, however, the emotive tone is apt to flip to the dangerous, repulsive, or rapacious. As Susan Bordo remarks, "hunger has always been a potent cultural metaphor for female sexuality, power, and desire—from the blood-craving Kali, who in one representation is shown devouring her own entrails, to the language of insatiability and voraciousness that marks the fifteenth century discourse on witches, to the 'Man-Eater' of contemporary rock lyrics": "Reading the Slender Body," in *Body / Politics: Women and the Discourses of Science*, ed. Mary Jacobus, Evelyn Fox Keller, and Sally Shuttleworth (New York: Routledge, 1990), p. 101. One could supply many other examples of female sexual desire as horrific gustatory appetite, including Richard Strauss's Salome, who hungrily kisses the bloody lips of the severed head of John the Baptist, declaring that she will bite them like ripe fruit.

[45] Schopenhauer, *World as Will and Representation*, p. 208.
[46] For instance, as the Madonna suckles the infant Jesus in Joos van Cleve's *Holy Family*, before them is an arrangement of food and drink, for which Bergström itemizes these symbolic meanings: "the apple for original sin, recalling the fall of man; the walnut symbolizing the *lignum crucis* and the divine nature of Christ; the 'mystic grape' for Christ's human nature; the beaker of wine for the blood poured out by Him; and a few cherries, the fruit of heaven": Bergström, *Dutch Still-Life Painting*, p. 10.

sexual appetite at all. Jehan Georges Vibert's *Marvelous Sauce,* for example, is gluttonously appetitive but hardly erotic (Figure 5.6). It portrays a cardinal who has come into the kitchen to sample the cooking. So tasty is the dish on the stove that he gestures in applause with his spoon.[47] In this case, the viewer is distanced from any appetite stimulation. We not only do not taste but cannot see what the cardinal has sipped; our appetite is safely tamped down, and we appreciate with amusement the relish of the man of God. Indeed, the appetite of the taster is something the viewer is positioned to hold in gentle disdain, perhaps with anticlerical overtones. His corpulence indicates not only a zestful relationship with the table but a degree of self-indulgence (especially in contrast to the leanness of the cooking boy). Given the fact that this is a well-fed cardinal, the distanced viewer might consider the irony present in his fulfillment of appetite through food, other appetites being prohibited a priest. Moreover, even when the gustatory and sexual appetites are presented together, the two are not always stimulated or indulged simultaneously. Not all intimations of lust need employ literal hunger, even when food is on the scene.

To switch art forms for a moment: the famous scene in Tony Richardson's film of *Tom Jones* during which Tom and Mrs. Waters feed their desire for each other while relishing a meal together is not matched in the novel. In the film, this is a scene of mutual seduction, and the two lustily devour huge trays of dinner, ripping apart roasted fowl with hands and teeth, sensually swallowing cool and briny oysters, tearing into fruits as the juices drip down their chins—all the while fueling their lust for each other. The equivalent scene in the book features an oblivious Tom who busily cleans his plate, while Mrs. Waters, lovesick and desirous, has no appetite at all.[48] She can only gaze at him hopefully, though he is so occupied with his food that she must wait for him to eat his fill before she can remind him of other appetites. The same context, the same setting, the same end, but different meanings assigned to eating and to the relationship between hunger and desire.

Nonetheless, though the links between the appetites are not invariably depicted, painting commonly pairs images of gustatory and sexual hunger with deliberately sensual effect. Paul Gauguin's painting *Tahitian Women with Mango Fruits* presents a plate of ripe mangoes, sliced and ready, along with the equally ripe body of a Tahitian woman, offering to the European man a distillation of appetite that is natural, primitive and exotic, sexual, and gustatory all at once.[49] In Edouard Manet's famous

[47] Vibert himself provides a more detailed story behind this picture: he suggests that the cardinal fancies himself a fine chef and, to the dismay of the cook, is interfering with meal preparations. See Eric M. Zafran, *Cavaliers and Cardinals: Nineteenth-Century French Anecdotal Paintings* (Cincinnati: Taft Museum, 1992), p. 116.

[48] Henry Fielding, *Tom Jones* (1749). This scene occurs in bk. 9, chap. 5, aptly titled "An Apology for All Heroes Who Have Good Stomachs, with a Description of a Battle of the Amorous Kind."

[49] Griselda Pollock's *Avant-Garde Gambits, 1888–1893* (London: Thames & Hudson, 1993) interprets the sexual and colonial politics of Gauguin's Tahitian paintings.

5.6. *Jehan Georges Vibert*, The Marvelous Sauce, *n.d. Oil on Canvas, 25″ by 32.5″. (Albright-Knox Art Gallery, Buffalo, New York, Bequest of Elisabeth H. Gates, 1899.)*

Déjeuner sur l'herbe the spilling picnic basket leads to the unclothed body of one of the female picnickers.

Perhaps the most blatant connection between eating and drinking and masculinity occurs in an entire genre of still life painting familiar not only in the artistic tradition but especially popular as decoration in American barrooms: the gamepiece. The gamepiece is a type of still life that features trophies of the hunt, birds or animals recently shot with arrow or bullet and presumably on their way to the kitchen or smokehouse. William Gerdts observes that as still life painting gained popularity in the United States in the nineteenth century, the genre became commercialized and institutionalized. Certain kinds of pictures were painted for certain rooms of the house or commercial establishments. Still lifes of food and game were considered appropriate for dining room decoration; indeed, chromolithographs of such scenes were marketed in the 1860s and 1870s as "dining room pieces." What is more, the barroom, an almost exclusively male place of entertainment, became another ideal area for decorative pictures of two varieties: the barroom still life and the barroom nude of a female figure. Of these two types of paintings Gerdst observes:

172 — *Making Sense of Taste*

If their compatibility appears questionable, consider that the two themes shared several common "aesthetic" qualities: a precise, factual delineation and a lack of ambiguity. The viewer knew exactly what he was looking at and why. And there was also the spirit of reality. The still life might consist of a peculiar conglomeration and the nude might synthetically sprout wings and be accompanied by cherubs and *putti,* but the former's factual content and the latter's anatomy were directly recognizable in experiential terms. Finally, both appealed to the male gender. The still life usually evoked the heat of the chase, hunting and fishing trophies, guns, knives, and hunting horns. The nudes were female. . . . The barroom nude became ubiquitous from New York to the Palmer House in Chicago and to the Palace Hotel in San Francisco.[50]

Such examples are almost enough to vindicate Schopenhauer.

The obviously social uses to which the visual representations of the gustatory and sexual appetites were put in the venue of bars presents an opportunity to ruminate further upon the visual and conceptual conventions that must be absorbed in order to find such scenes either "appetizing" or appropriate to hang in public view. What is a commonplace connection between eating and sex is explored variously in forms of representation, and these explorations in turn disclose more about the expressive possibilities of the representations of food. Pursuing the nude and the gamepiece in tandem reveals both commonalities and contrasts between these two appetites.

Earlier I noted that still life pictures of foods, flowers, and tableware are widely popular objects used for decoration, part of the ambiance of a place that enhances its purpose by intensifying mood and atmosphere. Still life pictures are often used for decoration, for they are relatively easy to detach from their long history of moralizing and to regard as visually interesting compositions. Fruits, plates, silver can be in themselves lovely to look at and therefore are the natural subjects of paintings that are pleasant accompaniments to eating and drinking. It is no surprise, therefore, to find them listed among the recommended decor for rooms dedicated to eating. Ripe fruit, dark, gleaming wine, and polished utensils within a frame appear the natural counterparts to what resides on table and sideboard for consumption by residents and guests. Certainly this use of such pictures is assumed to be obvious in this piece of household advice of 1889: "Our dining room should be one of the most pleasant rooms in the house; light, cheerful, nicely arranged, neat, clean and well-aired. A hardwood floor is cleaner than carpet for a dining room. . . . The pictures should be of fruit or game scenes. A wainscot of oak or of different colored woods, as maple, cherry and walnut, is very tasty."[51]

[50] Gerdst, *Painters of the Humble Truth*, p. 29.
[51] *Our Home Cyclopedia* (1889), p. 371.

5.7. *Jan Fyt*, Still Life of Abundant Game. (*National Museum, Stockholm. Erich Lessing / Art Resource, New York.*)

Once more, however, the appearance of natural connection is more complex than first it seems, as is dramatically evident in the recommendation to the nineteenth-century household that the dining room be decorated with pictures of "fruit or game scenes." Fruit is pleasant enough and not likely to be the target of extreme changes of attitude over the many centuries that it has figured in still life compositions, although its symbolic attachments vary considerably. Gamepieces, however, are another matter. They feature recently slaughtered animals and birds, sometimes arranged with other foods at more advanced stages of preparation, sometimes composed in an outdoor setting with tokens of the hunt, artfully dumped in the kitchen or hung for curing (Figure 5.7). Their animal subjects still bear feathers or fur. They may be pierced by arrows or blades, and trails of blood trace their painful entry into the picture frame. Entrails may spill from a slit belly, and occasionally a marauding cat, scavenging beneath the dark, dead eye of deer or hare, nibbles at the still-warm offal. The realism of a gamepiece can be startling, the dead animal seeming to breathe its last as the paint dries.

The squeamish may wonder at decoration that features slaughtered animals oozing trails of blood and spilled guts, especially if the illustrations are of one's dinner as it may have arrived at the kitchen hours earlier. Of course, not all people are put off by the sight or thought of the slaughter of the animals to be eaten (if indeed they consume meat at all). Such sensitivities vary hugely with local food economies, occupation, habit, and diet. Gamepieces were extremely popular for several centuries, particularly in seventeenth-century Holland and nineteenth-century North America, and indeed were (and still are) viewed as appropriate hangings for eating areas. Even granting the fact that different peoples are varyingly queasy about the edibility of animals, clearly the convention of such depictions must be absorbed thoroughly before they can be regarded as appetizing accompaniments to dinner. Indeed, gamepieces are rather like nudes in the need to get used to them before they can be regarded as routinely decorative. What is required is a degree of abstraction and distance from hunt to plate.

How does aesthetic distance come to be imposed between slaughter and dinner? Once we become accustomed to "realistic" pictures of dead animals, we tend to forget that the gamepiece is in fact a highly stylized genre. Classic versions tend to be dark in tone, with fur, scale, feather, and blood drops gently highlighted. Dead fowl are pinned to a wall by an arrow through their necks and their bright plumage falls like a sheaf of leaves that might be tacked to a door for decoration. The subjects of such paintings are clearly arranged for the eye. Not only the formal styles of depiction but the tendency to expect viewers to regard the formal elements of composition contribute to the abstraction with which gamepieces are approached. As we have seen, the art-historical apology for still life is geared to the painted image and its visual / intellectual appeal. The gulf between the aesthetic enjoyment of a painting and that of the subject as it would be "in life" is dramatically underscored by commentary on this genre. A gamepiece of a slaughtered deer by Jean Baptist Weenix, Bergström observes, "shows the carcass of a roebuck suspended by a hind leg so that its head and breast rest on a stone table, an arrangement permitting a rich and soft interplay of lines in the drawing of the body. A centre colour, of red, yellow, and orange, is formed by the entrails placed in the foreground."[52] Scott Sullivan voices the same kind of appreciation of the formal presentation of viscera: "Warm, resonant colors have been combined with a realistic sense of detail in the glistening red and brown entrails."[53]

This sort of appreciation is solely visual, and it is greatly aided by the formalist tendencies of art-critical commentaries that abstract color and composition from subject in the appreciation of the look of bloody intestines. It is evident that the ability to appeal to the eye and the tremendous formal complexity that objects of sight can possess is an important sensory factor in the achievement of aesthetic distance. The absence of smell may be particularly important to the aesthetic enjoyment of the gamepiece. The several angles from which gamepieces may be appreciated illuminate something of the variable qualities of food appreciation, for what is considered

[52] Bergström, *Dutch Still-Life Painting,* pp. 253–54.
[53] Scott Sullivan, *The Dutch Gamepiece* (Montclair, N.J.: Allanheld & Schram, 1984), p. 32.

appetizing will change too. A suckling pig with an apple lodged in its mouth is now altogether too brutal for many contemporary North Americans who have no trouble with the rubble of a Thanksgiving turkey carcass (though a sentimental few will not bite the head off a chocolate Easter bunny). Clearly the imagination plays a big role in what counts as appetizing, not only the olfactory, gustatory, and visual senses. Even granting this, however, the appreciation of the gamepiece thrusts to the foreground of our attention the degree to which it is our familiarity with the conventions of art that render these paintings decorative—that is, pleasant in the ambiance of the dining room. The aesthetic distance provided by interest in the formal values of painting and familiarity with the conventional compositions of the gamepiece permit us to find such pictures appropriate decorations for dining rooms, kitchens, and other places where art is not expected to tax the intellect or the heart.

Something similar occurs with the nude so that it can become the accepted sort of decorative garnish that it so often is. The nude female body is often regarded as naturally beautiful, and presumably natural beauty qualifies a subject automatically to be an item for public decoration. But as with the gamepiece, this highly stylized genre of art depends for its natural attraction on a host of conceptual conventions. The nude as an artistic genre bears similarities both to still life painting of fruit and to the gamepiece. Like fruit, the female body is perennially regarded as beautiful in its nakedness, a bounty of nature. Provided, that is, that like beautiful fruit it is ripe and well formed, but not overripe or rotten, smooth and unspotted, not wrinkled or decaying. Even Schopenhauer has a word of praise for paintings of fruit, because representations of fruit could embody the idea of fruition from the seed and hence convey a kind of completion and dynamism, thus furnishing the mind with the idea of natural development. Like the pleasant genre of still life paintings—fruits, flowers, and the lovely harvest of nature—the female nude of the pinup variety conventionally displayed in barrooms appears to us as naturally attractive to look at. Unlike fruit and flowers, however, the nude also titillates, and the stimulation of appetite that Schopenhauer criticized in many food paintings is likely to be even more an object of conscious awareness. The female nude may be thought of as an object of pursuit, and in this way it bears similarities to the gamepiece. Like the gamepiece, the nude is an icon of sorts for the hunt. It represents a trophy, the quarry run to ground. The female reclining above a bar has also been captured and tamed in a frame. Not killed, not maimed, but still prepared to satisfy appetite. It is an asymmetry between the two subjects that animals are more aesthetically pleasing when they are still sporting their fur and hoofs than after they have been skinned, whereas a woman's clothes can be removed with no damage to the body beneath. One could elaborate on this theme and speculate that the nude is in fact in a more advanced stage of preparation than the gamepiece, perhaps more like a dinner plate. (How ironic that "dressed" means the opposite in the two cases: with clothes for women, without fur or feathers and ready for cooking for game or fowl.)

The comparison between nudes and gamepieces also demonstrates emphatically how fluid is the notion of gender as an analytical tool. Still life may be "feminine" insofar as the polarity between rhopography and megalography is laid upon the template of familiar binary oppositions. But if gamepieces qualify as feminine in this sense, the spaces where they may appear are hardly uniquely comfortable for women in the way kitchens and parlors may be assumed to be. No space could be more blatantly masculine than a barroom. The portrayal of edibles from the hunt and of artfully posed female bodies does not feminize the space of a barroom but generally sexualizes it and charges it with appetites gustatory and erotic, both organized to satisfy a particular type of masculine taste. In counterpoint, the gamepiece (but rarely the nude) enters the feminine space of the dining room in a somewhat different guise. Kenneth Ames speculates on the reconciliation between civilized dining and the slaughter of the hunt, noting that hunting motifs signal masculine provision from bountiful nature in the artful, domestic dining room.[54] Gamepieces and nudes represent both a taming or corralling of appetites and a reminder or even a stimulation of them.

These comparisons between the representations of gustatory and sexual appetites invite reflection on the reverse as well: the contrasts and differences in the way the two phenomena are manifest in artistic representations. Although both the history of art and most of my discussion trades on the commonalities of these impulses, they are also distinct in a number of ways. Differences between the two appetites remind us that the standard sense hierarchy, despite bald overstatement of the lower status of the bodily senses, yet provides some insight into the way senses inform emotions, behavior, and cultural myth.

Most notably, the appetite for sex, but rarely for food, often possesses a tragic dimension evident in such figures as the doomed lovers Tristan and Isolde, enchanted by a love potion so strong that they violate the most sacred vows of fealty and marriage. The potion was drunk, but the attachment engendered was not for more to drink but for each other alone, forsaking all others. Had the love potion simply generated a desire for more of itself—for we may imagine that it tasted very nice—the story might have turned into one of gustatory compulsion rather than doomed love. Sexual appetite, if it develops into romantic attachment or even obsessive desire for another person, generates the themes of rejected love (Medea), desire employed as a weapon (Tosca), transgressive love (Phaedra), and so on. Food figures only slightly in tragic themes, though sometimes it appears as "forbidden fruits" or love potions,

[54] Kenneth Ames, *Death in the Dining Room* (Philadelphia: Temple University Press, 1982), p. 73. Not only pictures but also furniture for dining rooms featured game motifs. Carved furniture, especially popular in Victorian-era Europe and North America, often depicted stags being slaughtered as central decorative figures. Ames discusses the relation between civilized dining and hunting slaughter on pp. 67–68. He also quotes one Harriet Prescott Spofford, for whom the theme of death of such decor was repugnant: "The perpetual reminder of dead flesh and murderous propensities is not agreeable at table" (p. 92).

for aphrodisiac qualities have been attributed to an enormous number of foods.[55] But while the overwhelming appetite to satisfy the erotic desire for another may be rendered in tragic form, an overwhelming desire to eat is more likely to be found in comic renderings such as Rabelais's Gargantua than in tragic ones. Both gustatory and sexual desire may be portrayed as playful and witty and teasing. Both may be somewhat menacing; the Brueghel allegory of taste possesses this dimension. In and out of representation, both appetites may be overindulged or denied, reaching the extremes that Aristotle identified as types of vice: concupiscence and gluttony, asceticism and anorexia. But sex, with its connection to romantic love, to obsession, to excessive feats of heroism, may be either comic or tragic. Gustatory appetite when obsessive never becomes tragic but reverts to the gross or the comic. (Starvation, the inability to satisfy not only appetite but the bare sustenance of the body, is another matter.)

A distinction may also be drawn between the objects of the appetites. Of course, one is for sex and the other is for food, but in addition, the appetites themselves are components of different types of emotions. Sexual appetite can be considered a foundation for erotic love, love that plays a part in complex dramatic stories, including romantic and tragic narratives. The lover has as an object a unique individual, the person who satisfies a heart's desire. Gustatory appetite may be a foundation for sophisticated tastes as well as for rather ordinary likes and dislikes, but the objects of taste are not unique individuals. If one craves chocolate, any piece of candy in the box is equally good, provided they all are compositionally identical. It would be extremely peculiar to attach one's desire to *that* particular piece and not to another. Sexual desire may also be general and not specific, but in this circumstance we would not have the nobility of romantic love at all, only a brute promiscuity—just any body will do. The desire for another *person* is a desire for a particular individual. The desire to eat is ordinarily the desire just for food in general, or for a particular type of food, but not for an individual item of food. Gustatory appetite does not easily evolve into complex emotional attachments to unique individuals, and as a result the representational contexts in which it appears differ in this regard from the artistic renderings of sexual appetite. Ronald de Sousa argues that the more highly developed and purely "human" emotions are ones the intentional objects of which are nonfungible, which is to say, their objects are unique and not interchangeable.[56] The paradigm of such an emotion is love of a person. The objects of gustatory appetite are paradigm cases of fungible objects when those objects are of similar type and quality. This phenomenon of appetite accounts for the greater propensity of sexual desire to lend itself to grand or tragic narrative, in which the

---

[55] Philippa Pullar, *Consuming Passions* (Boston: Little, Brown, 1970), app. 1.

[56] Ronald de Sousa, *The Rationality of Emotion* (Cambridge: MIT Press, 1987), pp. 100–101 and chap. 3.

pursuit or loss is of a loved one for whom another very like him or her cannot be substituted.

Examples such as these from myth and art indicate the conventional, cultural shaping that surrounds what at first seems to be a natural drive or appetite, whether gustatory or sexual. What appears to be "appetizing" is heavily coded, and when these codes are exploited by visual art, with its potential for commentary, irony, reversal, and boundary-prodding, they are particularly apparent. Nonetheless, in exploring those paintings that take as subjects items that trade on the stimulation of actual appetites, I have had to cast a rather narrow beam on still life painting, as well as on nude figures in art. Difficult subjects such as death, ever present in the game-piece, are widely implicit in still life generally. As we have seen, the depiction of death requires a large measure of aesthetic distance before such pictures can achieve the pleasant status of the decorative. Ironically, artistic success in rendering them decorative results in a lower status for still life, so often conceived as *merely* decorative and therefore a minor genre. However, not all representations of either food or bodies make use of these distancing devices to shield the viewer from unpleasant reminders of the nature of food. Artists do not always disguise the more brutal aspects of slaughter and decay. Of course, the artistic representation of less pretty foodstuffs may still admit some degree of aesthetic delectability. The portion of beef carcass featured in Aertsen's painting (Figure 5.4) may present a difficult element in the composition, though the painting as a whole interests both for its narrative implications and for its intriguing illustrative details. But we cannot always transform difficult subject matter into the pleasant, the decorative, or even the narratively interesting. Aertsen's picture has kin that border on the revolting and lead us to another category of still life painting altogether.

Revulsion

Art and beauty are often too glibly linked. The expectation that somehow, in some way, a successful work of art will yield a positive aesthetic experience and that such experience will somehow be kin to the appreciation of beauty often leads us to consider disturbing, ugly, or horrific art as unusual or aberrant. This, however, is an effect of selection for pleasure or beauty among the items recognized as "great art"; if one shifts one's focus, the range of horrid and difficult paintings is clearly seen to be enormous both in number and in aesthetic power. And still life paintings, though so often dismissed as a minor genre because of their supposedly limited expressive range, are included among the powerful depictions that horrify and disturb. Let us consider just one example.

Chaim Soutine's *Carcass of Beef* (1925) is a large red and blue canvas featuring a butchered ox (Figure 5.8). The figure fills the rectangle of the frame, hanging near the front of the picture plane. The feet are splayed, the ribs cracked open, the

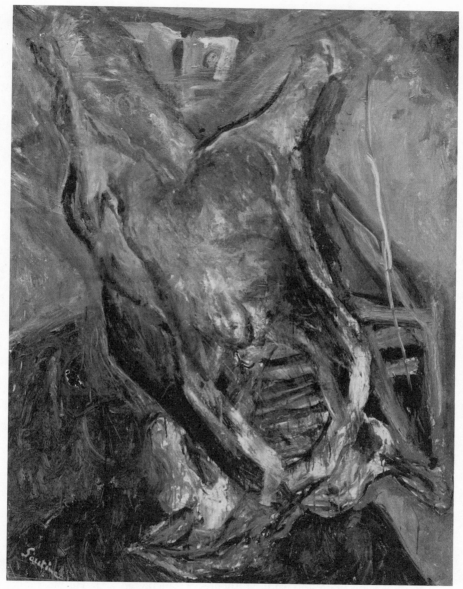

5.8. *Chaim Soutine, Carcass of Beef, c. 1925. Oil on canvas, 55 1/4″ by 32 3/8″. (Albright-Knox Art Gallery, Buffalo, New York, Room of Contemporary Art Fund, 1939.)*

interior cavity hollowed out. The head of the animal is missing. This carcass is the only thing to see in the picture; it is not an illustrative element of a narrative scene, nor is it a component in an artful arrangement that produces an overall decorative effect. The fact of death fills the frame. One could say even that we have here the *facticity* of death—the inert materiality of a corpse evoked in the materiality of the thickly applied paint. Moreover, it is death planned and routinized so that human carnivores may eat. In contrast to a gamepiece, this scene has no formal artfulness to mute its brutality, even though the form of the piece has standard precedents and the colors are carefully worked. (Soutine modeled it after Rembrandt's *Beef Carcass* of 1655, now in the Louvre.) Dark red predominates, and a brooding, intense blue makes up the background, forming an ambiguous cavernous space. The very frame of the picture contributes to its studied and contemplative horror, for the frame is incongruously ornate, featuring decorative, raised gilt openwork, the ground for which is a continuation of the paint: the red of dried blood featured on the canvas itself.[57]

This canvas is one of many that Soutine painted in the 1920s, during which time he also painted a series of other still lifes featuring hung birds, chiefly turkeys, fish laid out like sarcophagi, and even pigs. (Soutine, an expatriate artist living in Paris, was an Orthodox Jew from an impoverished Lithuanian shtetl. Biographers speculate that his preoccupation with dead and decomposing meat represents an encounter with the forbidden in the form of nonkosher meat, slaughtered improperly, left to rot.) He painted no fewer than eleven sides of beef, most of them close versions of the one reproduced here. During one infamous period of intense creativity, he installed a whole ox from a butcher shop in his studio and kept it there until the neighbors could stand it no longer. The colors of the carcass evidently fascinated Soutine, especially as they darkened and changed as his model rotted. Reportedly, as the meat dried and the colors faded, the artist had fresh blood splashed around to renew and enrich the reds. When the meat became so covered with flies it could no longer be seen, he paid an off-duty model to whisk them away so he could continue painting.[58] The visual focus on color in the painting matches Soutine's own interest in the decomposing meat, though his neighbors were vexed by assaults to other senses, complaining of stench and vermin and the danger to public health.

Perhaps even more relevant to the expressive power of this painting is Soutine's own account of his interest in painting still lifes of slaughtered meat. His biographer Emile Szittya reported this conversation with Soutine: "'Once I saw the village

---

[57] On these stylistic grounds I surmise that Soutine himself made the frame, though I have no confirmation of this conjecture. The present frame housed the painting at the time of its purchase by the Albright-Knox Gallery in 1939. Their records do not indicate the origin of the frame.

[58] Andrew Forge, *Soutine* (London: Spring Books, 1965), p. 41. Our contemporary art scene features a number of artists who work not only with the representation of dead animal flesh but with the actual carcasses of the animals; probably the best known of them is the British artist Damien Hirst.

butcher slice the neck of a bird and drain the blood out of it. I wanted to cry out, but his joyful expression caught the sound in my throat.' Soutine patted his throat and continued, 'This cry, I always feel it there. When, as a child, I drew a crude portrait of my professor, I tried to rid myself of this cry, but in vain. When I painted the beef carcass it was still this cry that I wanted to liberate. I have still not succeeded.'"[59]

This ambiguous comment invites several interpretations, which only on the face of it are mutually inconsistent: a cry of horror at the ease with which life ceases, a cry of joy echoing the expression of the butcher, a fascination with the horrible or the forbidden. Soutine is drawn to the blood and the death, to the loss, and to the heartless beauty of the color of rot.

Are we still in the realm of the visual representation of food with this example, or has the depiction of food become another genre of art and another aesthetic category altogether? While a side of beef is still food, albeit unprepared and as yet inedible, meat is now a vehicle for the representation of something other than itself as well. We are accustomed to discovering double meaning in still life: the bread and wine of Baugin's painting (Figure 5.3) are both table items and the Eucharist; Cranach's Eve grasps both an apple and a forbidden fruit. What exactly is the ambiguity present in Soutine's *Carcass of Beef*? Some commentators use the language of tragedy to describe the import of such splayed carcasses, so undeniably dead. However, tragedy requires a nobler narrative than these brute things can tell. Here we are witness to the ignoble fate of living bodies, at that point where a once-vital organism starts to lose not just its life—already long extinguished—but its very form; where it decomposes and begins to become something other altogether, suffering an irretrievable loss of shape and identity.

The objects we turn into food are not always immediately edible; once they are edible, they don't stay that way very long. They spoil. Once we begin to eat them, they are digested and transformed into less paintable substances. Food becomes a part of us; we are what we eat, and we are subject to the same process of decay, though our decline is slower. What memento mori motifs have in common with the brutal representations of Soutine is the reminder of the process of change and decay of any living organism. The depiction of this decay at certain advanced stages evokes a violation of order and classification that may be disturbing to the point of nausea. These objects are food and not food, no longer whole, disgusting. They represent rot and decay and uncleanliness that challenge our conception of order in the world and in our lives by violating the boundaries of living forms. They occupy the borderland of ambiguous identity, terrible transformation, what Mary Douglas characterizes as the essence of the unclean—that which violates its natural category by becoming its opposite. "Reflection on dirt involves reflection on the relation of order to

---

[59] Maurice Tuchman, Esti Dunow, and Klaus Perls, *Chaim Soutine* (Cologne: Benedict Taschen, 1993), p. 16. The text is quoting Emile Szittya, *Soutine et son temps* (Paris: Bibliothèque des Arts, 1955), pp. 107–8.

disorder, being to non-being, form to formlessness, life to death." The violation of order represented by the unclean and the fact that it draws attention to both the need for and the vulnerability of order are what keep the representation of these boundary experiences more than merely disgusting, what give them profundity as well as power over our sensibilities. "In painting such dark themes, pollution symbols are as necessary as the use of black in any depiction whatsoever. Therefore we find corruption enshrined in sacred places and times."[60]

This experience points to what may also be theorized as an encounter with the abject, the abhorrent, by means of which we may also understand unsettling borderline positions. Julia Kristeva analyzes the abject in terms of the confrontation with death and loss represented by a decaying body, a body that ought to sustain life but itself is inevitably corrupted. Much art and literature arises out of an awareness of the ever-awaiting disintegration of bodily integrity—and with it, personal identity: an awareness of "the fragile border (borderline cases) where identities (subject / object, etc.) do not exist or only barely so—double, fuzzy, heterogeneous, animal, metamorphosed, altered, abject."[61] The abject inspires horror and revulsion, but it also simultaneously draws us to the ever-fascinating edges of life. It is repellent to look upon, yet it represents something abyssal, inevitable, both universal and shockingly personal. And while it is presentable in art, it is ever lurking in the background of what we actually eat and drink, and it is what is in store for us as well.

Once we consider the undeniably disturbing, intense, and mysterious depiction of the abject, it becomes impossible to regard the visual representation of foods as a merely decorative and therefore minor art form. Still life and related genres of painting range through an enormous compass of expressive tones, as we have seen, depicting scenes from overt lust to the Last Supper. Still life with its edible subjects represents the peaceful and pleasant, the symbolic and spiritual, the moralistic and austere, the whimsical and witty, and the terrible and virtually ineffable glimpse of the end of the individual identity of an organism. The idea that still life pleases the visual sense rather than taxes the understanding is a charge that can be leveled only at painting in its narrowly decorative function. Other representations prompt thoughts along the most disturbing and terrible lines.

---

[60] Mary Douglas, *Purity and Danger: An Analysis of the Concepts of Pollution and Taboo* (1964) (London: Routledge, 1991), pp. 5, 179. An accident of metaphor makes Douglas's last comment seem more directly pertinent to Soutine than it actually is; she is talking not literally about painting but rather about the depiction of the unclean in religious ritual.

[61] Julia Kristeva, *The Powers of Horror: An Essay on Abjection,* trans. Leon S. Roudiez (New York: Columbia University Press, 1982), p. 207. Kirsteva makes extensive use of Douglas's anthropological research on dirt and disorder. Kristeva's psychoanalytic account of the abject roots the experience of abjection in the lost fusion between an individual and the maternal body, which continues both to threaten existence and individual identity and to exert a dreadful allure.

Defenses of still life that recognize the depth and elasticity of its subject matter have tended to emphasize the gulf between representation of foods and the practical commerce with food that occurs in actual eating. Representations have been vindicated because of their invitation to the viewer to reflect upon the meanings of bodily experience, its transience, deception, temptations—and its ultimate futility. As Michel Faré puts it, the painted table laden with foods "is less made to appease our mundane hunger than to arouse in us an appetite for a spiritual life."[62] Because these advocates have been extending their appreciation to paintings—that is, to representations of food, taste, and appetite—they have perhaps succumbed too readily to the assumption that the insight afforded by still life is not available from the subjects themselves. I myself justified the study of taste and food through painting on grounds that a greater range of expression is possible for representations than for real foods. Yet at the same time it is the nature of taste and appetite that makes possible the insights that vindicate their artistic counterparts, and now that this range has been laid out, we may ask: How does the artistic representation of the domain of taste compare to the actuality of its exercise?

The practical function of eating is certainly a factor in the undeniable fact that quite often one eats just to appease hunger. Few reflections or moral lessons about the mind and the body are likely to interrupt the daily round of hunger and eating. But this fact does not entail that the mode of sensory apprehension or the engagement in practical necessity actually prohibits reflection and insight (though practical necessity does severely restrict the amount and quality of what can be eaten). In fact, tasting and eating sometimes can deliver a heightened experience of what still life presents visually. Indeed, in being the more "subjective" and transitory experience, the messages that lurk in still life are all the more vivid, for one's whole body enacts the lesson of *vanitas*.[63] If this is rarely uppermost in the mind of the eater, that is a matter of attention and habit of thought, not of some intrinsic or inherent quality of the experience.

This chapter has closed on the sober topic of the abject, but it needs to be remembered that much of the representation of eating and of appetite is not moralizing but revel, and here as well the actual experience of tasting also furnishes both the pleasure and the invitation to reflect upon the pleasure. Admittedly, one is apt to dwell on the enjoyment rather than upon thoughts of memento mori. Nevertheless, against Schopenhauer, I suggest that when representations of food whet the appetite, they may do so in a way that conveys to that appetite all the understanding of its temporary and unstable nature that is revealed in the paintings that explore it. The actual experience of eating may but need not simply revel in pleasures of taste and satisfied

[62] Faré, *La Nature morte en France*, p. 105.
[63] Sloterdijk alludes to this vividly when he observes, "The arse triumphs secretly, conscious that without it nothing works": *Critique of Cynical Reason*, p. 149.

5.9. Roman mosaic fragment with refuse, shells, and a mouse. (Museo Lateranense, Vatican. Alinari / Art Resource, New York.)

appetite. Indeed, the appreciation of pleasure is heightened from a perspective that recognizes its transience and unpredictability. This view demands an understanding that participates in the senses without needing to be in thrall to them. No insight into the impermanence of life actually requires a rejection of the lower senses as blind to understanding, nor does it insist on the morbidity of *vanitas*.

If the ultimate insight requires that we confront the fact of death and decay, how ironic it is that the witty images of ancient mosaics of the type called "*unswept floor*" (Figure 5.9) remain on display today, their depicted detritus of nutshells and bones and chicken feet as distinct as ever such items must have been at the moment they fell to the floor. Actual sensuous embrace is in its passion an understanding of the transience that describes the nature of things, catching that transience at a point where pleasure is intense and therefore, inevitably, brief.

CHAPTER 6

Narratives of Eating

The variety of meanings we found assigned in visual art to taste, food, eating, and appetite is more than matched in the narrative arts, further attesting to the complexity of what we might label in shorthand "gustatory semantics." Because eating is a daily necessity, one finds scenes of food distributed liberally about the plots of stories, sometimes as the dramatic focus of an event, sometimes as background, sometimes as incidental detail, sometimes merely implicitly. Food invites such a variety of symbolic attachments that it may be employed to suggest opposite traits of fictional characters: Eating can signal gross indulgence and moral laxity or lusty participation in life's offerings. Attention to taste may indicate refinement of perception or silly preoccupation with superficial pleasures. Ascetic refusal can betoken lofty moral ideas and fine character, timid withdrawal and aversion to bodily needs, or religious extremism. The preparation and offering of food in gestures of hospitality may be manipulative, reluctant, generous, careless, or dangerous. Narratives may detail how food nourishes, heals, and comforts or how it dupes, poisons, or addicts. Food can be an offering to friends and an invitation to conviviality and conversation; or, as in the famous case of Plato's *Symposium*, food and drink may be those elements that must be withheld from the body to keep the mind in higher tune.

The hierarchy of the senses furnishes a general context within which many of these gustatory meanings emerge. Although I have ventured to argue that the demotion of the bodily senses is not justified on grounds standardly invoked, and that taste in particular qualifies as a fully cognitive experience, the fact remains that the values of the sense hierarchy have themselves entered our understanding of our sensory interaction with the world and the enjoyment and insight we are able to achieve. Yet sensuous awareness and bodily pleasures may be described with various normative vocabularies depending on the point that is to be made, an indication of the elasticity of attitudes toward the bodily senses even within the hierarchical framework. I take it as proven that foods and their consumption can acquire many meanings in both their practical and their artistic venues. I will not provide a catalog of the diversities in literature and film as I did for the visual arts. Rather, I shall explore a few narratives in order that some of the claims I have made about meanings of food may be considered in detail as they appear in fictional contexts.

Why turn to narrative for this purpose? Many philosophers have looked increasingly to fiction to guide and enhance their theoretical investigations. Some have come to see philosophy as a genre of writing that deploys literary devices, such as metaphor, irony, fable, and dialogue; therefore, they surmise, there is less distance between these two types of writing than once was believed.[1] Others, interested in questions about the nature of the self and of personal identity, have argued that discursive practices, including narrative, contribute to the very constitution of self and community.[2] Still others turn to fiction as an indispensable supplement to the abstractions, rules, and principles of standard ethical theories. This method is particularly congenial to those who argue that a reliance on general reasoning and rule-based moral theories produces incomplete accounts of the complexities of circumstance and the moral choices and dilemmas that human beings face. Fictional narratives, with their individual and distinct characters, their detailed particulars of setting, and their intricate plots, supply a network of factors relevant to moral assessment and furnish a wealth of detail that appropriately complicates and focuses salient facts and situations.[3]

Like a narrative, eating is an extended event: it takes time to accomplish. Its effects and enjoyments happen not all at once but sequentially. (Roland Barthes, we recall, compared sequence in a meal to plot in a story.)[4] Because of the temporal dimension of eating—and of tasting and the satisfaction of appetite—narrative contexts can furnish reflections on the meanings this activity avails. (Indeed, appetite itself has a plotlike structure with a beginning [hunger and the whetted appetite], middle [the process of satisfaction, sometimes lengthy], and end[satiation and satisfaction].)[5] It is the narrative artist who is likely to unpack and reflect upon the phenomena of tasting and eating and to record the sensations, thoughts, and recollections surrounding these events.

As we have seen, the experience of taste has frequently confronted a set of charges against its cognitive power on grounds that it yields too "subjective" an experience to be philosophically interesting. Taste has been understood as a sense that directs attention inward toward the state of one's own body rather than outward toward its objects, and hence it has not received credit as a sense that provides knowledge of

---

[1] See, for example, Jonathan Rée, *Philosophical Tales* (London: Methuen, 1987); Richard Rorty, *Contingency, Irony, and Solidarity* (New York: Cambridge University Press, 1989).

[2] See, for example, Genevieve Lloyd, *Being in Time: Selves and Narrators in Philosophy and Literature* (London: Routledge, 1993); Alasdair MacIntyre, *After Virtue* (Notre Dame: University of Notre Dame Press, 1981); Richard Eldridge, *On Moral Personhood* (Chicago: University of Chicago Press, 1989).

[3] David Novitz, *Knowledge, Fiction, and Imagination* (Philadelphia: Temple University Press, 1987); Martha Nussbaum, *Love's Knowledge* (New York: Oxford University Press, 1990) and *Poetic Justice* (Boston: Beacon, 1995).

[4] Roland Barthes, "Reading Brillat-Savarin," in *The Rustle of Language*, trans. Richard Howard (New York: Hill & Wang, 1986). See also Margaret Visser, *Rituals of Dinner* (New York: Penguin, 1991), pp. 196–210.

[5] This description obtains for gustatory and sexual appetites. The connection between the two is popularly exploited in such films as *Tampopo*, *Like Water for Chocolate* (based on Laura Esquivel's novel of the same name), and *Eat, Drink, Man, Woman*, to name but a few.

the world at large. The prominence of pleasures and displeasures—tastes and dis-
tastes—that accompany eating sustains the idea that taste is too subjective to warrant theoretical interest. Some reasons to dispute these judgments have already been
advanced in previous chapters, where I have argued that the complexity of the intentional objects of taste demonstrates the degree to which this sense directs attention outward as well as inward, affording cognition of the world as well as of the
state of one's own body. Moreover, I have claimed that the traits of taste that are labeled subjective should be understood in terms of the singular intimacy availed
through taste and by extension through eating. Here I continue the translation of
"subjectivity" into "intimacy" by exploring the role that *eating together* plays in the
formation and sustenance of community, in which the intimate and personal experience of tasting and eating takes place in circumstances that transform the event
into something shared, bringing into being, however briefly, a collective experience.
That eating and tasting require taking a substance into one's body is one of the features of the much maligned subjectivity of eating. But far from disqualifying taste
from significance beyond the sensations of an individual, this feature of subjectivity
actually betokens the community that eating together promises, becoming a source
of its powerful social—not merely individual—meaning. This is the eventual emphasis of this final chapter: food as formative of community, what makes it possible,
what it presumes, what it accomplishes.

Eating together is a common signal among most peoples for friendship, truce, or
celebration, and it is this social role of eating that I particularly target here. But just
how common eating transforms itself from fuel to feast, from satisfaction of need to
social bond, may not always be obvious. When one is used to these practices, when
such eating has become part of either the daily or yearly routine, the patterns of
meaning that eating attains may become hard to discern. Here the distillery of the
storyteller can refine and sharpen those shapes and bring them to clarity. I invoke literature to summon articulate allies in order to confirm and deepen my claims about
these matters, selecting narratives that provide especially dramatic epiphanies regarding taste and eating and that therefore bring otherwise unnoticed phenomena
into prominence in a story. Some narratives of eating illuminate relatively commonplace—and therefore familiar—experiences. Others pull the undertow of eating to
the surface and make us confront what is implicit or forgotten or willfully ignored
about eating, values both negative and positive. And finally, both eating and narratives are cultural practices. When food is treated in fiction, therefore, it brings to
light the way eating may achieve significance within the tradition the narrative in
question addresses or in which it participates.

What I have summarized as the intimacy of eating is part of what knits together
those who eat—the mutual trust presumed, the social equality of those who sit
down together, and the shared tastes and pleasures of the table. Shared eating is

commonly recognized as among the most enjoyable aspects of civilized food preparation and consumption, but what in fact must be presumed, subdued, or accomplished for this "civilized" activity to be possible?[6] Both the pleasures and the objects
of eating, as has been noted so frequently, are transient. Enjoyment of tastes is fleeting, and what is eaten perishes in the act of providing nourishment and delight. It is
this temporary quality of eating and the resultant need to fold it into routines of bodily sustenance that make food preparation a matter of repetition and necessity. Because both the moments and the objects of enjoyment soon vanish, food and eating
have been considered recalcitrant objects of aesthetic or social value. However, this
impermanence also contributes to a profound aspect of eating, which is an activity
that destroys its objects and requires an endless search for more to eat. There is
death in the act of eating—both the destruction of that which is eaten and the im-
permanent pleasures that foreshadow the ultimate death of the diner. Lurking in the
background of all acts of eating one can discover that which is destroyed or being
consumed, thereby losing its own identity while sustaining that of another. Hunger
and its satisfaction alternate perpetually in this realm of constant change. Mikhail
Bakhtin remarks that in the act of eating "the body transgresses . . . its own limits: it
swallows, devours, rends the world apart, is enriched and grows at the world's expense. The encounter of man with the world, which takes place inside the open, biting, rending, chewing mouth, is one of the most ancient, and most important objects of human thought and imagery."[7]

Because appetite is a drive to consume, it lends itself as a metaphor for power.[8] It
is also a drive that especially invites exaggeration in fictional treatment, and thus we
find excessive eating a familiar feature of comic writing. Rabelais's stories of Gargantua and Pantagruel, which are the focus of Bakhtin's meditations, exploit the trope of
appetite to ferocious excess, magnifying the "open, biting, rending, chewing"
mouths of these comic figures. The giants consume whole barnyards and remain un-
satisfied. These stories manifest a folk culture that turns the tables on the sense hierarchy and revels in the appetite for food without restraint. While these stories may
be read as a mockery of clerical Christian culture with its admonitions to moderation, they do so in terms that reinforce the associations of the sense hierarchy: the
gross excesses of the body are not only extolled, they are presented as irreverent reverses of the values of intellectual activity and temperance. As we found with visual
representations of food, the excesses of appetite may be rendered with different aes-

---

[6] This question also diverges to the subject of manners and their evolution. See Norbert Elias, *The Civilizing Process*, vol. 1: *The Development of Manners* (1939), trans. Edmund Jephcott (Oxford: Blackwell,
1994).

[7] Mikhail Bakhtin, *Rabelais and His World*, trans. Helene Iswolsky (Cambridge: MIT Press, 1968), p. 281.

[8] Ronald D. LeBlanc argues that this is a theme of Dostoevsky's novels in "An Appetite for Power: Predators, Carnivores, and Cannibals in Dostoevsky's Fiction," in *Food in Russian History and Culture*, ed. Musya
Glants and Joyce Toomre (Bloomington: Indiana University Press, 1997).

thetic tenors: erotic, comic, grotesque, horrible. All expose the cycles of destruction required by eating and the singular vulnerabilities that the use of the sense of taste and the satisfaction of appetites entail.

The objects of taste are taken into one's own body; they *become* one. Because tasting and eating alter one's very constitution, their exercise requires trust. We must trust that our foods are healthful and not poison, and thus we rely not only on the quality of the objects to be eaten but also on the kindly disposition of our eating companions and those who are responsible for preparing our food. This rather obvious fact occasions both the harmonious acts of eating and feasting that bind those who eat together in society and friendship and the most horrific acts of revenge and betrayal that occur when the trust presumed at table is abrogated. Both are to be found in narratives from the most ancient tales to contemporary fiction. In the dark side of eating we discover horrifying possibilities that are the counterpoint to food as a civil and binding aspect of society. Indeed, certain aspects of the dark side are actually presupposed by the transformation of this activity into a civilizing and unifying practice.

Terrible Eating

Revenge Cooking

Fairy stories and folktales are rife with terrible eating and hideous appetites.[9] The ogres that populate them are distinguished by their indiscriminate taste for human flesh and the canine acuity of their sense of smell. (English fairy tales are full of the ominous chant of wicked giants: "Fe, fi, fo fum. / I smell the blood of an Englishman. / Be he live or be he dead, / I'll grind his bones to make my bread.") Folk traditions abound in monsters who can be appeased only by a human meal: the Minotaur, the Laidly Worm, St. George's dragon. Vampires perpetuate their kind by sucking human blood and infecting their victims with their own insatiable thirst. Such monstrous appetites blend into stories in which hatred or rivalry induces the most fundamental transgression of the codes of edibility. The wickedness of a character may be signaled by his or her insistence that an enemy be served for dinner, as with the evil queen of the story of Snow White: after her stepdaughter has been driven into the forest, she has a woodsman bring back the girl's heart and demands it be cooked and served to her on a golden plate. As in many fables, Snow White is saved by the kindhearted woodsman, who kills a forest animal instead and substitutes its heart for hers. Such revenge eating is not confined to fairy tales. Herodotus recounts the story of Harpargus, who, having angered the Mede king Astyages, was

---

[9] These and other meanings of food in a set of French folktales are explored by Louis Marin, *Food for Thought*, trans. Mette Hjort (Baltimore: Johns Hopkins University Press, 1989).

served at a banquet the flesh of his own slaughtered son.[10] It is hard to imagine any more awful event. Shakespeare used the same theme as the final act of revenge in his bloodiest play, *Titus Andronicus,* in which at a feast supposedly celebrating truce, the Goth queen Tamora is served the heads of her two sons.[11]

Tales of horrific eating revive a question posed earlier concerning the profundity of the aesthetic character of the sense of taste and its exercise. As we noted in Chapter 2, Edmund Burke speculated that neither taste nor smell could occasion an encounter with the fearsome vastness or power that qualifies an experience as sublime. He surmised that the extremes of these senses are revolting or disgusting, but they do not attain the dimensions that produce awe on a par with the experiences that the distance senses can deliver. In Chapter 5 we saw a challenge to this generalization, for the abhorrent, a counterpart and contrary of the sublime, can be explored and presented compellingly by the artistic presentation of foodstuffs. Moreover, Burke also noted that when incorporated into poetic context, the description of stenches and noxious or poisonous foods can inspire the sort of awe characteristic of the sublime. Now we may add to this observation: If we consider the full experiences for which these senses operate—that is, experiences of eating—then the category of the terrible clearly comes into play. Terror is the root of sublimity, and the experiences attending terrible eating are hideous cousins to the sublime. As Burke puts it, "Whatever is fitted in any sort to excite the ideas of pain, and danger, that is to say, whatever is in any sort terrible, or is conversant about terrible objects, or operates in a manner analogous to terror, is a source of the *sublime;* that is, it is productive of the strongest emotion which the mind is capable of feeling."[12] Eating forbidden substances is unlikely to achieve the transcendence that characterizes sublimity, but it is fully capable of inspiring terror or horror, a capability exploited in narrative. The dreadful meal of Harpargus may not be sublime, but in its horror, cruelty, and utter transgression it is truly terrible. Harpargus not only sees the horror of his only son's murder (for the head and hands of the boy are delivered to him in a basket after the banquet is over), he is deceived into being an agent of the ghastly event, participating intimately in the destruction of the body of his child. Perhaps in recognition of the inexpressibility of such horror, Shakespeare gives Queen Tamora no lines to say after she is told she has eaten of her two sons. Titus Andronicus stabs her at the mo-

---

[10] Herodotus, *The Persian Wars,* 1:119. If Herodotus is correct in his account (some scholars believe he is repeating legend), this indulgence in a fit of revenge cooking cost the Medes their empire, for in retaliation Harpargus engineered the revolt of the Persians under Cyrus. (This theme certainly has precedents in myth, such as Uranus, who devours his children, the subject of a horrifying painting by Goya.)

[11] Act V, Scene 3. Tamora eats the dreadful dish containing the heads of her sons, now baked into a pie, while witnessing Titus Andronicus kill his mutilated daughter ("Why, there they are both, baked in that pie; / Whereof their mother daintily hath fed, / Eating the flesh that she herself hath bred").

[12] Edmund Burke, *A Philosophical Enquiry into the Origin of Our Ideas of the Sublime and Beautiful,* ed. James T. Boulton (Notre Dame: University of Notre Dame Press, 1968), sec. 1, p. 39.

ment of discovery, and his own lines ("'Tis true, 'tis true; witness my knife's sharp point") indicate her inarticulate, appalled reaction.

This ability to dupe the eater into complicity is a particular feature of the subjectivity of eating, as is the fact that the object of taste does not last, that it is destroyed in the exercise of the sense. The destruction of the object of eating is in a way a removal of evidence, for the eater has incorporated his prey, his victim, his dinner into himself. What that dinner was composed of is of grave importance. Familiar foodstuffs do not disturb, because we are used to the habits that incorporate them into our bodies. But discovery that we have eaten something we did not know we were eating, whether it be unusual, disgusting, or forbidden, makes the whole body quake with horror that something that ought not to have been eaten is irretrievably chewed, swallowed, and become part of one's own physical fabric. Perhaps even more than *doing* something that is forbidden, *eating* something forbidden may transform the very identity of the eater.[13] (Suspicion of his participation in cannibalistic rites is part of the "horror" that Kurtz alludes to mysteriously at his death in Joseph Conrad's *Heart of Darkness*.)

Recognizing that tasting and eating can summon up a dreadful range of aesthetic experience—at least as responses to art—suggests that the positive aesthetic values of these activities also sustain profounder possibilities than is usually acknowledged. As we have already seen, the accomplishments of food preparation and resulting taste experiences are customarily regarded as extending from the disagreeable or indifferent all the way up to the bland heights of the very pleasant. Our exploration of the visual representation of food has already complicated this picture, for depictions of foods extend from the spiritual to the abhorrent. The phenomenon of terrible eating similarly discloses an expanded aesthetic range. And the distance between terrible eating on the one hand and refined and civilized dining on the other suggests a depth of possibility for the latter that is hardly captured by values such as pleasant (Kant) and charming (Schopenhauer).

These terrible manipulations of the intimacy and subjectivity of eating do not represent ordinary experiences. They may well figure more prominently in fantasy than in reality, indicating an imagined horror that is more prevalent than the actual incidence of such transgressions.[14] (It is said that once wild animals taste human flesh, they become man-eaters, insatiably seeking after the succulent meat of the

---

[13] Eating may signal that one has taken an irreversible step. It was after Persephone carelessly ate some pomegranate seeds in Hades that she was condemned to spend half the year in the underworld.

[14] Freud judges that fantasies of devouring are among the most powerfully disturbing that the psyche delivers, because they are based on the earliest pleasure drive: oral gratification. The developing child desires to consume the parent, and this desire inspires fear of retaliation: that one will be devoured (*Totem and Taboo* [1918], trans. James Strachey [New York: Norton, 1950]);see also Bruno Bettelheim, *The Uses of Enchantment* (New York: Knopf, 1976).

human body. This may or may not be a case of anthropocentrism, whereby we humans are superior to beasts even in our flavor. But it surely signals the horror of being eaten.) Why, then, even consider such narratives to illuminate the social function of eating? When eating fosters the formation, revival, or intensification of community, of social relationships that bind people together in friendship or mutual respect, it is the obverse of the terrible, transgressive eating of fairy tale and ancient legend. But the possibility of the latter is what gives the former its depth. Eating can be dangerous. It can horrify and sicken as much as it can nourish and please. And it can be the locus of deception and betrayal.

The perverse transgressions of cannibalism are rare.[15] They inspire a particular revulsion because they violate a basic tenet both of what is edible and of what is acceptable conduct. The sort of trickery that Harpargus fell victim to is particularly horrifying, since he was made to devour his own son. Poisoning is another method of luring one's victim to eat, and far more common. Killing another with food or drink is also a time-honored theme of literature and legend, and poison too has become an emblem of revenge and betrayal, this time making its victim the target rather than the unwitting agent of destruction. Poisoning of one lover by another, a frequent theme in romantic literature, is particularly dramatic because it is such a betrayal of trust and love. The legendary death of Lord Randal was accomplished with ease, for he visited his lover, not an enemy, and with his guard lowered he met his doom. The ballad recounts his dismayed mother's colloquy with her son:

'Where gat ye your dinner, Lord Randal, my son?
Where gat ye your dinner, my handsome young man?'—
'I dined wi' my true-love; mother, make my bed soon,
For I'm weary wi' hunting, and fain wald lie down.'

. . .

'O I fear ye are poison'd, Lord Randal, my son!
I fear ye are poison'd, my handsome young man!'—
'O Yes! I am poison'd; mother, make my bed soon,
For I'm sick at the heart, and I fain wald lie down.'[16]

Because of the dreadful possibilities of the preparation and consumption of food, the meal of friendship and community is not a trivial affair. Tasting and eating alter

---

[15] Some anthropologists deny that any human society sanctions anthropophagy. Aspects of this controversy are reviewed in Lawrence Osborne, "Does Man Eat Man?" *Lingua Franca* 7.4 (April / May 1997): 28–38. Robert Louis Stevenson has interesting comments about cannibalism in his travel account *In the South Seas* (1896) (London: Hogarth, 1987).

[16] "Lord Randal," no. 66 in *The Oxford Book of Ballads*, ed. Arthur Quiller-Couch (Oxford: Clarendon, 1924), p. 292.

one's very body; their exercise requires trust. Eating may appear routine in the course of daily events, it may become a wearisome obligation to family or business relationships, it may seem at times a tedious call of the body that interrupts higher pursuits. But both the special and the mundane occasions of eating are built upon the profound foundation of trust that horrific and lethal possibilities dramatically illustrate when trust is betrayed. Forming friendships is no achievement if every person is a friend; functioning communities are precious because they are hard to come by. So in the course of considering narratives of communal eating, we should remember that their very possibility is premised on a trust that the obverse type of eating is safely tucked away in fable and ancient warfare.

The Paradox of Eating

The opposing poles of revenge, betrayal, and poison on the one hand and friendship, peace, and social harmony on the other have a middle term, and that is the peculiar phenomenon of eating itself. The examples of revenge cooking illustrate that companions are not just those who share bread but those who eat *together* foods that are *mutually nourishing.* In short, they do not eat each other and they eat the same things. (The poisoner refrains from sharing poison, unless he or she has both murder and suicide in mind.) These fairly obvious constraints are necessary because eating is by its very nature a destructive and risky enterprise. Hegel's observation that eating destroys the objects of taste may seem such a commonplace that it is hardly worth attributing to any particular author. However, the interference of taste with the object of its exercise has not only practical and aesthetic but moral consequences. Eating involves a paradox, and the enjoyment of the tastes of food participate in that paradox: it is a necessity for life to destroy life. Only a few of the things we eat are inorganic: salt, for example, is a mineral. Everything else is—or was—alive, although not necessarily sentient. (One of the basic moral reasons some people become vegetarians is to avoid taking the life of another sentient being.) The pleasant ability of meals to form communities and to bring peace requires that at some point in the relatively recent past there have been an act of violence that removed the food from its living site and set it, appropriately prepared, on a plate. Leon Kass refers to the "great paradox of eating, namely that to preserve their life and form living forms necessarily destroy life and form."[17] And Margaret Visser reflects on the gulf between feeding the body and preparing and serving food in a way that transforms that feeding into a civil act. The cultivation of manners, she argues, is a sober evolution premised on the dangers of eating, the insistent cycle of hunger, and the ever-present destruction required by the continuance of life.

---

[17] Leon R. Kass, *The Hungry Soul: Eating and the Perfecting of Our Nature* (New York: Free Press, 1994), p. 13.

Somewhere at the back of our minds, carefully walled off from ordinary consideration and discourse, lies the idea of cannibalism—that human beings might *become* food, and eaters of each other. Violence, after all, is necessary if any organism is to ingest another. Animals are murdered to produce meat; vegetables are torn up, peeled, and chopped; most of what we eat is treated with fire; and chewing is designed remorselessly to finish what killing and cooking began. People naturally prefer that none of this should happen to them. Behind every rule of table etiquette lurks the determination of each person present to be a diner, not a dish. It is one of the chief roles of etiquette to keep the lid on the violence which the meal being eaten presupposes.[18]

Even the most refined and delicate of meals presupposes a violent backdrop. Roland Barthes remarks that "if Japanese cooking is always performed in front of the eventual diner (a fundamental feature of this cuisine), this is probably because it is important to consecrate by spectacle the death of what is being honored."[19] Over millennia eating and the preparation and service of food became in many societies an elaborate, remote, and even elegant affair, the pinnacle and emblem of civilization. That there may be no clean, consistent, and uncompromised way to achieve this result is explored by Herman Melville in his meditative epic, *Moby Dick*.

Stubb's Supper

The famous novel of Captain Ahab's quest for the White Whale is not on the face of it an obvious narrative to consult about the meaning of eating. But it is directly about *devouring* and *being devoured*. The biblical story that is an emblem of the whole is that of Jonah and his sojourn in the belly of a whale. Whales and whalers alike must eat, and Melville confronts us with the awful kinship of man and beast, each in his own way a brute engine of existence. The crew of the *Pequod* represents the globe itself, its Yankee captain and mates, its aboriginal Polynesian, African, and Indian harpooneers, and its remaining crew from every corner of the earth.[20] Some of the crew, particularly Queequeg the Polynesian, have practiced cannibalism, but they are not thereby particularly set apart from the others. Eating other humans is not presented as markedly different from eating anything else—not because Melville is insensitive to the immorality of intraspecies consumption but because no one escapes participation in the cycle of life and death that eating entails. Cannibalism, in Melville's extension of the term, is not limited to anthropophagy but

[18] Margaret Visser, *The Rituals of Dinner: The Origins, Evolution, Eccentricities, and Meaning of Table Manners* (New York: Penguin, 1991), pp. 3–4.
[19] Roland Barthes, *The Empire of Signs*, trans. Richard Howard (1970) (New York: Hill & Wang, 1982), p. 20.
[20] Herman Melville, *Moby Dick* (1851) (New York: Penguin, 1978). Chap. 40, "Midnight, Forecastle," details the nationalities represented on the *Pequod*.

refers to the ineluctable destruction of living things to perpetuate the lives of those who consume them. Hence the famous rhetorical question of the novel: "Cannibals? who is not a cannibal?"[21]

Early in the novel Ishmael, the narrator, meets Queequeg, and the two strike up an improbable but trusting and intimate friendship. An early signal of this bond is the rather comic scene of eating at the Try Pots Inn, for they demand of the innkeeper's wife bowl after bowl of chowder, steamy and savory, full of the bounty of the sea on which they will soon sail.

> Fishiest of all fishy places was the Try Pots, which well deserved its name; for the pots there were always boiling chowders. Chowder for breakfast, and chowder for dinner, and chowder for supper, till you began to look for fish-bones coming through your clothes. . . . There was a fishy flavor to the milk, too, which I could not at all account for, till one morning happening to take a stroll along the beach among some fisherman's boats, I saw Hosea's brindled cow feeding on fish remnants, and marching along the sand with each foot in a cod's decapitated head, looking very slip-shod, I assure ye.[22]

When they embark, they sail amid the originals of their food, the fish of the sea, who, given the chance, would eat the sailors above them. They embark onto the world of the great predators, having first partaken of the bounty of the sea, their prey.

In the course of daily events, Captain Ahab and his mates eat in a formal, indeed rigid fashion.[23] One by one according to rank they are called into the cabin: Ahab; Starbuck, the first mate; Stubb, the second mate; and Flask, the third mate. It is not a pleasant dining experience, for Ahab is a silent and morose presider over the table. Their eating, however, is framed by restraint. Despite sometimes acute hunger, they do not fall upon their food, but pause after they are called before descending at a leisurely pace to the table. They wait to be served, observing strict deference to the captain at the expense of their own appetites. (When they are finished their places are occupied by the three harpooneers, who eat more lustily and tease the cabin boy by playing on his fears that they may prefer him for their supper.) The formalities observed over eating aboard the *Pequod* are detailed early in the novel, providing a backdrop for Stubb's macabre feast thirty chapters later. It is here that we discover Melville's extended rumination on human appetites and their affinity to bestial drives.

[21] Ibid., p. 406.
[22] Ibid., p. 162.
[23] Ibid., chap. 34, "The Cabin Table."

Stubb, the second mate of the ship, is introduced to us as a fearless and cheerful sailor. If he lacks the moral uprightness and religious vision of the first mate, Starbuck, he is not for that reason less likable, less fully a participant in the community at sea. None of this crew is exactly describable as an average citizen; they are all what Ishmael calls "isolatos" in their propensity for setting out on long sea voyages free from the fetters of city and town. Their liking for isolation is dramatized by the masculine world of the story, for the ship is populated entirely by men. The absence of women of course accords with the facts of nineteenth-century whaling, but in the medium of the novel it effectively emphasizes an absence of domesticity that is especially dramatic in the eating scenes, both the strained and awkward captain's table and the brutish feast in which Stubb indulges. The masculinity of the world of the novel and the loner propensities of the crew are background for the vivid individual personalities. And within this austere frame, Stubb is a jolly fellow, insouciant and sociable. "A happy-go-lucky; neither craven nor valiant; taking perils as they come with an indifferent air; and while engaged in the most imminent crisis of the chase, toiling away, calm and collected as a journeyman joiner engaged for the year. Good-humored, easy, and careless, he presided over his whale-boat as if the most deadly encounter were but a dinner, and his crew all invited guests."[24]

This convivial metaphor suggests a mealtime altogether different from the episode detailed in the chapter titled "Stubb's Supper." One evening, after his successful capture of a whale, Stubb is visited by an appetite for a whale steak. He sends Daggoo, the African harpooneer, down to the dead whale lashed to the side of the boat, to cut for him a piece of whale meat from the succulent spot near the tail. He awakens Fleece, the ancient cook, and demands that the whale steak be prepared for an impromptu supper. Stubb does not descend to the cabin table for his repast, nor does he invite anyone else to join him; he leans against the capstan on deck and devours his steak by the light of sperm-oil lamps. That he would eat a creature by a flame lit from its own body is already a kind of depravity, for the oil of the whale is made to abet the consumption of its own flesh. This sense of forced and perverse complicity echoes the biblical prohibition "Thou shalt not seethe a kid in his mother's milk" (*Exod.* 34:26), the wrongness of which is virtually self-evident. And yet the perversity of Stubb's action would hardly be noticeable absent the proximity of the whale flesh and the whale-oil lamp, for in fact he eats by flames that burn in every lamp on land, in every dining room of those civilized countries where whale goods are sold.

Stubb is not the only one to enjoy a cut of whale, for a marauding band of sharks have swarmed around the dead whale moored to the side of the ship, and they compete with Stubb in their display of appetite. The two dinners are presented as mir-

[24] Ibid., pp. 212–13.

ror images, inversions of each other. "Nor was Stubb the only banqueter on whale's flesh that night. Mingling their mumblings with his own mastication, thousands on thousands of sharks, swarming round the dead leviathan, smackingly feasted on its fatness."[25]

Sharks are not just any sea creatures, and Stubb's eating companions are among the most horrific denizens of the ocean. While the chief prey of the *Pequod* is the great sperm whale, and particularly the monstrous Moby Dick, whales as a species are presented in the novel with delicate complexity. They may be devouring beasts, symbols of nature's destructive power. But they also grow old and ill and provoke sympathy; they fear and suffer; they display canny intelligence. One ancient leviathan killed by the crew is a pathetic, blind, and withered whale who is slaughtered without mercy by a crew seen in the event not as triumphant entrepreneurs reaping the riches of the sea but as heartless killers carrying out their cruelty with the mindlessness of any brute swarm. And in the remarkable scene in "The Grand Armada," the crew of one of the small whaleboats drifts into the center of a whale nursery, and they mingle spellbound with mothers and their newborn calves, who snuffle at the sides of the boats like enormous puppies. The whalers put down their spears and reach out to touch the whales, just for that moment bridging the gulf between creatures of the land and sea, forgetful that they are predator and prey.

Such an encounter would be inconceivable with sharks. The sharks that surround the *Pequod* and feed from its capture are compared to dogs, to cannibals, to devils. But they are also likened to humans.

> Though amid all the smoking horror and diabolism of a sea-fight, sharks will be seen longingly gazing up to the ship's decks, like hungry dogs round a table where red meat is being carved, ready to bolt down every killed man that is tossed to them; and though, while the valiant butchers over the deck-table are thus cannibally carving each other's live meat with carving-knives all gilded and tasselled, the sharks, also, with their jewel-hilted mouths, are quarrelsomely carving away under the table at the dead meat; and though, were you to turn the whole affair upside down, it would still be pretty much the same thing, that is to say, a shocking sharkish business enough for all parties; and though sharks also are the invariable outriders of all slave ships crossing the Atlantic, systematically trotting alongside, to be handy in case a parcel is to be carried anywhere, or a dead slave to be decently buried; and though one or two other like instances might be set down, touching the set terms, places, and occasions, when sharks do most socially congregate, and most hilariously feast; yet is there no conceivable time or occasion when you will find them in such countless numbers, and in gayer or more jovial spirits, than around a

[25] Ibid., p. 398.

dead sperm whale, moored by night to a whale-ship at sea. If you have never seen that sight, then suspend your decision about the propriety of devil-worship, and the expediency of conciliating the devil.[26]

Stubb and the sharks, the voracious human and fish, are terrible mirror images of each other. Shockingly, the bits and pieces from the human table that the sharks are described as awaiting are compared metaphorically to human flesh. Later in the same paragraph the human flesh is literal, for sharks also congregate around slave ships with their human cargo and wait for the bodies of dead slaves to be jettisoned overboard. But this literal flesh is mentioned after the ordinary meat carved at the table, so that all eaters of flesh of whatever kind are likened to cannibals. The decorations of the civilized table do not markedly separate the domains of human and beast, for though the carving knives may be "gilded and tasselled," the sharks also have "jewel-hilted mouths." In fact, this section marks a hideous confusion of events, of allusions, and of tone of voice: the shark is domesticated in one phrase, diabolic in another; likened ironically to a useful companion ("in case a parcel should be carried anywhere"), to a fellow diner, to a devil—in fact, to virtually any species of animal, including the human. There is no separation of the brutish world of nature, where no moral code obtains, from the cultivated and ordered regulations of human society designed to quell the inner beast. All creation mingles, and the routine, daily, and ordinary evidence of that mingling is the common need to eat.

Stubb's supper, however, is no mere frenzied display of appetite. He does not devour his meal like a hungry animal. He does not eat out of need driven by starvation, as a consequence of which any creature might forgivably forget manners and simply fall upon its food. Stubb's supper is not even devoid of manners. Indeed, the formal, somewhat incantational speech that characterizes the exchanges among the characters of this novel imparts a degree of formality to this event as well. But Stubb stakes his claim to eating with sharks—above them, to be sure, but on a continuum, a higher end of the continuum of devouring that powers the very sustenance and perpetuation of life.

The noisy eating of the sharks prompts Stubb to command the cook, Fleece, to deliver a sermon to the fish, which he grumpily does, urging the sharks to govern their appetites and practice better manners toward one another. Through the caricatured dialect of Fleece we discover another expression of the continuum between bestial nature and human conduct: "Your woraciousness, fellow-critters, I don't blame ye so much for; dat is natur, and can't be helped; but to gobern dat wicked natur, dat is de pint. You is sharks, sartin'; but if you gobern de shark in you, why

---

[26] Ibid., p. 399.

den you be angel; for all angel is not'ing more dan de shark well goberned. Now, look here, bred'ren, just try wonst to be cibil, a helping yourselbs from dat whale."[27]

Fleece notes that the sharks don't listen until their bottomless bellies are full, so Stubb turns his attention to the condition of the whale steak he has just cooked. The steak, still red, seems nonetheless to be too well done for Stubb's taste. This human eater prefers his whale in much the same condition that delights the shark, for Stubb advises Fleece next time simply to "hold the steak in one hand, and show a live coal to it with the other; that done, dish it." The old cook returns to his bed, grumbling, "Wish, by gor! whale eat him, 'stead of him eat whale. I'm bressed if he ain't more of shark dan Massa Shark hisself."[28]

This comment, sobering enough in this context, takes on an even more horrifying suggestion a short time later when Queequeg and another crew member seek to drive the sharks away by plunging their whaling spades into the swarm at the side of the boat. Far from driving away the scavenging fish, the blood flowing from their own bodies stimulates another feeding frenzy, this time on their own kind. Even their individual identities are lost in this voracious delirium, and a shark may become so compelled to eat that it consumes its very self: "But in the foamy confusion of their mixed and struggling hosts, the marksmen could not always hit their marks; and this brought about new revelations of the incredible ferocity of the foe. They viciously snapped, not only at each other's disembowelments, but like flexible bows, bent round, and bit their own; till those entrails seemed swallowed over and over again by the same mouth, to be oppositely voided by the gaping wound."[29]

As many commentators have noted, this image of the shark devouring not only another shark but even its own entrails mirrors the *ouroboros*, the figure of the snake biting its tail, symbol of never-ending cycles. And the sharks are not just biting; they are actually consuming themselves, lending this cyclic image a dreadful cast. (Bakhtin claims that swallowing is the most ancient symbol of death and destruction.)[30] Once again, the topos of constant devouring is not confined to the creatures of the deep sea, but is mirrored in ourselves and on dry land. In the words of the novel's narrator:

Consider the subtleness of the sea; how its most dreaded creatures glide under water, unapparent for the most part, and treacherously hidden beneath the loveliest tints of nature. Consider also the devilish brilliance and beauty of many of its most remorseless tribes, as the dainty embellished shape of many species of sharks. Consider, once more, the universal cannibalism of the sea;

---

[27] Ibid., p. 401.
[28] Ibid., p. 404.
[29] Ibid., p. 408.
[30] Bakhtin, *Rabelais and His World*, p. 325.

all whose creatures prey upon each other, carrying on eternal war since the world began.

Consider all this; and then turn to this green, gentle, and most docile earth; consider them both, the sea and the land; and do you not find a strange analogy to something in yourself? For as this appalling ocean surrounds the verdant land, so in the soul of man there lies one insular Tahiti, full of peace and joy, but encompassed by all the horrors of the half known life. God keep thee! Push not off from that isle, thou canst never return![31]

Life aboard a whaling ship is difficult, and it may seem obvious that eating aboard a small vessel tossed on the waves of a remorseless ocean will be more brutal than dining on land. Certainly, we are far from the civilized dining room in which the gamepiece hangs so suspiciously. But if the horrors of the half-known life intrude into a sedate home more seldom than they visit the *Pequod,* they still lurk in the very fact of eating. This is the case even when the occasions of that eating represent the most refined and polished instances of haute cuisine, and the dining table is surrounded by guests in convivial gatherings.

What One Eats with Whom: Food and the Formation of Community

Shylock tells Bassanio in Act I, scene iii of *The Merchant of Venice,* "I will buy with you, sell with you, talk with you, walk with you, and so following; but I will not eat with you, drink with you, nor pray with you." His declaration reminds us of one of the most important social aspects of eating: its role in defining a community. Those who eat together are to some degree equals, alike, kin. Sometimes, as is the case with Shylock, a Jew speaking to a Christian, the defining powers of food concern what is eaten, kosher versus nonkosher foods in this case. Mutual recognition of what counts as proper food preparation and as conditions of edibility demarcates one group from another.[32] Those who choose to eat together tacitly recognize their fellow eaters as saliently equal. This practice underlies the root meaning of the Latinate word "companion," a person with whom one shares bread. Among those who acknowledge their community, eating together, whether in ceremony or informally, can serve to strengthen or renew the bonds of fellowship by bringing commonalities to the forefront of awareness. More rarely, a social bond may come into being from the mere act of eating together, in which case the relationship is a consequence of the food itself. The social acts on behalf of friends or of strangers that ride under the

---

[31] Melville, *Moby Dick,* pp. 380–81.

[32] See the essays in Mary Douglas, ed., *Food in the Social Order: Studies of Food and Festivities in Three American Communities* (New York: Russell Sage Foundation, 1984).

name of "hospitality" typically involve the offering of food and drink. Hospitality even enters into religious directives, as in the famous instruction of Saint Paul: "Be not forgetful to entertain strangers: for thereby some have entertained angels unawares" (Heb. 13:2). Indeed, the Bible is full of passages in which eating together is a sign of community.[33]

The power of food can be so profound that eating together may not only celebrate community but actually create a bond of kinship and obligation, uniting even enemies in the mutual intimacy of taking the same foods into the body. The societies in which this obligation obtains as an actual code of conduct are now exotic for many of us, though they can be revived through the medium of a vivid plot. This has aptly served a genre of adventure tale in which foods link people who would otherwise be adversaries. Such occurs in a novel popular in the early years of the twentieth century, *Siberian Gold*, by Theodore Acland Harper.[34] The hero, Stephen Wyld, is an American mining engineer sent by his company to explore for gold in the hinterlands of Siberia. Stephen earns a certain regard from the peasantry, and becomes fascinated by the lore concerning one Kubrik, an outlaw and horse thief. Kubrik is a dangerous man, and as events transpire he captures Stephen nosing about his territory and considers it necessary to kill him. Stephen, having sometime earlier discovered a picture of what looked like an old Bedouin chief in Kubrik's cabin, gambles on a guess about the background of his captor and asks for food. Kubrik obliges because he is hungry and was about to eat anyway, and they share a simple meal. By so doing Stephen saves his own life; he puts himself under the protection of the outlaw, for by Bedouin custom (the picture is of Kubrik's father), one who eats salt with another earns the latter's hospitality.[35]

In this episode eating brings into being a tie of obligation, in spite of the differences that separate those who eat together. And Kubrik and Stephen Wyld inhabit very different worlds: one an outlaw, a Muslim, and a Tartar-Russian, the other an educated engineer, a Christian, an American. The mere act of sharing salt forges a bond between them that, by the code of the Bedouin (and the equally important code of honor prominent in this type of adventure story), must be acknowledged. Stephen is saved by the capacity of eating to create intimacy even by trickery. And it is all to the good of the plot, too, for by another convention of the adventure tale,

[33] Abraham is the prototype for hospitality to angels: Gen. 18:8. Margaret Holland points out the following passages in the New Testament where eating signals Christian fellowship: Mark 14:22–25; Matt. 26:26–29; Luke 22:14–20 and 24:13–35; 1 Cor. 11:20–33; Acts 2:42 and 11:1–18; Gal. 2:11–14. In Mark 2:15–17 and Matt. 9:10–13 Jesus eats with "tax collectors and sinners," an indication that they are accepted by God.

[34] Theodore Acland Harper, *Siberian Gold* (New York: Doubleday, Doran, 1928).

[35] Eating salt with one's host puts one under his protection in many traditions. Additional symbolic meanings are discussed in Margaret Visser, *Much Depends on Dinner* (Toronto: HarperCollins, 1986), chap. 2.

Kubrik becomes a staunch ally of Stephen and a friend. While one must be duly cautious about drawing general conclusions concerning reality from this kind of story (or perhaps any kind of story), this plot clearly trades on practices that are familiar. When the anthropologist Jack Goody did his field research in West Africa, he was advised that if ever he felt in danger from the people around him, he had only to place some of the earth from the area of the village in his mouth, and he would be protected by those who lived there.[36] While this action is not properly eating, it shares with eating the gesture of trust and dependency presumed by physically taking a substance of mutually recognized significance into one's body.

The fact that eating together so often forms social ties provides a context in which to understand the different meanings suggested not only by shared meals but also by solitary eating. While the latter might indicate loneliness or isolation, it need not; nor does eating together necessarily indicate happy community. (There are entire societies in which eating is deemed a solitary function, not one to occupy social time.) But more important, because of the strong bonds implied by the social intimacy of eating, the choice to dine alone takes on special meaning by contrast. It might indicate an antisocial temperament or rejection—or the choice to interrupt a dependent relationship. Colette's lone woman in her story "The Other Wife," for example, who eats alone and at leisure at a resort hotel, signals independence and self-confidence, not rejection or incompletion. But this is obvious only because it is presumed that a woman ordinarily does not dine alone happily. The evident contentment of this lone eater stands out as a sign of her declared autonomy and inspires uneasy admiration on the part of another woman who watches from the table she occupies with her husband.

Eating together is often habitual, and, while custom itself takes place within social groups, mere habit can serve to obscure the presence of community. So familiar is group eating that it rarely stands out in a narrative as worthy of note, seeming merely a realistic note in the story.[37] Consider the ease and frequency with which the friendly and warmhearted characters in Dickens's *Pickwick Papers* repair to a tavern or inn, the repeated offerings of food to travelers in episodic narratives, the dinners signifying social acceptance in Jane Austen's novels.[38] One reason why eating serves to unite people concerns that other task of the mouth: speaking.[39] Diners sit or recline, disengaged from other practical endeavors. Their commerce with one another is oral—they eat, they talk: two activities that engage both the body and the mind (in spite of Plato's opting for only the latter in the *Symposium*). A meal lends itself to

[36] Jack Goody, *Cooking, Cuisine and Class* (Cambridge: Cambridge University Press, 1982), p. 75.
[37] For a discussion of food and realism in the novel form, see Gian-Paolo Biasin, *The Flavors of Modernity* (Princeton: Princeton University Press, 1993), Introduction.
[38] Though food is an important social ritual for Austen, appetite often indicates moral laxity, as Maggie Lane argues in *Jane Austen and Food* (London: Hambleton Press, 1995).
[39] This is a major theme of Marin, *Food for Thought*.

awareness of one's company and what is being shared. Ties with others are often re-vived through deliberate eating together; and the bonds may be renewed through ritual and ceremony, shared taste enjoyment, conversation, or some combination of them that kindles friendship. I turn now to two famous fictional dinner parties in which food is an agent that unites the assembled companies—albeit in different ways and with varying degrees of success. The scenes of these events present reflec-tion on taste and its pleasures, the transience of the experience, and the significance the occasions retain in memory long after they are past.

"Babette's Feast"

In marked contrast to *Moby Dick,* the characters of Isak Dinesen's short story "Ba-bette's Feast" are civil and proper, and they lead lives of narrow compass. Their world is small, confined, domestic, and feminine, for the three main characters form a household of women.[40] Within the local community, experience of the world is re-stricted. Devout Christians of an austere Protestant sect, they do all that is humanly possible to subvert and deny what they would regard as their "animal" nature. Yet they must eat, and in the most exalted act of eating that any of them will ever expe-rience there is still the shadow of the devouring world that Stubb embraces, albeit now it has been transformed into something wondrously removed from its original form. And this transformation makes all the difference between a lone devourer and a community of celebrants.

The fictional ethos of Dinesen's story presumes an extreme version of the deni-gration of the bodily senses, an ascetic variation on the hierarchy.[41] Most of the char-acters of the story are members of a pietist Lutheran sect who live in relative isola-tion in a small Norwegian village.[42] It is against this background of self-denial and disparagement of bodily pleasures that Dineson portrays food and the eponymous meal that is the story's climax.

Two of the main characters are daughters of the founder of the sect that consti-tutes their community. One of the chief precepts of their religion is denial of the pleasures of the flesh in any form, including of course the pleasures of the table. "Its members renounced the pleasures of this world, for the earth and all that it held to them was but a kind of illusion, and the true reality was the New Jerusalem toward

---

[40] Several novels by female authors mix domestic plots with actual recipes, thus blending two literary genres: the novel and the cookbook or book of household management. See, e.g., Ntozake Shange, *Sas-safrass, Cypress, and Indigo* (New York: St. Martin's Press, 1982); Laura Esquivel, *Like Water for Chocolate,* trans. Carol Christensen and Thomas Christensen (New York: Doubleday, 1992); Isabel Allende, *Aphrodite: A Memoir of the Senses,* trans. Margaret Sayers Peden (Pymble, N.S.W.: HarperCollins, 1997).
[41] Dinesen first wrote "Babette's Feast" in English; it was published in the *Ladies' Home Journal* in 1950 and later collected in *Anecdotes of Destiny* (1958). In 1987 it was rendered in an award-winning Danish film directed by Gabriel Axel.
[42] In Axel's film, the setting of the story is moved to Jutland.

which they were longing." As is evident in the perspective of this comment, the story is a mild comedy that portrays but does not embrace this rejection of sense pleasure, though it does so without burlesque and with touching sympathy for the characters. Conforming to fairy-tale convention, the two daughters are very beautiful, and they are sought after by young men of the village, but their father the Dean discourages marriage and they dutifully—and happily—stay by his side. Nonetheless, two men enter their lives and afford them a glimpse of romantic pleasures. A visiting soldier, Lorens Loewenhielm, nephew to a member of the local gentry, is sent to spend some time with his aunt and reflect upon the dissolute habits that have run him into debt and put his reputation in jeopardy. He meets the older sister, Martine, and is captivated by her, though he finds that her father's ascetic household represses his ordinarily easy skills of flirtation. Indeed, he uncomfortably decides he is unworthy of Martine and returns to his regiment both sadly chastened and a bit cynical, vowing to think only of the practical matter of his own career. Before he departs, he passionately kisses Martine's hand and declares in romantic despair, "I shall never, never see you again! For I have learned here that Fate is hard, and that in this world there are things which are impossible!"[43]

A year later romance touches the life of Philippa, the younger sister. Achille Papin, a French singer indulging in a solitary vacation, is sojourning in the tiny fjord village, and he hears Philippa's angelic voice as she sings a hymn of praise during a church service. He offers to coach her singing—professedly for the greater glory of God, but privately because he desires to introduce her to the Paris stage. As part of his instruction he teaches her selections from Mozart's *Don Giovanni*. Carried away after they sing the famous seduction duet together, he kisses Philippa and leaves, transported. His ecstasy abruptly ends when Philippa, disturbed by what this kiss has aroused, asks her father to tell M. Papin that she does not desire to continue her singing lessons. For Philippa is all too aware of the fine line between art and life that pleasure can cross. (Disappointed, Papin reflects, "Don Giovanni kissed Zerlina, and Achille Papin pays for it! Such is the fate of the artist!")[44] Papin returns to Paris and the sisters continue their quiet, pious life, tending to the needy and superintending the worship of the community after their father's death. Unfortunately, that community dwindles as it ages, and its members descend into squabbling and frequent acrimony.

Years pass. One stormy night the sisters are disturbed by a knock on their door and a strange woman collapses in their parlor. She bears a letter of introduction from Papin, who recommends to their mercy Babette Hersant, who has barely escaped France with her life, and whose husband and son have been murdered in the quash-

---

[43] Isak Dinesen, "Babette's Feast," in *Anecdotes of Destiny* (New York: Viking Penguin, 1986), pp. 23, 27.
[44] Ibid., p. 32.

ing of the Paris Commune. Papin takes the opportunity to remind Philippa of the musical career that she refused and to extol again her glorious voice. He ends his letter with a postscript, the printed notes of the opening bars of the duet of Don Giovanni and Zerlina. Almost as an afterthought, he notes, "Babette can cook." Out of pity the two sisters agree that Babette can make a home with them, cooking and serving in their meager household. Knowing the reputation of the French for perverse tastes, they carefully instruct her in the preparation of such trustworthy Protestant fare as split cod and ale bread, and "during the demonstration the Frenchwoman's face became absolutely expressionless." But Babette can indeed cook, and soon the sick whom the sisters tend are getting better and better, implicitly because her fine French touch improves the taste of even salted cod and soggy bread soup. She speaks little of her past and despite her daily activities among the people of the village (who regard her as "the dark Martha in the house of their two fair Marys"), she remains a somewhat exotic creature, a papist, alien to their stark brand of Christianity. Indeed, her mysteriousness is likened to "the Black Stone of Mecca, the Kaaba itself."[45]

More years pass, and Babette's one tie with her former life, a lottery ticket, unexpectedly pays off. She is suddenly the recipient of 10,000 francs, and the community anticipates with sorrow that she will soon leave and return to France. As a parting gesture, she begs that she be permitted to prepare dinner for the little community of the faithful on the upcoming hundredth anniversary of the Dean's birth. It will be a "French dinner," and with some trepidation the sisters agree to this unusual request.

This French dinner soon looms in their minds as a sinister affair. Babette must take a trip to France to order the ingredients, and when delivered they arouse horror: a cage of twittering birds, crates of nameless provisions, bottles and bottles of wine, and, most horrific of all, a hissing sea tortoise whose snakish head swings from the kitchen counter like an instrument of the devil. Martine, after a disturbed night of dreams that Babette is initiating them into a witches' sabbath, confesses to the community of the pious who were invited to the feast that she fears what they will be asked to eat. The group unites in a pact to *eat* but not to *taste*. They will attend the celebration to honor the Dean their founder, but they will secure their souls against the dangers that the table offers by not enjoying one mouthful, nor even speaking of what is placed before them. "On the day of our master we will cleanse our tongues of all taste and purify them of all delight or disgust of the senses, keeping and preserving them for the higher things of praise and thanksgiving."[46]

---

[45] Ibid., pp. 36, 37.
[46] Ibid., p. 47. In the film these lines are given to a different character with slightly different emphasis: "The tongue, the tongue. This strange little muscle has accomplished great and glorious deeds for mankind . . . but it is also the source of unleashed evil and deadly poison. On the day when we solemnly

On the day of the feast an unexpected guest arrives. Lorens Loewenhielm, now a general, is visiting his aunt, who writes to ask that he be included in the gathering. The table is now set for the auspicious number of twelve, and before the meal the guests gather in the parlor and sing a hymn of the Dean's own composition, a favorite of the community, which contains the lines: "Take not thought for food or raiment / careful one, so anxiously . . ."[47]

Spiritually bolstered, they enter a room transformed for the occasion with pressed linen, crystal and china, and more silver than anyone has ever seen on one table before—all of which Babette has procured for the occasion from France. Loewenhielm, anticipating frugal Norwegian fare, is astonished to discover with his first sip a glass of finest Amontillado, and he is even more transported by a spoonful of exquisite turtle soup. (Martine would later note with relief that the hideous tortoise was not in view; perhaps it had just been part of her nightmare.) But he is perplexed by the stolidity with which his fellow diners approach their extravagant meal. Not knowing of their vow, he can induce no comment upon the food, no praise of the wine. Course after course delights him, and no one else expresses enjoyment. However, the very taste and quality of the food begin to loosen the tongues of the guests, and while they do not speak of their food, they relate friendly and uplifting stories of their own pasts, their conversions, fond memories of the pastor. Gradually old friendships rekindle, wounds heal, irritations are smoothed and wrongs forgiven.

The main course is too incredible to remain unremarked. General Loewenhielm recognizes *cailles en sarcophage,* the unique creation of the genius chef of a famous Parisian establishment, the Café Anglais. He has had it once before at a dinner celebration, and he recalls the encomium to the chef—who was, unusually, a woman—which his host, Colonel Galliffet, had described in terms of transportive praise: "'And indeed,' said Colonel Galliffet, 'this woman is now turning a dinner at the Café Anglais into a kind of love affair—into a love affair of the noble and romantic category in which one no longer distinguishes between bodily and spiritual appetite or satiety! I have, before now, fought a duel for the sake of a fair lady. For no woman in all Paris, my young friend, would I more willingly shed my blood!'"[48]

Loewenhielm does not know, though by now the reader has guessed, that this accomplished female chef is now up to her elbows in the pots and pans of a rude Norwegian kitchen, conjuring up the magical dinner she used to serve in Paris. Loewenhielm makes a speech about human choice and divine grace that might have been made by the Dean himself; the guests feel a rush of love for one another, and Ba-

---

[47] Ibid., p. 50.
[48] Ibid., p. 58.

bette's alchemy completes what the late minister's preaching had not accomplished: a mending of the community and a sense of God's presence. But this is no longer a fearsome, self-denying effort. Their very pleasure in the food eaten and the wine drunk has loosened all the fears that tied them to selfishness, and their love flows with the effortlessness of children. In fact, they share a near-mystical experience in the subtle confusion of intoxication and love: "They only knew that the rooms had been filled with a heavenly light, as if a number of small halos had blended into one glorious radiance." As Loewenhielm leaves, he once again kisses Martine's hand, but he reverses his declaration of many years ago: "I shall be with you every day that is left to me. Every evening I shall sit down, if not in the flesh, which means nothing, in spirit, which is all, to dine with you, just like tonight. For tonight I have learned, dear sister, that in this world anything is possible."[49]

Belatedly, the sisters remember Babette. They enter the kitchen with smiles and thanks for the "nice dinner." They anticipate that soon she will leave, but she announces that she has no place to go and no money. With shock they discover that the entire lottery prize has been spent on their commemorative meal. They can barely comprehend the reason for this prodigality—but it has to do with art. Babette is an artist. She has created her finest meal not only out of affection for them but also for herself, for no artist wants to be unable to do her utmost. Philippa grasps this when she embraces Babette and repeats the words that Papin directed to her own singing. In Paradise, she says, Babette will continue her wizardry, and "how you will enchant the angels!"

Several themes of this story demonstrate a vision of food and of eating: the relationship between bodily experience and spiritual understanding, the status of cooking as an art, and the quelling of its original nature that Babette's meal underwent. The brand of Christianity depicted in this story is a particularly harsh one that regards pleasures of all kinds as invitations to wickedness, and the body as of little importance compared to the life eternal awaiting the pious spirit. This harshness is muted by the gentle comedy of the narrative and by the presentation of the characters as people of good intentions and virtuous efforts. However, the contrasts drawn between the familiar fare of the community and the meal Babette proposes underscore just how narrow and uncompromising are the habits of these pious people. As Babette assembles the ingredients for her feast, she not only resumes her alien, foreign countenance but becomes almost forbidding: "Babette, like the bottled demon of the fairy tale, had swelled and grown to such dimensions that her mistresses felt small before her. They now saw the French dinner coming upon them, a thing of incalculable nature and range."[50] Her cooking becomes mysterious, like something

[49] Ibid., pp. 61, 62.
[50] Ibid., p. 45.

that might emerge from a witches' cauldron.[51] The boy she engages as a helper is described as a "familiar," and despite their affection for their cook, the sisters approach the meal with dread. This is not merely a confrontation between sophistication and naiveté; it is a clash of value systems: ascetic denial of the body and its sensuous pleasures in contest with a recondite, purposive sequence of food and drink designed to raise those pleasures to their most refined pitch, to exercise the bodily senses in a recherché and extravagant style.

If the two sides are regarded as remaining in opposition throughout the story, then clearly Babette's enticement of the senses is the winner. In spite of themselves, the celebrants succumb to the pleasures she offers up, never quite realizing that their vows to deny the sense of taste are powerless before the delicious flavors set before them. At first hesitant to taste the wine, they take tentative sips. (It helps that they do not recognize champagne and assume it is some kind of lemonade.) But it is important to note that Babette is not setting out to make fools of her guests or to render them drunk. She instructs her helper to give each person only one glass of each wine, with the exception of Loewenhielm, who can be assumed to be able to monitor his own drinking. No one overstuffed and drunk enjoys a meal to the utmost; this is sophisticated fare, and only an accomplished chef can serve it so that it greets the mind at the same time that it pleases the palate. This it does, even though most of the diners are not aware that the meal itself has opened their hearts and caused them to cease their quarreling. Overpowering their abstemious vows, Babette's meal in fact fulfills the entreaty of their dinner grace:

> May my food my body maintain,
> may my body my soul sustain,
> may my soul in deed and word
> give thanks for all things to the Lord.[52]

At the same time, it would not be accurate to claim that Babette's magnificent dinner is wholly responsible for the transfiguration of this divided group into a spiritual community bound by love. Of equal importance are the character and habits of the people themselves, steeped in a lifetime of striving for goodness and spiritual transformation. ("The old Dean's flock were humble people. When later in life they thought of this evening it never occurred to any of them that they might have been exalted by their own merit.") But their striving had taken the form so frequent among very devout Christians: denial of the pleasures of their corporeal parts, figured for this evening in their vow not even to taste what they put into their mouths.

---

[51] See also Sara Stambough, *The Witch and the Goddess in the Stories of Isak Dinesen* (Ann Arbor; UMI Research Press, 1988).
[52] Dinesen, "Babette's Feast," p. 55.

Fear was as prominent a feature of their emotional lives as love, and it twisted their relationships into tense knots. One elderly couple, lovers a generation ago, continued to berate each other for the sin they committed and for which they lived in fear of everlasting punishment. The pleasures released by Babette's splendid meal replaced their fear, freeing the love and generosity of spirit long cultivated. (The two old lovers "suddenly found themselves close together in a corner and gave one another that long, long kiss, for which the secret uncertain love affair of their youth had never left them time.")[53]

If the pious members of the community discover their sensuous pleasure in life, the somewhat jaded General Loewenhielm discovers spiritual mystery and meaning previously absent from his worldly success. He makes a speech, and while it is true he is somewhat tipsy, his intoxication is as much of the spirit as of the body as he glimpses a vision of God's mercy:

> "Grace, my friends, demands nothing from us but that we shall await it with confidence and acknowledge it in gratitude. Grace, brothers, makes no conditions and singles out none of us in particular; grace takes us all to its bosom and proclaims general amnesty. See! that which we have chosen is given us, and that which we have refused is, also and at the same time, granted us. Ay, that which we have rejected is poured upon us abundantly. For mercy and truth have met together, and righteousness and bliss have kissed one another!"[54]

The Dean himself could not have been more eloquent. The story obliquely repudiates the necessity of asceticism for even the devout Christian. The film draws attention to this message when one guest observes of their vow to remain silent and suppress the sense of taste that "it will be as the wedding at Cana, where food and drink did not matter." But of course that account (John 2:1–11) has a different message, for Christ turned water into wine for that celebration. (Director Gabriel Axel subtly makes use of this theme in the film, where late in the meal one guest accidentally takes a drink of water, makes a face, and returns with gusto to her glass of Clos Vougeot '46.)

Dinesen's dislike of the pious, bourgeois Christianity of her youth in Denmark is well known, and this triumph of Babette's presents her own choice of a life in which the senses are honored, along with their pleasures. As with the feast, intense sense experience is not accurately described simply as bodily indulgence; it is a means by which spiritual, perhaps even mystical truths about life's transience and splendor are

---

[53] Ibid., p. 62.
[54] Ibid., pp. 60–61.

realized. This is perhaps a rather romantic picture, and it is matched by a view of art that in fact ends the story with some unsettling notes.

When the sisters enter the kitchen to praise Babette for her "nice" dinner, they find her sitting exhausted amid a towering wreckage of pots and pans. She declares to them, though they do not fully comprehend, that once she was the cook at the Café Anglais, and that she is an artist, a great artist. Her final triumph has been this extraordinary dinner, with which she brought peace and happiness into the reluctant and divided community. But one realizes that whom she has served is of little importance for Babette; the creation of the meal was an end in itself. She is thinking of the great figures of Paris who formerly patronized the Café Anglais, including dukes, princes, and one Colonel Galliffet, he whom Loewenhielm had quoted in praise of Babette, and also he who brutally fought the Communards and was responsible for the deaths of Babette's husband and son. They were evil, cruel men, grants Babette; but they were mine. They were the ones with the learning and upbringing to appreciate what a great artist I am. Babette has spent her last franc on a memorial meal (Martine thinks suddenly of a story she has heard of an African chief who in gratitude served up his baby grandchild for dinner to a guest). Babette cooks not only to commemorate the Dean's anniversary but also in memoriam to the aristocracy that developed the recherché taste that could appreciate her art, even while it could execute her family. This is a vision of art that is heavily romantic: art and the creative genius inhabit a plane that is loftier than daily life and its suffering. (Axel softened this aspect of the final portions of the story and the film omits some of these jarring notes.) But Dinesen's own ending is instructive when we consider this "narrative of eating," for it stays us from moving too easily from the beauty of the feast and its enlightening outcome in the story to the effects of fine dining in reality. At the same time, we need not confine our praise of feasting to the world of a tale. Food does have this function, eating together—enjoying together, conversing at table—does liberate friendship and unharness us from petty fears. It does this, so to speak, within our own stories, by which I mean within the fabric of understanding and traditions we carry with us ourselves. When those traditions are socially homogeneous and unquestioned, they become virtually invisible. An advantage of fiction such as "Babette's Feast" is that the treatment of food is both familiar and removed: the sense hierarchy is extreme among the Norwegian pietists, and it is treated with the distance of gentle comedy. It therefore both is familiar and carries a certain truth to readers who share the larger philosophical tradition of the sense hierarchy, but also it is visible because they probably do not fully participate in this version of it. The same holds for the high romanticist view of art, disturbing because it places artistic creativity even above familial loyalty. All these factors permit a distance that aids recognition of the conceptual framework that bestows meaning on this type of meal.

More subtle is the echo of Stubb's supper in Babette's feast, but it is there. The amassing of ingredients for the commemorative dinner is a task as enormous as the preparation of the table itself, and it includes a cage of quail and a huge sea tortoise that swings its head in helpless struggle, so hideous and alien a beast that Martine dreams of devils. By the time the food is delivered to the table, the tortoise is so transformed that it is unrecognizable, for who could see in delicately flavored soup a heavy, carapaced monster? The disposal of the inedible body parts left after the tasty portions enter the cooking pot is implicit in the story; in the film we see the kitchen helper wheeling away a barrow filled with bones, shell, feet, heads, offal. The dreaded tortoise has left only its flavor behind. The little birds are harder to disguise, and in the film their sacrifice is displayed as Babette carefully positions each little roasted head on the edge of the pastry "sarcophagus."[55] General Loewenhielm crunches a tiny skull between his teeth, sucking out the brains, and closes his eyes in ecstasy. Intricate preparation intervenes between the living creatures, their slaughter, and subsequent presentation to the dinner guests, preparation framed by the structured set of the table and the pace and form of the meal itself, and by accompaniments of baked, ground, seasoned, stuffed, sautéed, and variously arranged edibles similarly removed from the condition in which they entered the kitchen. Given the occasion and the reverent commemoration of their founder's birth, these diners might even be seen as acknowledging a holy sacrifice in the service of their religion. (Though should anyone point out that in their numbers they match the apostles, a comparison that would cast Babette as Christ, they would be horrified by the blasphemous parallel.) The brutal necessities of the preparation that brought them their mystical communion through the delights of the sense of taste are virtually invisible, the evidence of bone, gristle, and shell safely hidden in the kitchen or already disposed of. It is a very long way from Stubb's supper to Babette's feast, but the paths between the two begin at the same place.

To the Lighthouse

There is another dinner party at the center of Virginia Woolf's novel *To the Lighthouse* (1927). Fourteen people—Mr. and Mrs. Ramsay, their older children, and six guests—sit down to an evening meal in a summer house in the Hebrides. As in "Babette's Feast," the meal serves to unite a disparate and quarrelsome crowd, though not without a rocky start. And again the sense hierarchy provides a context within which the meaning of the meal unfolds. With this scene as well the pleasure of the meal and its centerpiece dish, *bœuf en-daube,* serve as a catalyst for conversation and

---

[55] Preparations of this sort remind us of the importance of food's visual presentation. In the film, Babette (played by Stéphane Audran) positions the quail right side up in their pastry sarcophagi, with their heads peeking over the sides in the position a bird assumes when roosting. In Molly O'Neill's pictured version of *cailles en sarcophage* in a *New York Times Magazine* tribute to movie meals (Nov. 16, 1997), the quail is positioned in the pastry shell on its back with its roasted feet sticking up sharply, rather as if it had just slipped and fallen stunned in the bathtub.

good feeling; but this story is far more than the triumphant merger of sensuous pleasure and spiritual exaltation. The meal demonstrates Woolf's great preoccupations: time, its passage, and the changes it wreaks; memory and forgetfulness; the irreconcilability of our shifting perspectives on reality. The experience of the meal represents a moment in which bodily awareness temporary arrests what the mind knows cannot be halted: the heartless disintegration that time visits upon all living things. Indeed, this novel not only demonstrates the formation of community through eating but also captures other features of tasting and eating, such as the ephemeral nature of taste, the temporary existence of foods, and the relentless necessity of eating, features that lend a singular importance to the sense of taste and its activities.

Mrs. Ramsay is the hostess, and she has had to exert some persuasion over her guests to bring the party about, for several of them are heedless of either social obligations or gustatory enjoyment, and the children would prefer to wander off by themselves. But she prevails, convinced of the importance of such an event even if it must be prompted by insistence. Mr. and Mrs. Ramsay preside over the gathering and sit at opposite ends of the table. Mr. Ramsay is a philosopher, an academic, a man of keen mind and quirky personality who, despite a stern adherence to "facts," is prone to sentimentality and given to dramatic bursts of poetry that startle his companions. The dinner party was not his idea, and he is put out by the constraints of polite and social eating, leaving the conversational burden to his wife as the meal commences. Mrs. Ramsay is repeatedly described as astonishingly beautiful, and her occupations are domestic and generous—her garden, her knitting, her distribution of goods to "the poor." She is beloved of her children and a bit meddlesome in the lives of others, urging them (in spite of their own wishes) to marry. A woman who does not marry, she asserts, has missed the best of life. She herself has had that best, summed up in her marriage and the eight children it has produced. Mr. and Mrs. Ramsay explicitly represent "feminine" and "masculine" attitudes, and Woolf invokes these oppositions in her presentation of the dinner.[56]

Their guests include Charles Tansley, a young philosopher and disciple of Mr. Ramsay, who is feeling prickly and out of place because he is too poor to own dress clothes. Tansley spends much of the meal in a private fume of irritation. He sits near Lily Briscoe, a painter, who is a somewhat resistant target of Mrs. Ramsay's matchmaking endeavors. William Bankes, a botanist and widower; Augustus Carmichael,

---

[56] Woolf modeled Mr. and Mrs. Ramsay on her own parents, Leslie and Julia Stephen. Entries in her diary chronicle her development of the characters and the reaction of her sister Vanessa, who found them so exact that painful ghosts were awakened. See Suzanne Raitt, *Virginia Woolf's To the Lighthouse* (London: Harvester Wheatsheaf, 1990), p. 36. For a critical discussion of the relationship between the Ramsay characters and the real Stephen family, see Alex Zwerdling, *Virginia Woolf and the Real World* (Berkeley and Los Angeles: University of California Press, 1986), chap. 7.

a poet and sometime opium addict; two younger guests, Minta Doyle and Paul Rayley; and the six oldest Ramsay children complete the party.

Although they are spending some time together for the summer, this group does not regularly dine together, so the dinner party is a special occasion. It begins poorly. Several of the younger diners are late. Minta and Paul have been dallying on the shore, pursuing a romance despite the encumbering presence of Nancy Ramsay, and these three are further delayed because Minta lost her grandmother's brooch and they pause to search for it in the darkening evening. But the food is ready, and Mrs. Ramsay directs that dinner be served before everyone is seated at the table. This indicates a certain, perhaps familiar coerciveness to the social occasion, for the meal demands its own schedule, and if the wishes and convenience of the guests were accommodated, it might not happen at all:[57] "Everything depended upon things being served up to the precise moment they were ready. The beef, the bayleaf, and the wine—all must be done to a turn. To keep it waiting was out of the question." Tansley is irritated because he is socially at sea and cannot figure out how to make himself appear worthy in this company. Lily, who dutifully comes to Mrs. Ramsay's aid in the feminine obligation to pursue social small talk, is nonetheless feeling distant from her and critical of her narrow vision of a life worth living; she contents herself with thoughts of how she will revise the painting she has in progress. Bankes likes Mrs. Ramsay and converses politely, but he prefers eating alone and has agreed only reluctantly to attend the party. Mr. Ramsay is feeling customarily impatient and disgruntled. When Carmichael asks for another plate of soup, it is all Ramsay can do to keep his temper, for eating is an annoying necessity to him and he hates to be kept waiting. Mrs. Ramsay is herself privately feeling remote and disconnected, wondering if all life has left to her is "an infinitely long table and plates and knives."[58] She realizes that the evening is off to a bad start and experiences a sense of failure even as she stubbornly keeps up polite exchanges with her guests, for the dinner is launched and has demands of its own that must be met: "The room (she looked round it) was very shabby. There was no beauty anywhere. . . . Nothing seemed to have merged. They all sat separate. And the whole of the effort of merging and flowing and creating rested on her. Again she felt, as a fact without hostility, the sterility of men, for if she did not do it nobody would do it, and so, giving herself the little shake that one gives a watch that has stopped, the old familiar pulse began beating, as the watch begins ticking—one, two, three, one, two three."[59]

---

[57] Su Reid discusses the coercion present in this enjoyment: the guests must come, must eat together, to please Mrs. Ramsay: Su Reid, *To the Lighthouse* (Houndmills, Basingstoke: Macmillan, 1991), pp. 82–83.
[58] Virginia Woolf, *To the Lighthouse* (New York: Harcourt, Brace & World, 1955), pp. 121, 125.
[59] Ibid., p. 126.

This bad start to the dinner occupies roughly half of the scene, some twenty pages. During it we visit the thoughts of the various guests, all in their own way occupied with themselves and the failure of those assembled to coalesce into a convivial gathering. Bankes and Tansley are each imagining how much more enjoyable it would be to eat alone in his room, turning quickly to books and to work. "How trifling it all is, how boring it all is, [Bankes] thought, compared with the other thing—work." Tansley is whipping himself into a fury ("They did nothing but talk, talk, talk, eat, eat, eat. It was the women's fault.").[60]

Three things all at once bring the company together: the candles are lit, the missing guests take their seats, and the main dish is served. Thereafter, both visual and gustatory relish combine to ease the social tension, conversation flows more readily, and Mrs. Ramsay feels the occasion begin to take shape. When Paul and Minta arrive, they bring with them the glow of their romance and new engagement, though they do not speak of it. But just before their entry, when the tension around the table is at its height, Mrs. Ramsay interrupts what she senses may become an explosion of temper on the part of her husband (over Carmichael's extra plate of soup) and orders that the candles be lit. The somewhat ritual fire brings a pause in the conversation, and with the darkening sky outside the windows, the glow of light defines the space they occupy, drawing them together in contrast to the surrounding shadows. The candlelight falls upon the table and focuses attention on the centerpiece: an elaborate bowl of fruit that her daughter Rose had carefully arranged.

Now eight candles were stood upon the table, and after the first stoop the flames stood upright and drew with them into visibility the long table entire, and in the middle a yellow and purple dish of fruit. What had she done with it, Mrs. Ramsay wondered, for Rose's arrangement of the grapes and pears, of the horny pink-lined shell, of the bananas, made her think of a trophy fetched from the bottom of the sea, of Neptune's banquet, of the bunch that hangs with vine leaves over the shoulder of Bacchus (in some picture), among the leopard skins and the torches lolloping red and gold. . . . She saw that Augustus too feasted his eyes on the same plate of fruit, plunged in, broke off a bloom there, a tassel here, and returned, after feasting, to his hive. That was his way of looking, different from hers. But looking together united them.

Now all the candles were lit up, and the faces on both sides of the table were brought nearer by the candle light, and composed, as they had not been in the twilight, into a party round a table.[61]

---

60 Ibid., pp. 134, 129.
61 Ibid., p. 146.

It is a visual composition that is effective here: the bowl of fruit that draws their attention like a work of art, a still life painting that catches and holds for a moment the fragile life of ripe fruit. The candlelight makes them conscious of their position indoors in unified arrangement around a table, in contrast to the amorphous dark gathering outside. The narrative point of view is Mrs. Ramsay's, but it is a powerful one that seems to describe a general knitting together of the previously shredding fabric of the party. To the reader and the imagined onlooker, the candle glow unites them into a scene itself, as though they too were arranged for the painter's brush.

But the pièce de résistance is to come, the main dish of the evening, which has required three days of preparation and has commanded the assembled company to dine. A heavy earthenware dish filled with *bœuf en daube* is set before Mrs. Ramsay. Finally, enjoyment visits the table. The dish is described in terms that make it faintly mysterious and exotic: "An exquisite scent of olives and oil and juice rose from the great brown dish." Serving, Mrs. Ramsay must peer into the huge, earthenware pot as if into a cavern, "with its shiny walls and its confusion of savoury brown and yellow meats and its bay leaves and its wine."[62] The dish is (like Babette's) French, a recipe from Mrs. Ramsay's grandmother. It loosens the tongues of conversation, and the dinner party moves from tension to success. Mr. Bankes, who has been drawing away from the invitation to conversational intimacy launched by his hostess, thaws and expresses his appreciation as she helps him to especially tender morsels of beef. "It is a triumph," says Mr. Bankes.

And it is a triumph, albeit we are not given a scene of harmony and unity to equal the company of Babette's feast. Private thoughts continue to disconnect individuals from one another, and Paul Rayley thoughtlessly rebuffs Lily Briscoe's offer to help in the continued search for the lost brooch. But the ritual of dinner has prevailed, and almost in spite of themselves the assembled company acquiesce in Mrs. Ramsay's desire that the meal be a pleasurable occasion. One might go so far as to say that the *bœuf en daube* has exercised as much social force as she has.

Immediately following her pleasure with the success of this dish and the enjoyment of her guests, however, Mrs. Ramsay is suddenly conscious of the fact that a preparation of such care, that has taken such time and yet that will be consumed in such short order, calls forth sentiments both solemn and comic. For with all the effort of its preparation, the pleasure it delivers is soon spent. The beautiful dish set before them puts her in mind of Paul and Minta, for she senses that they are probably now engaged, a prospect about which she feels both reverence and cynicism:

This will celebrate the occasion—a curious sense rising in her, at once freakish and tender, of celebrating a festival, as if two emotions were called up in her, one profound—for what could be more serious than the love of man for

[62] Ibid., pp. 150–51.

woman, what more commanding, more impressive, bearing in its bosom the seeds of death; at the same time these lovers, these people entering into illusion glittering eyed, must be danced round with mockery, decorated with garlands.[63]

These thoughts capture the density of Mrs. Ramsay's character, the qualities that keep her from becoming a stock figure of sentimental maternity. She is a match-maker intensely interested in couplings and progeny, yet she casts a clear eye on the fact that as time passes the hope of permanent happiness is always betrayed. If the moment is to be celebrated, it also is to be recognized as simply a *moment*. Her meal is the perfect token of this recognition: it is a "triumph" both gastronomically and socially; and it is quickly finished. The scene opens with Mrs. Ramsay sitting down at the table and wondering, "But what have I done with my life?" and it ends with her consciousness that this domestic triumph of the party is rounded out, finished: "it had become, she knew, giving one last look at it over her shoulder, already the past."[64]

This scene from *To the Lighthouse* lends itself to analysis according to the oppositional concepts that Bryson employs with painting; that is, between preoccupation with matters of lasting historical drama and importance and the domestic and quotidian round of necessary preparation, cooking, feeding, and cleaning. The respective interests of Mr. and Mrs. Ramsay fall more or less completely into these categories. Mr. Ramsay is concerned about the dubious value of his work, about any fame he may achieve that will endure long. Mrs. Ramsay is occupied with the details of domestic life, with the rhythm and change of growth and decay, of cooking and cleaning up. (She superintends a small staff of servants. She provided the recipe, but it is not she who made the meal; her cook spent three days preparing the meat.) She is fully aware of the temporary quality of all she has laid upon the table, indeed of life itself. Nonetheless, as the meal draws to its close and the guests begin to eye the fruit as a finishing course, she experiences an almost comical desire that they stop eating and leave the beautiful composition to last a little longer. "Her eyes had been going in and out among the curves and shadows of the fruit, among the rich purples of the lowland grapes, then over the horny ridge of the shell, putting a yellow against a purple, a curved shape against a round shape, without knowing why she did it, or why, every time she did it, she felt more and more serene; until, oh, what a pity that they should do it—a hand reached out, took a pear, and spoilt the whole thing."[65]

---

[63] Ibid., p. 151. Maria DiBattista presents a complex analysis of the dining room scene and Mrs. Ramsay's character in *Virginia Woolf's Major Novels* (New Haven: Yale University Press, 1980), chap. 3.
[64] Woolf, *To the Lighthouse*, p. 168.
[65] Ibid., p. 163.

It is almost an enactment of the memento mori implicit in still life painting that Mrs. Ramsay's serenity at savoring the beauty of the fruit composition should be disrupted by someone eating a pear. This sentiment can be read as a desire to fix that which cannot last in an enduring form—a tension between food and painting, perhaps, for Mrs. Ramsay savors the fruit as if it were painted, while her hungry guests relish it more literally. At the same time, she knows more than anyone else that the moment is passing, and that this evening of fellowship and unity will last no longer than the beauty of her daughter's still life arrangement. Still the temptation to want it all to last is unavoidable. It is reflected in the doubled, opposing emotions that she is aware of throughout the meal: the sense that this is a celebration for Paul and Minta, and at the same time that the occasion requires a mockery of their betrothal. A sense that love is the most important thing in the world, and that love is untrustworthy—for what they look forward to in the glow of their romance will soon encounter compromise and disappointment. She takes pleasure in the well-prepared food, its transformation into delight; and she insistently acknowledges its impermanence. But while it lasts, the moment of community and of shared pleasure seems to have found a point of rest, of beauty. At moments during the dinner party, Mrs. Ramsay senses the constancy that eludes most experience and is exhilarated by the somewhat inchoate awareness of something enduring emerging out of the cohesion imposed on the company by her dinner.

> (The Boeuf en Daube was a perfect triumph.) Here, she felt, putting the spoon down, was the still space that lies about the heart of things, where one could move or rest; could wait now (they were all helped) listening; could then, like a hawk which lapses suddenly from its high station, flaunt and sink on laughter easily, resting her whole weight upon what at the other end of the table her husband was saying about the square root of one thousand two hundred and fifty-three. That was the number, it seemed, on his watch.[66]

The food—delectable, temporary—and the number—abstract, permanent. How fitting that Mr. Ramsay's attention to his watch should be in terms of a mathematical relation, whereas at the start of the meal, stubbornly promoting the lackluster conversation, the aspect of a watch she thinks of is the steady tick of its action. He considers his timepiece by way of a number. She thinks of the tick of its gears, which not only measure the passage of minutes but will inevitably run down and break.

The first section of *To the Lighthouse* covers a span of scarcely twenty-four hours, but during the middle section of the novel some ten years pass and three of the characters die suddenly, unexpectedly, and in parentheses. The house is attended only by

[66] Ibid., pp. 158–59.

the sweeping beam of the lighthouse and Mrs. McNab, an elderly cleaning woman, who sees the rooms fill with sand, damaged by rain and vermin, the books grown frosty with mold. Then at the unexpected request of one of the Ramsay daughters she must see that the house is put in order again for a summer visit. She enlists the help of a friend in cleaning and sweeping and putting all to rights again, and to her she describes the family that used to visit here. The dinner party has become in her memory something even finer than it was: "They had friends in eastern countries; gentlemen staying there, ladies in evening dress; she had seen them once through the dining-room door all sitting at dinner. Twenty she dared say in all their jewellery, and she asked to stay help wash up, might be till after midnight." Mrs. McNab's recollection echoes Mrs. Ramsay's sense of their unity when the group finally merged into harmony with the lighting of candles: she could see the pattern they temporarily made up in their eating together. It gave an impression that both marks the moment and distorts it. And as such it is rather like Mrs. Ramsay's vague sense that there is meaning just beyond her grasp, an insight that she cannot quite grip that would help her catch "the heart of things" and hold time still.[67]

These impressions mark off a segment of experience that attains shape and form, "making of the moment something permanent."[68] Lily Briscoe the artist attempts something similar with her painting. She places shape upon shadow, color upon color, in plays of form and line like those that entrance Mrs. Ramsay in the fruit arrangement. Although the painting has greater power to last, the moment is never permanent; and yet the event itself has shape, and one may glimpse it and realize that something meaningful has been brought into being. The intensity of such awareness impresses the moment in memory, making it stand out from the continuous flow of life that passes by with less notice. During the dinner party Mrs. Ramsay vacillates between being charmed by the beauty of the illusion that she has caught the moment and sustained it as something that endures, and the realization that it *is* an illusion:

Everything seemed possible. Everything seemed right. Just now (but this cannot last, she thought, dissociating herself from the moment while they were all talking about boots) just now she had reached security; she hovered like a hawk suspended; like a flag floated in an element of joy which filled every

---

[67] Ibid., p. 211. Mrs. McNab's remembered scene is reminiscent of a later writer who also described, though more wryly, the feminine world of food. Two of Barbara Pym's characters, looking into the lit window of a hotel dining room, sense the "still space that lies about the heart of things" in almost those very words: "A middle-aged couple, looking like people in an advertisement—she in pearls and a silver fox cape over a black dress, he in a dark suit—sat at a table in the window. A waiter bent over them . . . helping them to some fish—turbot, surely? Its white flesh was exposed before them. How near to the heart of things it seemed!" (Barbara Pym, *No Fond Return of Love* [1961] [New York: Harper & Row, 1984], p. 180).

[68] Woolf, *To the Lighthouse*, p. 241.

nerve of her body fully and sweetly, not noisily, solemnly rather, for it arose, she thought, looking at them all eating there, from husband and children and friends; all of which rising in this profound stillness (she was helping William Bankes to one very small piece more, and peered into the depths of the earthenware pot) seemed now for no special reason to stay there like a smoke, like a fume rising upwards, holding them safe together. Nothing need be said; nothing could be said. There it was, all round them. It partook, she felt, carefully helping Mr. Bankes to a specially tender piece, of eternity; as she had already felt about something different once before that afternoon; there is a coherence in things, a stability; something, she meant, is immune from change, and shines out (she glanced at the window with its ripple of reflected lights) in the face of the flowing, the fleeting, the spectral, like a ruby; so that again tonight she had the feeling she had had once today, already, of peace, of rest. Of such moments, she thought, the thing is made that endures.[69]

Examined and analyzed, this combination of sentiments will not cohere. The moment both passes and endures; time slides by and remains suspended; she understands, she is deceived. The thoughts that pass through Mrs. Ramsay's mind are strictly speaking inconsistent, but the impression she obtains and its lingering memory continue to press her heart despite her inability to state any grounds to justify her feelings. And a portion of her impression is the harmony and cohesion among her company that the dinner has brought into being.

The ultimate effect of this dinner party on the assembled company is more difficult to assess than that of Babette's dinner, not least because this novel is a considerably more complicated piece of literature, involving as it does the perspectives of the multitude of characters and Woolf's philosophical interest in the difficulty of achieving stable and reliable access to reality. These issues exceed the purpose to which I employ the dinner party, but they inevitably make this scene in *To the Lighthouse* more difficult to discuss in isolation than even Stubb's supper in the much longer *Moby Dick*. From the perspectives we are presented, however—chiefly those of Mrs. Ramsay, Lily Briscoe, Mr. Bankes, Mrs. McNab—as well as the overall import of the dinner in the whole narrative, we can see several factors at work that contribute to molding this company together in an event that retains some special meaning. Foremost is the very fact that Woolf chose a *meal* as the plot device with which to unfold this drama of isolation and communion. Food and its place in the sense hierarchy are at issue both in the ways the characters respond to the occasion and in the dense meanings Woolf layers into the scene. She takes advantage of the familiar social practice that a dinner represents and plays against it the individual consciousness of each guest.

[69] Ibid., pp. 157–58.

The dinner nearly fails, but in the end "it is a triumph"—at least from Mrs. Ramsay's point of view, for this novel does not permit us a general or omniscient assessment. To be sure, in this case there is a dose of coercion, and hence some irony in the fact that the diners are united with one another almost in spite of themselves. It is not that they are otherwise adversaries, so this bond is not forged in the rule-governed manner of the bond between Kubrik and Steven Wyld. It is closer to Babette's event in that the pleasure taken in the food, though a more forced and gradual process, finally draws them from their isolation, permitting the social efforts of Mrs. Ramsay and Lily to succeed. It is easy to imagine that the union of the group is not entirely complete; it is certainly not as wholehearted as Babette's almost magical effect. Tansley, in particular, is portrayed as nursing his grievances so assiduously that we cannot assume he could be wholly won over by the food. But is this not a familiar situation, and one that demonstrates that the very structure of such a meal and the formalities it imposes have the capacity to effect unity by virtue simply of demanding participation in the ceremony?

The tastes of this meal are only implicit, and it is the *bœuf en daube* that is chiefly described. Yet the taste of that noble dish is imprinted on the memory of at least one of the diners so vividly that it fixes the moment with all of its associations long after the event itself has passed. The remembered taste rushes into Lily Briscoe's consciousness as, ten years later, she returns to the painting that preoccupied her throughout the dinner party, and she stands once more on the windswept lawn outside the Ramsay's summer house. She stands before her canvas with the house in view, emptier now, for Mrs. Ramsay is dead along with her children Prue and Andrew. Mr. Ramsay is on his way to the lighthouse with his youngest two, Cam and James, and the boat in which they travel is a diminishing speck on the sea. The only other guest from the past is Augustus Carmichael, an enigmatic presence resting on the grass nearby. The place and her meditation on the past cause Lily to be visited by a rush of memory in which the taste, or more precisely the smell, of the *bœuf en daube,* an imagined vision, and an onslaught of emotions are bound together in recollection so vivid it is lived afresh:

> (Suddenly, as suddenly as a star slides in the sky, a reddish light seemed to burn in her mind, covering Paul Rayley, issuing from him. It rose like a fire sent up in token of some celebration by savages on a distant beach. She heard the roar and the crackle. The whole sea for miles round ran red and gold. Some winey smell mixed with it and intoxicated her, for she felt again her own headlong desire to throw herself off the cliff and be drowned looking for a pearl brooch on a beach. . . .)

Anguished and shaken, Lily can only put the phenomenon she has just experienced in terms of her very body's ability to grasp what her intellect fails to formulate in sufficiently exact language. She ponders her struggle over her painting and the placement of colors and shapes that would capture the summer afternoon as Mrs. Ramsay and her youngest son sat in the window of the house—the very window in which the candles shone throughout the dinner party. Missing Mrs. Ramsay, wanting and not having, she thinks: "The urgency of the moment always missed its mark. Words fluttered sideways and struck the object inches too low. Then one gave it up; then the idea sunk back again; then one became like most middle-aged people, cautious, furtive, with wrinkles between the eyes and a look of perpetual apprehension. For how could one express in words these emotions of the body? Express that emptiness there? . . . It was one's body feeling, not one's mind."[70]

"It was one's body feeling, not one's mind" captures the inchoate combination of emotions and impressions that flood Lily's consciousness and invade her very physical frame. This turn of phrase is particularly adaptable to describe the kind of sense experience for which propositional understanding remains elusive. It reminds one of another famous literary account of how a simple sensation can catch and keep the intensity of past experience, calling it up so vividly that the original is lived again. In what is probably the best-known passage of the first volume of Marcel Proust's *Remembrance of Things Past*, the character Marcel tastes a madeleine cake dipped in lime-flower tea and a powerful memory-laden experience is aroused.[71] It is triggered directly through his taste sensation, for his mind cannot at first interpret what he tastes or determine the source of this intense encounter. His taste of the little cake summons up the past, recalling the experience as vividly as when it was first impressed. Lily's experience is not quite parallel, for her memory is not triggered by a taste from the past. Rather, the rush of memory and emotion concerning that evening ten years before carries with it the sensory remembrance of the dinner mingled with her nostalgia and regret. In both cases, however, the immediacy and vivacity of the recollection takes the form of bodily experience virtually reenacted: *it was one's body feeling, not one's mind.*

Ironically, such vividly relived moments are just the ones that rely most on senses often denigrated for the ephemera of their proper objects. And as we have seen repeatedly, they are credited as affording the most subjective of experiences. But shared meals, the ceremonial or hospitable or ritual events such as those that form the stories of Babette and Mrs. Ramsay, ideally harness the subjectivity of taste and in so doing bind together those who share food in an intensity of experience—in which pleasure is often no small portion. The very brevity of the experience contributes to its depth of meaning, locking it into memory, which, though it lingers considerably longer than the original tastes, fades and disappears just as they do.

---

[70] Ibid., pp. 261, 265.
[71] Marcel Proust, *Swann's Way*, trans. C. K. Moncrieff (New York: Modern Library, 1956), pp. 62–65.

In this assessment, we must again bear in mind the many meanings of "subjective" discussed earlier. Like Marcel's, Lily's experience is highly personal. It is occasioned not only through memory and rekindled sensation but also through the combination of her peculiar nostalgia and grief, her uneasy desire for an independent career, her loneliness, her rejection of the choice of marriage on which Mrs. Ramsay insisted, her search for her own vision—all the events of her past that culminate in this moment. It is emphatically a singular experience that only Lily could have.

At the same time, this portion of the novel and the kind of event it describes appropriately complicate the distinction between subject and object, which is considerably more blurry than at first it seems. On the one hand, this experience is uniquely Lily's. The revival of memory is an overwhelming experience for her. It does not touch Augustus Carmichael, dozing obliviously nearby. Grief, regret, loss, yearning, all flood her consciousness along with intense sense memory ("the sky and sea burned red; some winey smell . . ."). And yet—everything that she experiences concerns herself not as an isolated individual but in relation with others: Mrs. Ramsay, Paul Rayley, the assembled company at the dinner party. Insofar as this complex memory—taste is but one component—directs attention toward her own condition, it is subjectively and "inwardly" directed. But even so her attention is not directed simply toward her own private inner self, for the objects of consciousness summoned up include those with whom the dinner party connects her. As we have seen, a classic charge against the subjectivity of taste involves the claim that this sense directs attention only to the state of one's own body. But Woolf conjures Lily's experience in terms that complicate body and mind, subject and object, self and other, for the intentional objects of Lily's awareness link her with others, and it is her body feeling, not her mind. Or, more exactly, her awareness, understanding, and insight arise from the experience of inseparable conscious mind and responsive, sensing body. The complexities of selfhood and the relations between self and other are topics that must be pursued far beyond the covers of this book. But it is noteworthy that a consideration of the maverick philosophical topic of taste has led us to the threshold of these traditional subjects of philosophical inquiry: the relationship of mind and body, subjectivity and objectivity, the identity of self.

This book began with an analysis and critique of the sense hierarchy and the demotion of taste that it entails. It ends with a more robust understanding of this bodily sense and its capacities, from lusty pleasures to spiritual insights; but aspects of the hierarchy are still importantly present in that understanding. Taste and the enjoyments of eating have traditionally been accorded less philosophical weight than other sensory experiences because they have been interpreted as merely pleasant at best and self-indulgent at worst. This mistaken assessment, I hope, has been dispelled. Other traditional characterizations of taste remain intact, however, although the value assigned to them has been substantially revised. The objects of taste not only are fleeting, they participate in the necessary repetition of the practical world of daily life. Eating and all the work that is required to make it possible is a repetitious and perpetual exercise. But this practical fact does not mean that when eating is conducted with reflection and grace it manages to be only pleasant, nor does it mean that its pleasures do not reach beyond themselves to anything more profound. Scrutiny of taste, of foods, and of eating, for all their domestic and quotidian context, does not sustain the assumption that attention directed to these things must be trivial or superficial. Nor does it reclaim a view of the world that is gentler or more comforting than the austere intellectual concerns with which philosophy is customarily occupied. The fictional worlds of Dinesen, Woolf, and Melville evoke in their different ways insights that are uncompromising, clear-eyed, and unsentimental: nothing lasts. And there is no more direct realization of this verity than reflection upon the very taste of things.

Index

Abject, 182–83
Absolute Spirit, 60–62
Ackerman, Diane, 74n, 84n, 85–86
Ackerman, James, 26n
Addison, Joseph, 42
Aertsen, Pieter, 154, 155, 178
Aesthetic Taste, 4–6, 38; artistic senses and, 60–63; gustatory metaphors and, 38–40, 50, 66–67, 100–101, 104–5, 111–14; judgment and, 41, 43–44, 49–50, 111; language of, 41–42; objectivity and, 107, 110–11; problem of, 46, 50–51; rationality and, 42–43, 48–49, 55; standards of, 52–53, 54, 69, 112; subjectivity of, 51–54, 134
Aesthetic theory, 1–2, 4; cognitive dimensions, 4, 6–7, 114–18, 128, 144; eighteenth-century, 5–6, 38–45; food as art form, 6–7, 103, 108–9, 130, 140–45; values, 6–7, 33, 45, 46, 48. See also Aesthetic Taste; Beauty; Language; Metaphor of taste; *individual philosophers*
Agreeableness, 54–55
Alcmaeon of Croton, 13n
Allegories of the senses, 150–51
Allegory of the Five Senses (Brueghel), 151–55
Allen, Prudence, 31n
Allende, Isabel, 203n
Alpers, Svetlana, 159n
Ames, Kenneth, 176
Angier, Natalie, 79n
Anthropology, 129–30
Appetite, 1, 5, 13, 56; gender and, 167–70, 175–76; objects of, 177–78; overindulgence of, 14, 22–23, 170, 188–89; sexuality and, 152, 168–71, 176–78
Applied arts, 130

Aquinas, Thomas, 26
Arenal, Electa, 37n
Aristotle, 5, 11, 18–24, 31–33, 53
Armelagos, George, 89–90, 168n
Art, 11; cognitive theory of, 4, 6–7, 114–18, 128, 144; decorative arts, 109, 126; fine arts, 62–63, 141, 143; food as, 6–7, 103, 108–9, 130, 140–45; hierarchy of senses and, 146–47; historical context, 143; major vs. minor, 109, 144; pictures and representation, 115–16; *rasa* and, 44–45; themes, 157. See also Still life
Artistic senses, 60–63, 103
Asrat, Tereffe, 139n
Augustine, 35
Austen, Jane, 202
Axel, Gabriel, 203n, 209, 210

"Babette's Feast" (Dinesen), 9, 203–11, 220
Baillie, John, 59
Bakhtin, Mikhail, 188, 199
Barnes, Jonathan, 19n
Barnouw, Jeffrey, 41n
Barroom paintings, 171–72, 175–76
Barthes, Roland, 18, 82, 186n, 194
Bartoshuk, Linda, 76n, 83n, 87
Basket of Fruit (Caravaggio), 166
Bass, Alan, 39n
Baugin, Lubin, 153, 155
Baumgarten, Alexander, 42, 117
Beardsley, Monroe, 75n, 108n
Beare, John I., 12n, 13n, 17n
Beauty, 24; Absolute Spirit and, 60–62; agreeable and, 54–55; as mixed mode, 47; ontological status of, 46–51; perception and, 48–49, 61; as pleasure, 48–49, 53; sexuality and, 56–57; taste metaphors and, 40–42, 50
Beck, Lewis White, 56n

Gleitman, Henry, 84n
Gluttony, 15, 23
Gombrich, E. H., 22n, 158n
Goodman, Nelson, 7, 115–18, 128, 132, 141, 158n, 168n
Goody, Jack, 69n, 92, 93–94, 202
Gorman, Warren, 85n
Goswamy, B. N., 45n
"Grand Chinese Pavilion," 123–25
Green, T. H., 51n
Grice, Paul, 25n
Grontkowski, Christine, 28n, 34
Grose, T. H., 51n
Gustatory semantics, 185

Habitus, 64
Haller, Albrecht von, 76
Hamilton, Edith, 13n
Hamlyn, D. W., 13n, 16n, 19n, 25n
Harpargus, 189–90, 192
Harper, Theodore Acland, 201–2
Haute cuisine, 93–94
Hearing, 28, 110, 149, 154; classical views, 12, 17, 19, 24
Hegel, G. W. F., 5, 60–63, 99, 110, 117, 145, 193
Heldke, Lisa, 37n
Henning, Hans, 77
Herodotus, 189–90
H factors, 95
Hierarchy of senses, 2, 5, 11, 185; Aristotle's view, 19–21; in art, 7–8, 146–47; artistic senses and, 60–63; complexity of, 155–56; continuity of tradition and, 26–27; disinterest and, 105–7; gender and, 30–37, 147; Hegel's view, 5, 60–63, 99, 145, 193; Kant's view, 57–60; in narratives, 211–12, 219, 222; Plato's view, 13–18, 30–31; Scruton's view, 110. *See also individual senses*
Higgins, Kathleen M., 45n
Hippias Major, 24
Hirst, Damien, 180n
History painting, 8, 158–59, 162–63
Hobbes, Thomas, 47–48
Hogarth, William, 52n
Holland, Margaret, 201n
Hospitality, 201
Howes, David, 14n, 79n, 133n, 168n
Hughes, Emma, 26n

Human Senses (Geldard), 75
Hume, David, 51–54, 57n, 111, 112
Humphrey, Nicholas, 25n, 26n
Hutcheson, Francis, 48–50, 52n

Iconography, 153–54
Idealism, 60–63
Illusion, 120–21, 158–59, 218–19
Indian aesthetics, 44–45
Inés de la Cruz, Sor Juana, 37
Inquiry into the Original of Our Ideas of Beauty and Virtue (Hutcheson), 48–50
Intellect, 13, 16–17, 23–24
Intentionality, 96–97, 110, 187
Internalism, 111–13
Intimacy, 101, 187
Irigaray, Luce, 30n, 33–35

Jacobus, Mary, 32n, 169n
Janin, Jules, 121
Jaucourt, Chevalier Louis de, 44
Jay, Martin, 10n, 16n, 26n, 27n, 34
Jeanneret, Michel, 26n
Johnson, Mark, 39
Jonas, Hans, 27–29, 33, 37
Jowett, Benjamin, 13n
Judgment, 25, 41, 43–44, 49–50, 111

Kahn, Charles H., 19n
Kant, Immanuel, 5, 42n, 43, 48, 54–57, 63, 64, 99; hierarchy of senses and, 57–60
Kasparek, Christopher, 22n
Kass, Leon R., 132n, 193
Keller, Evelyn Fox, 28n, 34, 169n
Kelly, Michael, 41n
Keuls, Eva C., 16n, 30n
Kivy, Peter, 48n, 49n
Knowledge, 11, 23–24; vision and, 18–19, 34
Korsmeyer, Carolyn, 30n, 46n, 108n, 114n, 157n, 159n
Kristeva, Julia, 182
Kuipers, Joel C., 133n, 168n

Lacan, Jacques, 33
Lady with the Unicorn, The, 147–51, 155
Lamphere, Louise, 36n
Language, 35, 38–39, 94. *See also* Metaphor